CAMBRIDGE BOOK DEPOT
Mall Road, Mussoorie

British Lions and the Indian Tigers

Triumph of the Sepoy against the British Sword

To Sharo

With best wishes and kind regards,

Nirm Jadoon
30 Oct 04

British Lions
and the
Indian Tigers

Triumph of the Sepoy against the British Sword

Brigadier Kim Yadav
(ADC to the Last Viceroy of India)

Manas Publications
New Delhi - 110002

Manas Publications
(Publishers, Distributors, Importers & Exporters)
4858, Prahlad Street,
24, Ansari Road, Darya Ganj,
New Delhi - 110002 (INDIA)
Ph.: 23260783, 23265523
Fax: 011 - 23272766
E-mail: manaspublications@vsnl.com

© Brigadier Kim Yadav

2004

ISBN 81-7049-140-1
Rs 495/-

No part of this book can be reproduced, stored in a retrieval system, or transmitted in any form, by any means, including mechanical, electronic, photocopying, recording, or otherwise, without prior written permission of the publisher.

The views expressed in this book are those of the author and not necessarily of the publisher. The publisher is not responsible for the views of the author and authenticity of the data, in any way whatsoever.

Typeset at
Manas Publications

Printed in India at
Nice Printing Press
and Published by Mrs Suman Lata for
Manas Publications, 4858, Prahlad Street,
24, Ansari Road, Darya Ganj,
New Delhi - 110002 (INDIA)

To

Ann

My wife for 52 years who witnessed many of the events in history with me and without whose support, love and inspiration I would not have survived to write this book

and

Arun

Our son, a Colonel in the Army when he died, whose life of dedication to his profession and his Country gave me a reason to write this book.

Gratitude

My gratitude to

- Our daughter, Maya Lydia, my indispensable fortitude and companion through terrible family bereavements; and for her love, support and unyielding ardour to get this book published early
- Our Grandchildren, Nisha, Karen and Sasha for their enthusiasm for the stories in the book.
- Admiral of the Fleet the Earl Mountbatten of Burma, KG, for accepting me as a Liaison Officer in 1943 and subsequently; and in particular, for asking me to be his ADC when he was appointed as the Last Viceroy of India in 1947, which provided me with all the grit I needed for writing this book. Also for his recommendation to Prime Minister Indira Gandhi and a letter to the Chief of the Indian Army to recall me from retirement to command troops for the liberation of Bangladesh in 1971.

- General Sir Montagu Stopford, GCB, for selecting me as his only ADC through 1945-1946, during his High Military Command Assignments and Diplomatic Missions in Burma, Indonesia and South East Asia and for pampering me as an adopted son and a friend.

- The Countess Mountbatten of Burma, GCVO, who was my role model of a truly Great Person with compassion and concern for the sick, the handicapped and the deprived and who was a friend in need in my complex and irrational personal life.

- Sir Winston Churchill, JFC Fuller, BM Kaul, SL Menezes, Ram Gopal, Rudyard Kipling, Arthur Swinson, Tara Chand, Sardar Khushwant Singh, Pundit Jawaharlal Nehru, Ishwari Prasad, RB Deeds, Penderel Moon, Rico Holmes and others from whose books, essays and diaries I have quoted or gained knowledge for writing this book, and Karen Wennerstorm for help in compilation of data on my life.

Synopsis

There is no historical evidence to suggest that anyone on the Indian Subcontinent had any notion of democratic freedom for India before the British Raj. The Moguls certainly did not believe in any kind of democracy and, perhaps, it was fortunate that their imperious rule provoked anti-Mogul movements led by the Mahrattas and the Sikhs to preserve indigenous faiths and culture. These movements had the trappings of nationalism, but were severely limited by regionalism and inadequate resources to overwhelm numerous small and large kingdoms in an India, which was hopelessly divided on religious, ethnic and regional basis. These acute differences could only be bridged by a powerful 'third party' from Christian Europe, who would have to conquer the whole Subcontinent and consolidate it for convenience in governance to exploit its fabulous wealth. There was no other way, which could bring the diverse people together to constitute a nation state.

The British happened to come to India as the 'third party'; they were the first conquerors of India to come by sea. In due course they evolved a brilliant strategy to conquer the Subcontinent from powerful bases in the west, the south and the east – the book gives details of how this was done.

The British came to the Subcontinent not to stay, but to exploit and milk its vast resources and to create a controlled market for British manufactured products. For the first time in history a trading company, the East India Company, fielded its own Army, conquered territory and established its own administration; it became the sovereign ruler of a vast Subcontinent. To consolidate and integrate its huge Empire, the East India Company found that common laws and procedures, common civil, judicial and police services were imperative for convenience in administration and maintenance of law and order. How this was done is explained in the book.

As security of the Empire, both internal and external, was paramount, especially to counter the real and perceived threats from France and Russia, the British were constrained to raise and train the Indian Army, with soldiers from all regions of the Subcontinent, to engage in battle against the most modern European troops. The Indian Army thus became the true representative of all the Indian people – and the instrumentality through which the British ruled India and defended their vast overseas possessions. Little did the British realize at the time that in doing so they had, for the first time in history, laid the foundation of an Indian Nation State and that the Indian Army they had created would one day defy them and seek independence. The role of the Indian Army in impelling the British to concede independence is the main theme of the book

The Indian Army was recruited from defeated armies of Indian rulers, or from all British regions of rural India. The soldiers from defeated armies, however, created serious loyalty problems, as they regarded themselves as Soldiers of Fortune. So long as the service conditions were favourable, the Soldiers of Fortune remained loyal, but when the British deviated from the 'contract', the Soldiers revolted. The recruits from the rural areas were usually from zamindar (or land-owning) families who were conscious and proud of their heritage, religion and status; if the British intentionally or inadvertently offended the soldier on these issues, he revolted. The great Indian Sepoy Mutiny of 1857, the harbinger of eventual freedom to the Subcontinent, and numerous other mutinies, which eventually made Britain to quit India, have been examined in the book on the basis of these characteristics of the Indian Soldier.

The inhabitants of the Indian Subcontinent were (and are) largely farmers or agricultural people who lived in remote villages across India. Till after Independence in 1947, these village folk, mostly illiterate, were not easily accessed or addressed, as communications were poor. The only influential link these village folk had with the outside world was the soldier of the Indian Army who travelled widely not only in India but abroad to garrison British possessions, or to fight in wars against enemies of the United Kingdom. Through contacts with his British Officers, who were by and large liberal and democratic, and from the experience gained in overseas assignments, the soldier had a clear vision in his mind of the import of political freedom. He shared these visions and thoughts with his colleagues from all parts of India and, when he went back to his village, with the folk there. These links of the soldier were the first warps and wefts of the vast lattice of Indian unity and integrity, which took shape during the British Raj. The soldier's vision of freedom also laid the foundation of Indian Nationalism. He revolted whenever British hauteur and racial discrimination hurt his pride. In fact, if the British progressively conceded self-governing institutions to their Indian Empire, it was to placate the Indian Soldier as they could not stay on without his support – nor could the British fight their wars without the manpower of India and the renowned valour of its soldiers. The political concessions conceded by Britain to the self-governing institutions in India from time to time were dependent on the need to deploy the Indian Army to contain the threat implicit in international situations. This aspect is discussed in the book.

Britain was compelled to replace the horrendous casualties in the First World War by Indian Soldiers. But as sufficient volunteers were not willing to join the Army, the British resorted to the 'carrot-and-stick' mode and in August 1917 promised, through the Montagu Declaration, that their aim was 'progressive realization of responsible government in India'. In the event, when volunteers were not forthcoming, despite the Montagu Declaration, the Government in India had to resort to very coercive and oppressive methods to enlist Soldiers for the War. The consequences that followed from these inordinately savage methods are discussed in detail in the book

The general impression conveyed by historians that freedom came to India through a political struggle, or that independence was conceded by Britain because a few political leaders of one or two parties could make enough noise to intimidate the British, is seriously challenged in the book.

The Congress, was founded by Allan Octavian Hume, a Scot in the service of East India Company, founded the first organized political party, the Congress. Hume had been a district officer during the 1857 Sepoy Mutiny. He was thoroughly acquainted with the rampant poverty and consequent disaffection among the people in Bihar and elsewhere. He was convinced that if the discontent among the people could be consolidated and exploited by rabble-rousers and politicized, a revolution was possible in some parts of India. He had seen the terrible mayhem and savagery of the Sepoy Mutiny in 1857 and he was determined to create an organization, a sort of National Parliament, where Indians could learn to think 'constitutionally' to avoid revolutions or mutinies. Those Indians who attended the first meeting of Hume's Indian National Congress at Bombay on December 25, 1885, were only those who were 'well acquainted with the English language' and were listed as politicians, a status the British respected but did not fear till much later, as, at the time, these politicians were as far removed from the people of India as the Moon is from the Earth. So, till the Montagu Declaration in 1917, Hume's party was just a talking shop which gave the 'politicians' an opportunity to blowhard on their knowledge of the English language and eloquently air the political mumbo-jumbo from here and there which was in vogue at the time. Nobody had a clear vision of how to seek independence from the British, or how Indians could administer and defend a country so vast and diverse as the Subcontinent.

After the Montagu Declaration in 1917, the intelligent politicians realized that if Britain's need for the Indian Soldier persisted it was just possible that out of sheer compulsion the British may concede 'responsible government in India'. Those who knew Britain and her democratic traditions realized that if Britain were to hand over power to Indian hands, it would be to the politicians and not the Army. So now there was an opportunity to convert Hume's talking shop into a viable political movement without resorting to violence – and let the Soldier carry on in his firm resolve to oppose British racial discrimination and oppression with mutinies and violence. The book elaborates on these aspects.

The British Indian Government's highhandedness in forcible recruitment of young Indians as cannon fodder and in pressing all Indians to contribute financially for the First World War evoked widespread disaffection and even violence especially in Punjab. A Special Commission under Justice Rowlatt, sent from England, recommended additional powers to the Indian Government to deal with lawlessness and terrorism after the expiry of the Defence of India Act six months after the War. The recommendations were transformed into the oppressive Rowlatt Acts in 1919. Mahatma Gandhi, an outstanding leader of Hume's Indian National Congress, who had been loyal to the Government and involved in encouraging recruitment for the War, at once saw the opportunity to bring his party into active politics by opposing the infamous Rowlatt Acts thorough non-violent methods. This was the beginning of his legendary non-violent methods to gain political freedom.

But Gandhiji's non-violent methods did not pacify the on-going violence and lawlessness. In any case, the Government had already resorted to terrible acts of repression and punishment to contain the increasing acts of violence. The people were subjected to insults and humiliation, widespread arrests were made and mobs were slaughtered ruthlessly. This was the background of the tragedy at Jallianwala Bagh in Amritsar on 13 April, 1919, where a large peaceful crowd, presumably pilgrims who had come from outside celebrate the great festival of Baisakhi, had gathered there as in previous years. Brigadier General Reginald Dyer entered the Bagh through its only gate with two armoured cars and ninety soldiers and opened fire on a peaceful, unarmed and unsuspecting crowd without let or hindrance for ten minutes. Over 2000 innocent people were slaughtered. The book gives details of the tragedy.

Britain sought to contain the disaffection and lawlessness in India by offering a carrot in the shape of the Government of India Act of 1919. The Legislative Assemblies in the provinces, to which less than 5 per cent of Indians were eligible for election, were given a few innocuous democratic powers, but the ultimate authority of the Governor-General was not touched. The new politicians now in the fray demanded independence but, of course, India was totally unprepared for independence, as 95 per cent of the people could not be addressed or easily accessed for any political dialogue and there were no infrastructures of any kind, or leadership with experience for governance of a country as large as the Subcontinent of India without European presence.

The British, always so contemptuous of non-violence, thought the movement was opportunistic and farcical and reneged on their promise made in the Montagu Declaration of 1917, but they continued to be apprehensive of another mutiny as in 1857. So they dragged their feet till the Second World War, conceding only superficial freedom to placate the Soldier whenever war-clouds were in sight on the international horizon. Everything, they said, was hunky-dory till unexpectedly the Central India Horse, a Cavalry Regiment converted to light tanks, mutinied in 1940, demanding equality in status and service conditions with the British. The Governments in London and New Delhi were appalled and frightened and although they ruthlessly executed the mutineers, they also hastily changed such rules and regulations as were discriminatory or humiliating. But these measures were not obviously up to the expectations of the Indian Soldier, as there was another mutiny in Cochin Coast Artillery where the Bengali Gunners demanded the same pay and perks as their British counterparts in the Regiment in 1941. Soon thereafter the Indian National Army was raised under Mohan Singh in Feb/Mar 1942 in Singapore, from POWs as they were outraged by the British Commander's racist remarks; it was the largest mutiny since 1857 and it completely unhinged any British design to perpetuate their rule in India. For the first time in history, independence for India appeared in sight though a little blurred and distant. The Author's personal experiences at the time are related in detail in the book.

The War map was dismal and bleak in 1942. There in Europe the British were forced to flee from France through Dunkirk to the safety of their island home. France lay prostrate and bleeding. The German Panzer Forces and the Luftwaffe just streaked through East Europe and the Balkan States and then into Russia. In a surprise attack the Japanese destroyed a major portion of the US Pacific Fleet on the 7th December, 1941, and occupied most of South East Asia within three months. The only sunny side, and which sparkled, was in Africa and the Middle East, where thousands of redoubtable Indian Soldiers blocked the Axis blitzkrieg; and when they were unleashed they smashed the Italian Armies and rushed to Egypt to blunt German General Rommel's streak eastwards through the north African coastal desert. And when Japan treacherously joined the Axis powers only India had the manpower and the formidable Indian Soldier to stall the Japanese Juggernaut from overrunning most of Asia. It was obvious that if the War had to be won by the Allies without further losses, the participation of the Indian Soldier was imperative. This could only be ensured by a promise of independence to India on the successful conclusion of the War. The book elaborates on the uncertainties of the War situation.

Sir Stafford Cripps was sent to India in March 1942, to offer partial freedom straightaway with the promise that after the War Indians could frame their own constitution. But the politicians demanded total independence and rejected the offer. There were also serious differences between Congress and Muslim leadership, which could not be bridged. The British were quick at evaluating the political situation as very superficial and Cripps returned to England in April without any commitments on independence to India. The rejection of Cripps' offer by some prominent Indian leaders was one of the great political blunders of the Twentieth Century, as its acceptance may well have saved a partition of the British Indian Empire into India and Pakistan in 1947.

To redeem the political blunder in rejecting Cripps 'offer' the Congress passed a resolution on 8th August. 1942, in Bombay calling upon the British to quit India. Ram Gopal writes in '*How India Struggled for Freedom*', "There was no hope of settlement left, and he (Gandhiji) asked Britain to 'leave India to God and if that be too much, leave her to anarchy'. But he advised the people not to 'lean on the Japanese to get rid of the British power'." As a consequence, in Eastern United Provinces and Bihar over 250 small railway stations were torched and 500 Post Offices were attacked by angry mobs; some railway track, rolling stock, and engines were wrecked; but the vast majority of the Indian people did not participate in the 'Quit India' movement. The British response to the 'Quit India' movement was, however, immediate and brutal. All the top Congress leaders were arrested and imprisoned and all protests and demonstrations against the Government were crushed ruthlessly.

It must be noted, however, that the 'Quit India' movement had no impact on recruitment or the outstanding performance of the Indian Armed Forces in the execution of the War against the Axis powers. There were endless queues of volunteers from rural India to fight for the survival of freedom and democracy in the world. In fact, more than 90 per cent of the troops deployed against the Japanese were Indian. There were substantial Indian Forces engaged in the War against Germany and Italy in the Mediterranean. India had made a very valuable contribution for the survival of freedom and democracy in the First World War (1914 – 18) – and did it again in the Second World War (1939 – 45). Sadly this vital role played by India in the two World Wars of the Twentieth

Century has not received the encomium it deserves in history. The Author explains why Japan lost the War in Burma before the Atom bombs were dropped on Hiroshima and Nagasaki in August 1945.

After Germany and Japan had surrendered, the Indian Troops continued to be deployed in the Middle East and the whole of South East Asia, i.e., Burma, Malaya, Thailand, the French Indo China, the Dutch East Indies, Singapore and Hong Kong as the British Troops were anxious to join their families in the United Kingdom and did not consider a war outside Europe as of their concern any more—some even mutinied to urge the Government to respond. Without European Troops Britain could not retain its Indian Empire–in any case, Britain had a promise to fulfill to give freedom to its subjects in the Indian Subcontinent.

Lord Wavell was the Viceroy of India when the Second World War ended. He was resolute in his pride in British achievements in India and therefore loathed the idea that the unity and integrity of the Indian Empire, an historic British accomplishment, would have to be split on communal basis before power could be transferred to Indian hands. But his mentors in Britain, with greater political acumen, could see clearly that, after Mr. Jinnah's call in August 1946 for Direct Action, the conflagration of communal riots threatened to engulf the whole Subcontinent. There was thus urgency in conceding independence to the Indian Empire, as the Indian Soldier had already expressed his desire for freedom through numerous mutinies. The fear that the communal virus may afflict the soldier was real, as also the apprehension that in the absence of sufficient European Troops a large scale mutiny, such as the one in 1857, could not be contained. Britain had to leave India before mutinies and anarchy intervened. The Author's personal experiences at the time are recounted in the book.

Synopsis

So pressing were the political exigencies in the Indian Subcontinent that Lord Wavell had to be replaced by a younger and more receptive Viceroy. Lord Mountbatten, who had extensive experience of dealing with situations in South East Asia as the Supreme Allied Commander during the Second World War, was appointed to replace Wavell. As the last Viceroy of India, Lord Mountbatten was given a clear brief that power had to be transferred to Indian hands by June 1948. But why were two new countries, India and Pakistan, carved out of the British Indian Empire and why was it done on 15 August 1947? Kim Yadav, the Author of this book, then serving with 1 Royal Garhwal Rifles at Peshawar, was appointed ADC to Lord Mountbatten when he took over as the last Viceroy. The story of Indian Independence in the book is recounted from his personal experiences and from his perception of the events leading up to 15th August, 1947–and he answers why India and Pakistan had to be created from the British Indian Empire.

Did we ape the British in our life-style before the War and what were the imperial discriminations that humiliated us? What was the social life like in Indonesia and Malaysia after the War? How were the Indian Officers and Soldiers treated by the British during the Raj and in particular during the War? Kim Yadav answers these questions in the book

Kim Yadav recounts : "But really speaking all ADCs had a wonderful time at the Viceroy's House. There were horses to ride and hounds to take out for fox-hunts with Champagne breakfast and the prettiest girls in town as our guests. Facilities for almost all games were on a lavish scale. During summer we would have huge slabs of ice floating in the swimming pool and we would try to balance our cocktail glasses on them—and then serve ourselves a delightful buffet lunch— better than any restaurant or hotel could produce. Just floating around in the cool water with a girl friend was great fun that would have made the richest tycoons round the world green with envy. The finest wine, liquor and liqueurs were on the house and the ADC bar was perhaps as well stocked as best in the world. The cigars and cigarettes were of the finest quality and all on the house, and if we wanted to buy any they were at custom-free prices which were ridiculously low. There were the Mughal Gardens with finely manicured lawns and trees and splendour of roses that filled the air with fragrance that inspired love and romance, which, was perhaps denied to Mughal Emperors Babar and Aurangzeb, but not to us. It was there, in the fairyland of the Mughal Gardens, resplendent in the pale silvery light of a September full moon, like an exquisite painting in soft water-colours, that I proposed to my wife Ann. When she said yes we danced round the roses and saw them nod their beautiful heads in approval and open their petals in smile to share our joy. That painting, etched forever in our minds, was the most beautiful memory of our stay in the Viceroy's House and my wife Ann and I shared it lovingly for the rest our lives."

Were the Mountbattens a happy and loving couple? Is there any truth in the gossip on Lady Mountbatten (regarded by the Author as one of the truly great persons he ever met) and Pundit Nehru?

What were the celebrations like on 15 August, 1947 in New Delhi? Kim Yadav recalls, "Obviously it was just not possible or wise for Lord Mountbatten to attempt to get out of the Carriage, walk to the dais and unfurl the Tricolour. So he said to me, 'Come on, Kim, you are young - go and unfurl the Flag for me.' I stepped out of the Carriage and from that moment I was literally tossed and flung by the crowd to the Flagpole. I managed to grab the halyard and pull it to unfurl the second Tricolour on that day—and made history! I doubt if an ADC had ever been ordered to carry out such an onerous and historical mission. The Guns boomed to proclaim the new Flag of Freedom as I stood to attention and proudly saluted our new ensign of Independence—and cried unashamedly with a rare thrill and joy in my heart. On that first auspicious day of liberty whoever thought that there would be a supernal design to create a situation where a Soldier, a representative of the Army that ushered in freedom, would be favoured to unfurl the National Flag near India Gate, the splendid memorial to brave Indian Warriors who sacrificed themselves to save democracy in the First World War (1914 - 1918)! That moment of ecstasy inspired all the thoughts for this book. I knew I was born lucky but I could not even dream that my lucky stars would hurl me to those lofty heights."

Did Pundit Nehru and Sardar Patel get on well together? How well was the Army doing in J&K against Pakistan before the cease-fire was imposed? Kim Yadav answers these questions.

The Army had literally to be reorganized as the Muslim elements had to go to Pakistan and the Hindu-Sikh Soldiers there were to come to India. The process of reorganization had hardly begun when the call came to send troops to fight the invaders in J&K. The troops had no equipment or clothing to wage war in very difficult mountain terrain under snow conditions. But their morale as Soldiers of Free India was so high that they wanted to achieve the impossible on a shoestring and prayer and did overwhelm the enemy entrenched in very difficult mountain terrain. The Author commanded a column in a unique operation over the Umasila (pass) 17,400 feet high under heavy snow conditions and smashed the enemy troops on the other side. Read the story of how the much-revered deity in the mountains, Chandi Devi, was invoked and contributed to the remarkable success of this unique and apparently impossible operation.

The Author recounts his personal experiences from the time he was in Woodstock School before the Second World War till the cease-fire in J&K December 1948 in his chapter on Reminiscences.

Contents

	Gratitude	7
	Synopsis	9
1.	Part I	25
2.	Part II	65
3.	Part III	121
	Index	227

Part I

On August 15, 1947 Great Britain decided to wind up her Indian Empire. Nearly two centuries earlier, Major Hector Monro of East India Company had, in a decisive battle at Buxar in 1764, defeated Prince Mir Kassim of Bengal and the Nawab of Oudh. The reluctant Mughal Emperor, Shah Alam, who had supported the Nawab, was taken prisoner. The British occupied and ransacked the great Indian Kingdom of Oudh. Thus the decisive victory at Buxar confirmed the prestige and might of British arms throughout the Indian Subcontinent. A solid foundation for building the British Indian Empire was now firmly laid and in due course India became a Jewel in the British Crown.

The reason why India became a Jewel in the British Crown was because India could provide the finest soldiers in the world to fight and win wars for Britain round the globe. Notwithstanding the American might and help in the latter part of the two World Wars of the Twentieth Century, it would have been well nigh impossible for Britain to survive the mighty onslaught of her enemies in the initial stages of these wars without the tenacity and legendary valour of the Indian Soldier. But the British took the fidelity of the Indian Soldier for granted till the mutiny in Central India Horse in 1940 and the Cost Artillery in Cochin in 1941; till, in the greatest revolt since 1857, the Indian Prisoners of War captured by the Japanese raised the Indian National Army in Singapore under

Captain Mohan Singh in Feb 1942 to fight the British as a protest against the humiliation heaped on them by the British racist Theatre Commander and the fact that they had suffered a terrible defeat and many casualties because the British, in their imperial arrogance, had planned the defences in South East Asia on the premise that no non-European power could match the invincibility of the Royal Navy and that no army could penetrate the jungles in Malaya and attack Singapore from the north. In 1945, the Royal Indian Navy and the Royal Indian Air Force also mutinied against racial discriminations just to confirm that they felt the same way as the Army. Thus it became abundantly clear to the British that the Sepoy was no longer willing to tolerate their imperial hauteur or racial discriminations and that colonial indignities in status and lack of political freedom were just not acceptable in any guise to the Indian Soldier who had helped the British in dominating the World for over a century. As Britain, shattered in economy and manpower, could not deploy large armies of European Troops to repress the defiant Indian Soldier and tame the increasing political unrest, there was no option but to quit. The only questions that remained were: How? and When?

Sir Stafford Cripps had offered substantial autonomy to India in 1942, but with subtle clauses, which cleverly preserved British paramountcy over the Subcontinent. Lord Wavell, the second last Viceroy, who was keen to go all the way to independence, was not willing to surrender to Mr. Jinnah's machinations. But the impasse had to be resolved and resolved quickly if India was to be saved from the terrible communal holocaust, which was inflicted on the simple Indian people through Mr. Jinnah's decree to the gullible and the bigots for Direct Action in Aug 1946. Thus a British Prince of Royal blood, later a Five Star Admiral and Chief of the British Defence Staff, who had been a Supreme Allied Commander in the Second World War, was commissioned as the last Viceroy to hand over power to such politicians as came forward to receive it.

There was, of course, no question of handing over power to the Army. Such an act was unethical to the British democratic psyche and imperial ego, although it was the Indian Soldier who had made unimaginable sacrifices, on low pay and despite racial indignities, to defend the British Empire in India and elsewhere. Indeed the Indian Soldier was the guardian angel of Western Democracies during the two Great World Wars in the Twentieth Century, but he was denied the encomium he so richly deserved for his legendary valour and unmatched fortitude in battle against the enemies of Great Britain and her Allies, as he was only a subject of the British Indian Empire and not a free citizen.

For over a hundred years, the British and the French had wooed India and fought each other with all the venom of colonial suitors, but after Buxar, Britain's brilliant three-prong strategy to conquer the Subcontinent prevailed. Some of the world's greatest administrators, Clive, Hastings, Hardinge, Dalhousie, Canning, Lytton, Minto, Curzon, Irwin, Wavell, Mountbatten and others were selected and appointed Governor Generals or Viceroys of Imperial India. They pursued the British policies with remarkable acumen and vigour though not always with commendable impartiality, honesty or tact. They conquered, integrated and organized congeries of innumerable Indian kingdoms, who were always fighting each other endlessly, into provinces and native states. Land reforms, a common penal code, criminal and civil law were evolved from Britain's legacy as a Roman colony, but without impinging on Hindu or Muslim susceptibilities. The evil practices of 'thugee' and 'sati' were suppressed and forbidden. Universities were established to impart modern education and efficient government hospitals were opened in all districts. Newspapers were freed from censorship and telegraph and a cheap postal system were introduced. An extensive construction of roads and railways was undertaken. To obviate famine, extensive irrigation projects were launched and wells and canals were constructed in the Ganges and the Yamuna Valleys and in the Punjab and other provinces, while a vast network of tanks harvested rainwater for irrigation in the South.

The weakest link on the Indian Subcontinent had been the lack of unified and homogenous system of defence, civil administration and the police. To the everlasting credit of the British they structured the Indian Army, the Indian Civil Service and the Indian Police as the finest instruments of governance ever contrived by man. These pillars of security, administration and law and order sustained and consolidated India through some difficult and lean years after Independence.

Although the young British Officers would brag and say that they took pleasure in training Indians in the same way as one would a monkey, the fact remains that skills acquired by Indians under their guidance were par excellence. It must be noted that by 1947, the Post and Telegraph Services, the Railways, the Customs, the Indian Civil Service and indeed the Indian Army, which had fought and saved Western Democracies in two global wars, were rated among the finest in the world. No wonder that in 1946, Field Marshal Lord Wavell, the Viceroy, was opposed to splitting the British Indian Empire. He felt strongly that the vast Subcontinent with its diverse ethnic, cultural, linguistic and religious population, which had been diligently and fearlessly pieced together like a jigsaw puzzle, for the first time, must never be cleaved so that the avowed and unique British achievements could endure for ever. Indeed the British Indian Empire was a glorious realization of British military prowess, administrative skills, wisdom, an incomparable sense of duty to serve the King and Country and dreams. Wavell did not want these dreams consigned to oblivion!

The British Officers used to boast that their Indian Empire was a cut above the great Roman Empire of which Britain herself had been a colony. In fact, most British Officers of the Army were averse to any division of the Indian Empire in

1947, as that would also break up the Regiments in which they had served with enormous pride, camaraderie and professionalism.

But the Viscount Mountbatten of Burma, the last Viceroy, had no option, as he was constrained by uncompromising circumstances to split the British Indian Empire and create two new independent countries—India and Pakistan. This unfortunate partition became necessary as the available leaders were unable to convince the Muslim leaders that the Hindus and the Muslims did not (and DO NOT) constitute two separate nations. There was urgency in the transfer of power as the instrumentality through which Britain ruled India, the Indian Army, wanted freedom at one jump, which had been amply demonstrated in the numerous mutinies during the War. After his decisive contribution to victory in the Second World War, the Indian soldier was justifiably impatient to realize his dream of independence.

Notwithstanding British colonial postures in India, there is no doubt that they were 'democrats' at heart. The British Officers, perhaps the finest leaders of colonial troops in history, thought it was their prerogative to get acquainted with their Indian soldiers 'better than their mothers'. Consequently the Indian soldier also became familiar with the 'thinking' of his British Commanders and wanted to be as 'politically' free as his Officers. To meet this aspiration of the Indian soldiers, the British had embarked on a series of constitutional reforms the like of which the Subcontinent had not seen under any foreign ruler before. During the First World War, when the need for Indian soldiers in great numbers was imperative to protect and defend the British Empire in Asia and Africa, or to conquer enemy territory in Africa, west Asia or Europe, as Britain and European Commonwealth Countries lacked the necessary manpower, the British Secretary of State for India, Edwin Montagu, declared in August 1917, that the policy of the British Government was "the increasing association of Indians in every branch of the administration and also the granting of self-governing institutions with a view to progressive realization of responsible government in India..." Although this Declaration did not entirely overcome the problems of recruitment, especially in the Punjab, where coercion continued to be used till the War was over, Indians educated in British institutions, however, sensed at once the opportunity to have a political organization in being to participate in any 'responsible' government that Britain may decide to concede after the War. Thus came into being 'political' leaders who declared that their demand was complete independence for India although 99 per cent of Indians living in the rural areas, which were difficult to access, except through the ex-servicemen, had not the vaguest notion as to what 'independence' meant. There is substantial evidence that India had numerous and beneficial religious movements, but there is nothing on record to suggest that India ever had a political movement to demand any federation of or freedom for the Subcontinent.

It is to be noted that self-governing institutions were conceded by Britain to meet the aspirations of the Indian Soldiers who were required in increasing numbers to garrison the vast British Empire and to fight Britain's wars in China and elsewhere. Apart from the Sepoy Mutiny of 1857, there was no political movement in India to press for Indian Independence till the Montagu Declaration of 1917, which was intended to attract recruits for the savage War in Europe. In fact, the Declaration 'kick-started' an organized political movement in the British Indian Empire for the first time. There is, therefore, no substance in the exaggerated claim that freedom came to India exclusively through the so-called non-violent revolution, or that any political party had such a sway over the people of India that the British were forced to quit. It should also be noted that almost half of India was 'native' states or tribal reserves where loyalties were limited to their own rulers or state and any concept of a free united Subcontinent could not even be dreamed of.

Of course, it is true that from time to time some intellectuals who were offended by British arrogance and indignities demanded freedom as a birthright. But it must be noted, however, that such demands gained momentum and credence only after the Montagu Declaration of 1917, which was a constraint to attract more recruits and donations in India for British victory against the Germans and their allies in World War I. But there was no political revolution in the same sense as the American War of Independence of 1776, or the French Revolution of 1789. This is the basic reason why today, 55 years after Independence, voting patterns for election to Parliament and Assemblies are based on caste, community, religion and regional basis. In fact there are more 'disgruntled' leaders actually waging war or fighting political battles against the Establishment than during the British Raj. The Kashmir issue is a hangover of this reality. As a subcontinent, India had never been a single compact political or religious entity. India was really a hotchpotch of invaders, migrants, tribes and indigenous peoples, who were hopelessly divided on ethnic, racial and religious grounds. As far as history has been able to reach and investigate, only differences in persuasion, allegiance and disunity have been confirmed – there is no evidence to suggest that there was ever a political movement to unite and consolidate the Subcontinent for democracy. Unfortunately through most of its history the Subcontinent was a random collection of small states as India was subjected to innumerable invasions through the Hindukush Mountains by Aryans, Turks, Greeks, Persians, Afghans, Mongols and, later, by Europeans who came by sea.

Muslim influence was established in Northern India only after Qutab-ud-din Aibak was declared the Sultan of Delhi in 1206. This had a profound effect on the people who sought to take refuge in remote and often inaccessible villages to escape the horrors of alien conquest and forced conversions. Thus came into being the self-contained 'independent village republics' whose social and political structures were based on the vocational pursuit of the people or the much maligned 'caste system'. Of course, the Muslim rulers sought to bring unity and harmony in the states they ruled on the Subcontinent through conversion to Islam, but this irreconcilably antagonized the people of indigenous faiths. So, India was in turmoil when the British came. It is to their everlasting credit that they managed to consolidate a fissiparous people into well-organized provinces and states under common laws, administrative procedures and powerful defence and security systems, as explained earlier, which endure to this day. What is not generally known is that India today would be congeries of Islamic Republics like Pakistan, Bangladesh, Malaysia and Indonesia had the British not conquered India in the nick of time to save those who today constitute a majority in the secular Republic of India.

Great Britain had to quit India as in a competitive World it was not economically viable to garrison and defend far-flung empires of alien peoples who had acquired hi-tech resources and enlightened military leadership to fight for their independence. Moreover, at the outset of the Second World War both the President of the United States and the Prime Minister of the United Kingdom had declared in the Atlantic Charter of August 12, 1941, Para 3, that 'they respect the right of all peoples to choose the form of government under which they will live; and they wish to see sovereign rights and self-government restored to those who have been forcibly deprived of them.' India, of course, had no self-government when the British came. Nevertheless, the Atlantic Charter was an international and moral commitment on which Britain could not renege.

But events in India were moving to an unhappy conclusion. The Viceroy, Lord Wavell, had proposed to convert his

Executive Council into an Interim Government in July 1946. He had hoped that the Interim Government would comprise well-known Indian political figures selected by all parties to replace serving members nominated by the Viceroy. Mr. Jinnah did not accept the proportional representation offered to the Muslims by the Viceroy and announced that a 'Direct Action' day would be observed on 16 Aug 1946, to protest. Members of the Muslim League interpreted this as a signal to attack the Hindus. The conflagration started in Calcutta, but soon spread to all parts of the Subcontinent. The holocaust later blazed through independence celebrations and claimed over two million lives – probably two or three times as many, as no census was ever undertaken to determine the exact number. And all this terrible and avoidable carnage took place only because Mr. Jinnah wanted to show that Hindus and Muslim were two separate nations that could not live together because the Hindus worshipped the cow and he ate it!

Lord Wavell, an outstanding General, was appointed Viceroy in 1943, to help with the war effort. He had a very high sense of duty and loyalty and he read poetry to sustain his patriotism and pride in the historical greatness of Britain and her culture and arms. He saw India as a wonderful creation of those brave British men and women who had perished six thousand miles away from their home, so that the British Indian Empire might live in all its splendour. He could hand over power to a united India, if the politicians agreed among themselves, and then make a neat withdrawal to Britain like a military operation without denting British pride and honour in handing over freedom to the Jewel in the British Crown. He was too old (64) to mellow to Hindu-Muslim rivalries, or the rhetoric of Direct Action, Quit India or the Two Nation Theory – it did not fit into his format of a military appreciation. The Prime Minister of Britain, Clement Atlee, was shrewd enough to see that the Old Warrior Field Marshal Wavell had these inhibitions in transferring power to Indian politicians by

June 1948. So Wavell had to be replaced by a brilliant young man, preferably a Soldier who should have had experience of handling situations in Asia. Rear Admiral the Viscount Mountbatten of Burma, who had been the Supreme Allied Commander of South East Asia during the Second World War, and who had voluntarily stepped down two notches in rank to command a Squadron of Destroyers in the British Royal Navy, was the obvious choice. The British King gave his assent. Lord Louis Mountbatten took charge as the last Viceroy of India on 22 March 1947.

Clement Atlee, the Labour Prime Minister of Britain, had already committed himself to Indian Independence by 1 June 1948. It was now Mountbatten's historic assignment to hand over power to Indian or Pakistani politicians by that date. After a tour of the North West Frontier on 21/22 June, 1947, (on advice of the Author who had seen the carnage there before he joined the Viceroy as ADC. Of course, he accompanied the Viceroy on the tour), Lord Mountbatten found that the British writ had ceased to matter with the Muslim or Hindu/Sikh Soldiers there. The British General Officer Commanding in Chief of North West India, General Sir Frank Messervy, told the Viceroy at Rawalpindi that Indian Soldiers were unwilling or reluctant to fire on rioters of their own community and that 'the sooner we get out of India to avoid another 1857, the better'. (When asked the Author told the Viceroy and Messervy that a civil war was possible if immediate steps were not taken for an early political solution, as there was tension even between Hindu and Muslim Army Officers.) Messervy's assessment was particularly relevant as most of the British troops normally stationed in India for a contingency such as the 1857 Mutiny, were clamoring for repatriation to England to start a new life after demobilization; they were war-weary and homesick and they longed for a 'White Christmas' with their families. In fact, the RAF had mutinied in north India and British Paratroopers in South

Malaya early in 1946 to press their demand 'for early return to Blighty'. Only the Indian troops continued to remain on 'imperial duty' overseas even after Indian independence!

In India the only viable political party that could handle the proposed transfer of power was the Indian National Congress. The birth of the Indian National Congress was conceived by Allen Octavian Hume, a Scot in the service of East India Company as the Chief Civil Officer in charge of Etawah district during the 1857 revolt by Indian Soldiers of the Bengal Army of East India Company. When Hume constituted the Indian National Congress in December 1885, it was in the hope that it would be a sop to the growing possibility of a revolt greater in magnitude than the one in 1857. The Congress was intended as 'a kind of unofficial Parliament' and in the utterances of its founders there was no suggestion of opposition to British rule, and sentiments of loyalty were expressed. In fact, Hume's aim was to 'create a constitutional way of political thinking', as, apparently, the discontent among the Indian Soldiers had spread to the people – obviously through the Soldiers who had been recruited from all parts of India.

In analyzing any movement for 'freedom' it must be clearly understood that in the entire history of the Subcontinent there had never been any 'politics' or 'political' movement as understood today; nor was such a movement possible, as the Subcontinent was hopelessly divided into small kingdoms where rulers often changed without the immediate knowledge of the subjects who lived in villages which were difficult to access. In fact, most villages were self-contained 'republics' with their modus operandi based on rituals and caste. Even today the vast majority of Indian people cannot comprehend the political mumbo jumbo flung at them by clever politicians, who have eventually to rely on communal, caste, regional or financial manipulations and temptations to win an election. During the British Raj, more particularly during the days of the East India Company (which, incidentally, had the prefix 'Honourable' to inspire awe among the 'natives') the commonality in thinking on any kind of 'freedom' first took shape in the minds of the soldier who came together in the Army from the remotest parts of the Subcontinent. Harsh and often savage British dictums imposed by haughty, authoritarian and racist European Officers of those days, who seldom paused to understand Indian customs and traditions, antagonized the Muslim Soldiers as much as the Hindus, thus forcing a union among them to face the British as a 'common' enemy. Of course, the European Officers were encouraged in their contemptuous behaviour by the terrible communalism, casteism and regionalism and manifest disunity among the Indian people.

As the Congress was conceived as a 'talking shop', its membership was confined largely to intellectuals most of whom were Indian elite educated in British institutions. The lines of communications beyond cities were non-existent in those days. The elite and largely urban members of the Congress were, therefore, constrained in the choice of crowds, as it was difficult to address those outside the city areas. Unless there was manifest discontent among the people for a particular reason, which could be exploited for 'political' gain, or more often for self-aggrandizement, the response from the people was generally inconsequential, as the people had no background of 'freedom' or political thinking and therefore did not understand its import. Some revolts, which erupted periodically, were purely local in nature and had little or no impact in other parts of the Subcontinent. There were educated individuals who protested from time to time against denial of some privilege or right, which they felt was their birthright—such protests continue even today as no democracy can deny its citizens the right of 'dissent'. Obviously, no serious note can be taken of those who have been projected as great freedom fighters only because of their personal grouse against the British Administration.

The fact remains that apart from lack of unity among the hundreds of little kingdoms in the Subcontinent the concept of freedom for India could not be determined in political or geographical terms. For this reasons there was no 'political' movement till the British were desperate to recruit Indian Soldiers to win the First World War, as severe casualties had very considerably depleted their own manpower. To attract more recruits to the Army the British made a solemn pledge in the Montagu Declaration of 1917, as stated earlier, to progressively give Dominion Status to their Indian Empire after the successful conclusion of the War. The fact that the British dragged their feet to redeem this pledge even partially suggests that they were encouraged to stay on in India as the politicians then in the field did not have a sufficiently strong country-wide clout to force the British to quit. In fact, the Congress, which was till then a talking shop, was hastily dressed up to launch a non-violent 'freedom' movement in 1919, presumably in the hope of filling the ministerial posts that would fall vacant when Britain honoured her pledge – the appetite to be a political-somebody at any cost persists to this day. But Britain could face a passive movement in its stride— the only turbulence she feared was another 1857 Mutiny. So freedom to India was delayed till the Indian Soldier could assert himself again in the Second World War and once again save Western Democracy from annihilation at the hands of the brutal totalitarian regimes. Unfortunately, after Independence, the politicians made sure that the Indian Soldier was denied all credit and encomium for saving the institutions of Democracy through unprecedented valour and sacrifice; he was reduced in status and his British awards for exceptional valour were degraded vis-à-vis the Indian decorations. The Sepoy Mutiny of 1857, was projected as the First War of Independence in which the civilian 'nationalists' (as if nationalism was a common trait) fought to evict the British from India—a fantasy without any trace in history!

Nevertheless, credit must be given to Mahatma Gandhi for converting Hume's 'talking shop' Congress into a viable political party with an agenda for freedom. There is no doubt that Gandhiji was entirely responsible for spreading the agenda of the Congress, which he had inspired. His message to the people he could access drew exemplary responses and his charisma made a lasting impact on the hearts and minds of the common people largely because Gandhiji's 'spiritual' and moral approach to a political issue were readily understood by the God-fearing Indians. Lack of communications, of course, made it difficult for him to reach the rural people, but his name and fame reached all corners of the Subcontinent by 1947, and beyond with the passage of time.

Although Hindus and Muslims had been treated as two distinct people by a majority of Muslim rulers, curiously their common antagonism towards the British brought them a little closer together in the Armed Forces than at any time previously. Apart from common antagonism, the British enforced a common Penal Code and equality under the law for all their subjects in the Indian Empire—this in itself was a uniting factor. Notwithstanding this newfound unity, the religious differences remained among the people. The Muslim League was able to exploit these differences in their demand for a separate homeland for the Muslims in 1947.

The Soldier, who was recruited by the British from the 'Martial Class', had a strong rural and peasant background. As the 'Martial Class' had a distinct status in the village vis-à-vis the lower castes, he joined the British Indian Army with a good deal of family pride and hauteur, which were his emotional engine for all mutinies during the British Raj. In fact, the Soldier was the only 'native' who, by the nature of his profession, came in very close contact with the European Officers and their habits, characteristics, idiosyncrasies, religious faith and love for freedom. Although the majority of the British were arrogant and supercilious, some of them were friendly and they did impart the values they cherished as citizens of an industrialized, civilized and progressive country to the Indian Soldiers they commanded and on whom they were almost totally dependent for the defence of their Indian and overseas Empire.

In any Army field formation, one third of the soldiers were usually British. Our soldier was therefore also able to observe the behaviour and characteristics of the British Other Ranks from very close quarters. As fighting was almost routine in those days, the first thing that came home to the Indian soldier was that he was better in endurance and fighting than the European. And yet the European was provided with greater creature comforts and status than he, as he was a 'subject'. The Indian soldier was thus able to see what it meant to be a 'ruler' and the 'ruled'. With experience he realized that the British were holding on to their Empire through 'his' valour and sacrifice for which he was not only paid poorly but also treated as an inferior. On numerous occasions he was paid the allowances due to him only after vigorous protests. The British were inclined to treat these protests as 'mutinies'. The bossism and racism irked the Indian soldier enormously and he became very sensitive to British discriminations. Whenever the British were arrogant and blustering in dealing with the soldier's personal beliefs and customs, he revolted. It was in these revolts that the soldier expressed his vision of 'freedom' i.e., unfettered freedom in the pursuit of personal beliefs and rituals and equality in status without any discrimination—what else could be the constituents of freedom but these!

When the soldier went to his remote rural home, he used his exposure to the European thinking and life-style to shape his own way of living. The deep-trench latrines, sterilized water, fly proofing, mosquito nets, smokeless 'chulas' and other health and home comforts were introduced into village life long before the urban people got to hear of them. And, of course, the soldier also communicated to his fellow villagers his understanding of liberty, fraternity and equality. As British Expeditionary Forces comprising Indian soldiers were employed overseas with increasing frequency, the soldier's understanding of political systems and freedom widened. This understanding translated itself into a wholly new sense of patriotic feeling for his origins and faith. In the minds of the Hindu soldiers, India or Bharat was worshipped as 'Bharat Mata' in the same sense as 'Dharti Mata' on which he and his forbears were born and nourished. He accepted 'Bharat Mata' as a goddess who had not only given birth to the jawans but had nurtured warriors who had no match for endurance and bravery anywhere in the World. Thus, 'Bharat Mata Ki Jai' was the Indian soldier's fierce battle cry—and the first expression of 'nationalism' as we know it today.

Sir Winston Churchill describes the Indian soldier thus in his books on The Second World War: "The unsurpassed bravery of Indian Soldiers and Officers, both Moslem and Hindu, will shine for ever in the annals of war." This was a tribute from a leader who possessed proven outstanding physical courage himself. Except for the Indian soldier, he regarded all other things Indian as inferior! He was opposed to freedom for India for a long time. He knew history and he knew that India was in a terrible shape before and after the Mughals.

Let us open our history book. Dr. Ishwari Prasad says, "India was a congeries of states at the opening of the 16th Century and likely to be easy prey of an invader who had the strength and will to attempt her conquest." Ibrahim Lodi was the Sultan of Delhi in 1517; his authority did not extend beyond Agra, the Doab, Jaunpur and a part of Bihar. There was widespread indiscipline and confusion; in fact, his uncle, Alam Khan Lodi, also claimed the throne of Delhi! The situation in other components of the Subcontinent, viz., Mewar, Vijayanagar, Khandesh, Kashmir, Orissa, Gujarat, Malwa, Bengal and Sind was not such as could promote the unity of India. Babar says in his memoirs, "The five kings who have been mentioned are great princes and are all Mussalmans and possessed of formidable armies, the rulers of vast territories. The most powerful of pagan princes, in point of territory and army, is the Raja of Vijayanagar. Another is Rana Sanga who has attained his present high eminence only in these latter times by his own valour and his sword. His original principality was Chitor.". The Hindus pursued a faith, which had been honed and profoundly reasoned over three thousand years. The faith sustained the spirituality of an agrarian people who had to battle against natural disasters and countless invasions of their land by predators. To call such people pagans was not only pretentious but also a sad display of bigotry and ignorance, which could only be justified through the power of a gun.

Notwithstanding the 'formidable armies' possessed by various rulers of a divided India, Babar, in his fifth attempt, streaked through Punjab and reached Panipat on April 12, 1526, with an army of 12,000. An alarmed Ibrahim Lodi rushed to Panipat from Delhi with an army of one lakh comprising infantry, cavalry and elephants. For a week the two armies lay facing each other. Babar had artillery, which was new to battlefields of India. With great skill and foresight, Babar used his artillery against the elephants and the cavalry of Ibrahim Lodi. Frightened by the solid balls of artillery, the elephants stampeded. In the ensuing chaos, Babar's cavalry and light infantry drove the enemy away from the battlefield like a herd of cattle. Ibrahim Lodi was killed. Babar stood triumphant at Panipat on April 21, 1526, and dreamed of an empire in India that no one could traverse on the fastest horse in a day. He was fond of wine in those days but not withstanding the celebrations of victory he hastened to Delhi to crown himself as the 'Badshah' of India.

On March 3, 1707, Aurangazeb, the last of the great Mughals died, a hundred and eighty-one years after Babar's great victory at Panipat. Aurangazeb was a religious and learned man, but there were many serious flaws in his character, which led to the disintegration of his army and administration. In a way it was fortunate as it gave rise to new powers like the Maharattas and the Sikhs who pursued martial traditions with enormous respect for the Soldier. It was here that the seed was sown for the revolt of 1857, and the eventual freedom of an India carved out of the British Indian Empire.

During the reign of the Mughals the Subcontinent of India experienced a totally new kind of invasion—an incursion into India by sea by Britain, France and Portugal, who were able to establish firm bases in various parts of India on the coasts ostensibly as 'trading posts'. Till then all the conquerors of India had come through the passes in the Hindukush Range of mountains. Consequently, most of ancient culture, buildings, history, art and traditions were totally or partially destroyed in northern India, though, fortunately, the South was not so savagely ravaged.

But the Europeans ingress was by sea as they had powerful navies. Britain had the most remarkable strategy to penetrate the hinterland from firm bases in the east, south and west. Historians have never touched upon this brilliant strategic plan. In 1608, Captain William Hawkins landed at Surat and travelled to Agra as Ambassador of the English King James I to the court of Emperor Jahangir at Agra. The Portuguese who had preceded Hawkins frustrated his efforts to obtain trading privileges in the Mughal Empire. Four years later, in 1612, Captain Thomas Best commanding four of the Company's man-o'-war defeated a stronger Portuguese fleet in the battle of Swally Roads, thus gaining ascendancy in the Subcontinent. Mughal permission soon followed for a British factory at Surat (north of Bombay). In 1615, Sir Thomas Roe obtained more privileges from Emperor Jahangir. In 1622, the Masulipatam factory came up on the Golconda Coast. A need was felt to check the French, so an island, Fort St George, with a coastal strip comprising Madras (now Chennai) was taken on lease for a settlement from an Indian prince. A trading post was set up on the Hoogly in 1640, with an eye on Bengal. When Charles II married Catherine of Braganza in 1662, Bombay came as a part of the dowry; the Port was handed over to East India Company in 1668. It took the British eighty years to consolidate their position as traders on the Subcontinent.

For the first time in 1684, the British in India took up arms against the Mughals although they had clashed with Shivaji's troops at Surat in 1664. At the time Aurangzeb was the Emperor. The powerful Mughal Army defeated the British and annexed the Hoogly settlement and the factory at Masulipatam. For some years thereafter the British presence on the Subcontinent was shaky especially as the French were anxious to strengthen their gains in India. But the British, with their vast experience in Europe of endless wars, intrigues and peace treaties, regained their position; Fort William was established on the Hoogly, which founded Calcutta, and Fort St. David was set up south of Madras in 1690, to counter French ambitions in India. After Aurangazeb's death in 1707, the Mughal Empire disintegrated rapidly and gave the Europeans the opportunity they needed to enlarge their bases. Thus came to a halt for 150 years the 'martial' movement initiated by the Maharattas and the Sikhs to rid India of foreigners.

In the wake of their advance into the hinterland, Britain, the predominant sea power in Europe, used all coercion and oppression she could muster, as had been done by the Muslim conquerors earlier, to impose her culture and faith on the conquered people of India. In examining this attitude of coercion it must be remembered that politics and religion were in tandem in Europe, in India and elsewhere for centuries. In fact, from the reign of the Roman Emperor Theodosius I (AD 379 -395) religion was used very effectively as the 'policeman' to maintain law and order through peaceful means throughout the vast Roman Empire. Europeans were converted to Christianity and the Church of Rome was established as the supreme spiritual centre in the realm. The

Hindu, Jain and Buddhist rulers in India also followed this practice, as did the Muslim rulers in various parts of the world including India. South Indian Pallava King Mahendravarman (AD 600 -630) was a Jain and persecuted followers of other religions; when he converted to Saivism he destroyed Jain temples, executed 8000 Jains and decreed that his subjects follow him. Some Muslim rulers and the Portuguese were intolerant of India's local faiths! In Britain, Henry VIII had renounced the Church of Rome and established the Church of England; the British King was head of the Church and 'Defender of the Faith'; for years members of other faiths were excluded from exercising the rights of a British citizen unless he (and much later she) was a member of the Church of England. With that background it was not unreasonable for an Englishman to expect that the same coercion could also be applied in India where people were hopelessly divided by caste and religion. The British encouraged European Christian missionaries to come to India to convert the 'heathens' and garner a rich harvest for their Faith to give the British a 'spiritual hold' over the people, which would be more peaceful and effective than a political hold through military power and intrigues. Just as the Romans expected others to do as the Romans did, the British, absolute rulers of a mighty Empire, expected their subjects to do what they wished. The British had imbibed Roman customs and tradition and they wanted Indians to do the same. In fact, the Romans had shaped religion, rule of law, language and philosophy on the British Isles. Latin was a compulsory subject in many British schools till late 1930s. The British were keen to replicate these experiences in India. So eternal was their dictum that even today, after more than 55 years of Independence, people emulate them for good life. More people speak English today -and are proud of it than at any time during the Raj. The entire basic structure of administration and jurisprudence, political norms, commerce, education, the Armed Forces, Police and the Civil Services remain the same in substance and practice as evolved by the British during the Raj.

Through close association, the Indian Soldier had realized that the Europeans had acute religious differences among themselves. Till recently the British treated the Roman Catholics shabbily and lauded the Great Reformation which became necessary as the Popes took bribes and had a large number of illegitimate children in defiance of the oath of celibacy and accumulated vast riches in total disregard of Lord Jesus Christ's celebrated exemplum that only the poor shall inherit the Kingdom of God. Martin Luther was honoured for defying the practice of 'indulgences' whereby a Catholic could seek redemption from sins by giving money or property to the Pope or the Roman Catholic Church. The Protestant British warned their Indian soldier against evil practices pursued by the Portuguese in imposing inquisition in India and elsewhere when they had slaughtered those who opposed conversion to Christianity. Thus, the Indian soldier was fully fortified and inspired to retaliate if his religious freedom was violated. And coercion or slight was all that was needed to arouse the proud Soldiery of India to revolt for freedom at Vellore 1806, Barrackpore 1824, Meerut 1857, Hyderabad 1940, and Singapore 1942.

The axiom is that history is written to please and flatter the ruler of the day. After power was transferred to Indian politicians in 1947, it was but natural that historians were hired to justify how and why the British transferred power to a certain coterie of political leaders. It was made out that these leaders carried out an intense struggle for freedom for 26 years or so and preached high politics which was totally alien to 99 per cent of Indians, and forced the British to quit India after 192 years of rule! This is not true. Pure fantasy. It took the French Revolution nearly 200 years to erupt when France was a much smaller and homogeneous country than India. The Subcontinent, vast and diverse, with exceptionally poor communications with the rural hinterland where the bulk of the Indian people lived in abject ignorance, poverty, superstition and irreconcilable social divisions could not be aroused to a political revolution in 26 years. It was physically impossible for any political leader to address and arouse a non-political people with whom communication was well nigh impossible or impracticable.

Of course, there were numerous wars in India waged against the British from time to time to gain territory or to regain lost territory; but these were not wars for the freedom for India. Such conflicts had been going on since times immemorial. There is no historical evidence to suggest that these conflicts were struggles for freedom or democracy for the Subcontinent of India.

The British had to deal with numerous wars against small kingdoms to stay in India. Of course, it was impossible for the British to bring huge armies from Europe to fight wars on the Subcontinent to gain and sustain ascendancy. The only sensible solution was to recruit from the excellent manpower available within the country to fight for the British Empire. The Afghans, the Turks and the Mughals had done the same. No ethics were involved as India was only a geographical entity and not a political or a united nation and therefore there was no violation of an individual's pride or nationalism. So long as the Indian Soldier was taken care of, the British felt they were quite secure in India. They recruited mainly from a class of Indians who had a tradition of soldiering. Some ignorant commentators say that the recruitment from the 'Martial Classes' was carried out to ensure 'loyalty'. Certainly loyalty was not a very reliable factor as the Soldiers revolted time and again to preserve their cultural beliefs and dignity, which they regarded as fundamental to their perception of freedom. In fact, no other army in the world had mutinied so often as the Indian Army during the British Raj. In any case, for whatever reasons, the so-called 'Martial Classes' were dominant in the rural Indian social structure and they extracted subservience from the weaker castes ruthlessly. Perhaps it was this sentience of pride and hauteur of the 'Martial Class' in the rural environment, which made the Indian Soldier such a skilled and dauntless warrior in battle and unquestionably a revolutionary at heart.

But the increasing number of mutinies in the Army in the first half of the Nineteenth Century alarmed the British. They felt that the only way they could placate the Indian Soldier was to create a more liberal attitude among the people, so that the soldier could feel that he was fighting for certain universally accepted values, which were also dear to the British psyche. Thus was born the institution of 'Local Self Government', which was based on concepts which existed among the tribals and few progressive kingdoms in India, e.g., during the reign of Emperor Ashoka and later the Chola Kingdom of the South. It is significant to note that whenever there was an upheaval in the Army, the British found it prudent to respond by administrative reforms for more 'self-government'. The British used the soldier in India and in their colonies elsewhere to bolster their power and wealth. As mentioned earlier, an aspect, which needs to be emphasized, is that the Indian soldier saved Democracy as an institution, as the Allies could never have won the two World Wars in the Twentieth Century without our soldier's tenacity and valour.

Perhaps Rudyard Kipling's 'The Ballad of East and West' explains why the Indian soldier, despite all the manifest differences, fared so well in battle with his British Officers:

> "Oh, East is East, and West is West, and never the twain shall meet,
> Till Earth and sky stand presently at God's great Judgement Seat;
> But there is neither East or West, Border nor Breed, nor Birth,
> When two strong men stand face to face tho' they come from the ends of the Earth!"

These verses explain why the Indian soldiers and their British Officers were such formidable companions in battle. Each had enormous respect for the other in war; there was a superb and tacit challenge between the two as to who could do better than the other in fierce battle against an enemy. But back in the barracks, the life-style and thinking of each was miles apart. Racial origins, religion, education, cultural background, traditions and status made sure that 'never the twain shall meet'.

Off parade the British Officer lived as close to his life-style in England as the local conditions would allow. A few indulgences were permitted as aberration in the tropics; for example, 'chhota hazri' or a cup of steaming hot tea served ceremoniously by a bearer or a Sepoy Orderly first thing in the morning to awaken the sahib. When down South, a few sweet bananas with the cup of tea were good for acidity. In battle an enamelled mug replaced the cup of tea. After a good thrash at the bar or in a party, a bowl of hot Mulligatawny soup, prepared like the Madrasi 'rasam', with black coffee and dry toast, was as good an antacid as Alka Saltzer or ENO's Fruit Salt. If the sahibs had a very late night and came home in the wee hours of the morning, normally after a hearty breakfast of bacon, sausages, ham, a slice of tomato and eggs and coffee, Mulligatawny soup was served at lunch with roast beef, Yorkshire Pudding, one or two green vegetables, a salad, banana fritters and fruit in season. All meals were sit-down meals in the Mess at highly polished dining tables, preferably oak, with white linen mats embroidered with the regimental crest. Cutlery of pure silver or a good silver-plate and fine China usually Royal Doulton, Chelsea, Wedgwood or Dresden adorned the exquisitely polished dining table. Indian servants who served the meals were always in impeccable uniform and turbans with regimental colours and badge.

There was, of course, the custom of toasting the Sovereign's health usually at a Regimental 'guest night' once a week in either Port or Madeira; some Regiments raised a loyal toast to the Sovereign every day at dinner. When King George IV discovered that officers could not afford to drink a loyal toast to the Sovereign, he decreed that a bottle of Port and a bottle of Madeira be provided free for the occasion to each regiment; this was later converted to a Mess Allowance, but the wines continued to be provided free of cost for the royal toast at Jamrud Fort situated strategically at the mouth of the famous Khyber Pass (now in Pakistan). Apparently the Duke of Wellington introduced a custom for a toast for every day of the week: Mondays-Our men; Tuesdays-Our women; Wednesdays-Our swords; Thursdays-Ourselves; Fridays: Our religion; Saturday To Sweethearts and Wives with the wish "May they never meet!"; Sunday was reserved 'For Absent Friends'.

Some Regiments were permitted to toast standing on the dining chair with the right foot on the dining table—which wasn't easy after a fling at all the wines! By custom the Royal Navy drank their toast sitting down for fear of being swept off their feet if the ship pitched or rolled, or having their heads bang on the low ceiling of the ward-room! King Edward VII decreed that the toast could also be drunk in water! But the Indian Soldier had no such option. On an out-pass he could drink the local brew; on days determined as 'cold' in certain stations, a tot of rum was issued; those found inebriated were, of course, dealt with severely.

An interesting custom at the long drunken sit-down regimental dinners was for the servant to bring the chamber pot or the bidet for those who had a weak bladder! There was always the rose garden just through the dining room doorway; this arrangement was found necessary as few, if any, were able to navigate to the toilet without falling flat on their face; those who did make it, fell asleep in the anti-room or the ladies room! Also, if there was only one toilet in the Mess, it was reserved for ladies, if they were present at a party, and the men used the rose garden.

As social intercourse with the natives was taboo, almost all cantonments on the frontier or in peace-stations had exclusive clubs for Europeans. The Clubs usually had facilities of a well-stocked bar, indoor-games, billiards, tennis, squash, polo, pig-sticking, ballroom dancing, golf and a swimming pool. Some Clubs also had residential quarters where married Officers could find accommodation on a temporary basis. An attempt was always made to create a home away from the home in England. The life-style pandered to the British ego and arrogance and inflamed the sensitive nature of the Indian Soldier whose board and lodging had no extravagance or frills.

There were special brothels for British Other Ranks. The Duty Officer of the Week and a Medical Officer were required to inspect these brothels and submit a report on them to the Station Commander. The British Other Ranks were also permitted to visit dances and social evening in the local Railway Clubs run by Anglo-Indians. It was not unusual for British Officers to have an Indian mistress, but such liaisons were always very hush hush. In a number of stations the civilian bearer provided a 'bibi' for the sahib's pleasure. Those Officers who married Anglo-Indian or Indian women were ostracized. Close to a Regimental Centre there were often quite a few Eurasian children in the habitation. Illegitimate children of British Soldiers were recognized for certain allowances and education. Towards the end of the Second World War, when British Soldiers were being repatriated to England, their abandoned 'wives' in India was a problem for the Administration.

The British had a very high regard for the Indian Soldier. General Charles Cornwallis. Governor General in 1786, (remembered for his surrender to General Washington at Yorktown in 1783!) wrote to the Duke of York, C in C in Britain, 'A brigade of our Sepoys would easily make anybody emperor of Hindustan.' But there were warnings also. Lord Metcalf, a Member of the Governor General's Council, wrote in 1828, 'We can keep India in order by its instrumentality, but if the instrument should turn against us, where would be the British power? Echo answers, Where?' In 1852, a correspondent of the Delhi Gazette, who believed that the government was to blame for the mutinies in the Indian Regiments, wrote about the government that 'most assuredly (it will) turn itself out of the country (India) at no distant period by its own repeated acts of gross mismanagement and of bad faith to its own native troops'—a prediction which was to come true ultimately after many mutinies.

The important landmarks, which brought about freedom through the Indian Soldiers, are discussed below.

Vellore-1806

After defeating Suraj-ud-Daula at the Battle of Plassey in 1757, the British established a firm base to destroy what remained of the Mughal Empire. This historic victory and subsequent victories in the hinterland were unexpectedly easy, which was unfortunate, as it gave the British reasons to feel contemptuous, superior and arrogant towards the people who caved in so easily. From this stance of superiority and arrogance the British felt that the Soldier's faith, traditions and rituals were based on superstition and sorcery and sullied the image in which the British wanted to see the men they were training for war. After all, politics and religion were in tandem in Europe. Elsewhere conquerors had imposed their faith on their subjects as religious harmony simplified administration and was considered more important to sustain law and order than to save the soul of individuals. This approach evoked a great deal of hostility among Indian Soldiers of the Madras Presidency Army and later the Bengal Presidency Army.

Vellore lies sixteen miles from Arcot. Ram Gopal writes in *How India Struggled for Freedom*, "There was a mutiny at Vellore in 1806. Its cause was an innocuous order." Some historians have referred to this mutiny as 'the First War of Independence'. Of course, mutinies are not rare in the armed forces of any country, but the causes are different. In fact, the

British Gunners, all Europeans, mutinied at the Mount just outside Madras in 1798, not far from Vellore. Four British mutineers were executed for unlawful protest. This may have provided the role model for mutiny by the Indian garrison at Vellore.

But the order, which provoked the Indian soldiers of the Madras Army to mutiny, was not entirely innocuous. The Commander in Chief of the Madras Army was General Sir John Cradock. As an Officer from the British Army (as opposed to the Indian Cadre which comprised East India Company Officers), General Cradock was not sufficiently informed to be sensitive to the cultural susceptibilities of the Indian Troops under his command, but the Governor Lord Bentinck (age 32!) and the Madras Government ought to have known better. As a keen soldier General Cradock issued an order to smarten up the troops under his command. A new type of 'turban', leather cockade and leather stocks were required to be worn by the Indian soldier; caste marks, earrings and beards were no longer permitted and if a moustache was kept, it could only be to a regulation pattern. A leather headdress made of cow or pig hide was, of course, repugnant to both the Hindus and the Muslims. The removal of caste marks and earrings violated a ritual sanctified by hundreds of years of religious tradition. Muslims kept their beard as an Islamic tradition.

The orders to smarten up were received with alarming resentment by the Indian Troops of the Madras Army. A Regiment stationed at Vellore in May 1806, declined to wear the new 'turbans'. Later, on the 10th July, 1806, the Indian soldiers, 1500 or so, garrisoned in the Vellore Fortress, opened fire on the Europeans, about 350 strong, while they were still asleep in their barracks in the early hours of the morning. Over a hundred Europeans were killed. When the Officers rushed out to see what was happening, more then ten were shot dead. The British were taken completely by surprise despite early warnings.

Of course, British Troops stationed at Arcot were rushed to Vellore to crush the mutiny ruthlessly and 350 Indian soldiers were killed in the encounter. A number of mutineers were tried summarily—eight were hanged, six were tied to a cannon and blown and five were executed by a firing squad. A few were sentenced to life imprisonment. The offending order to smarten up the Indian soldiers was cancelled.

Tipu Sultan's sons and their families were imprisoned in the Vellore fortress after Tipu's defeat and death in the Battle of Seringapatam in 1798. An attempt was made by the Officers of the Madras Army to spread the rumour that the imprisoned sons had incited the Indian Sepoys to mutiny especially as one of the Regiments that mutinied was enlisted from Tipu's defeated army. This rumour was a ploy by the British Officers who wished to conceal the fact that their man-management was poor and their attitude towards the Indian Sepoys was generally contemptuous and condescending. An experienced British Officer, General Sir Thomas Munro, was of the opinion that the mutiny was not political and he wrote to Governor Bentinck that, 'However strange it may appear to Europeans, I know that the general opinion of the most intelligent natives in this part of the Country (South India) is that it was intended to make the Sepoys Christian.' Conversion was not, of course, the intention of the British then, but certainly it was believed, as indeed all conquerors believed, that conversion would simplify administration and sustain law and order, as the Sepoys would then owe allegiance to the same faith as their rulers and Officers and would not object to inconsequential susceptibilities like cow or pig hides for the 'turban'! But there is no evidence to suggest that the conversions were intended to save the soul of the Sepoy or to enhance the spiritual standing of the rulers! In practical terms, rulers through the ages have always looked upon religion as a good policeman; spiritual frills and mysticism were woven into the religion only to lure the gullible. But in India the freedom to practice one's religion was the only freedom universally understood by the people—the majority was not willing to compromise on any aspect of it! As politics was not known, the mutiny had no political overtones other than a strong desire to serve a clear quit-notice on those who thought they could coerce or threaten the Indian Sepoy to compromise on his faith.

Barrackpore-1824

The Burmese had conquered Assam in 1822. In 1824, they declared war against the British and advanced towards Cacha, but were repulsed. The Burmese Commander, Maha Bandula, threatened to capture Chittagong and Decca. To meet this threat, three Bengal Army Regiments, who had recently arrived in Barrackpore after a very long march from Mathura, were ordered to march down to Chittagong to counter the threat posed by the offending Burmese. As Hindu Soldiers of the Bengal Army had mutinied earlier when asked to go by sea, the British decided to march the three Regiments to the Burmese border in the Arakan.

Of course, in those days the Army did not provide transport to carry the heavy baggage of soldiers who had to find their own means of transport—at the time bullocks. Contingents of the Madras Army, who did not object to a journey by sea had already been shipped to the Rangoon front and with them all suitable load-carrying and meat-on-hoof bullocks. The three Regiments were now in need of transport, as the Government turned down their request for Army transport or extra allowance to pay for the hiked rates for hiring the bullocks that remained in Bengal. The Muslim Subedar Major of the 47th Regiment also intimidated the mostly Hindu Soldiers by saying that if they did not march they would have to go by sea. So, when the 47th was ordered to assemble on the parade ground to prepare to march off, they did not fall in as they complained that although their pay had been deducted for new knapsacks, no new ones had been issued; the old ones were worn-out and unusable. The Commanding Officer informed the Commander-in-Chief, General Paget, that his troops had mutinied. On the following day, Paget, having surrounded the parade ground with two European Regiments, some European Artillery and Indian Cavalry, addressed the Indian troops. The 47th Regiment and elements of 26th and 62nd explained to Paget on the parade ground that the Indian soldiers had no means of transport for the arduous journey and that they feared that they may be forced to go by sea. But when ordered the Indian Soldiers declined to ground their rifles. General Paget and his entourage galloped off the parade ground and ordered the European Artillery to fire on the assembled Indian Soldiers without any warning. Those who tried to escape, after throwing down their arms, were shot or sabred. Later it was found that the rifles were not loaded, but by then more than sixty Indian Soldiers had been slaughtered mercilessly. General Paget was of British Army; he did not know anything about the Indian Soldier, nor did he care. Herbert Spencer, the British philosopher thought that Paget's action was 'a despotism under which a Regiment of Sepoys was deliberately massacred.'

As if the massacre was not enough, the Commander-in-Chief assembled a Court Martial the following day. Twelve Indian soldiers were hanged and twenty-nine sentenced to 14 years RI, but this sentence of imprisonment was later remitted. Paget's brutality was censured in Britain and India. Obviously the General had no knowledge of the Bengal Army which had won the Indian Empire for Britain. His folly embittered the Indian soldier who treated those killed and executed in the mutiny as martyrs. There is reason to believe that there was a design to avenge this massacre in the 1857 Mutiny.

Mutiny at Meerut-1857

The first Burma War lasted till 1826. Although troops of the Madras Army did not resent going abroad to fight for the British, e.g. in East Indies (now Indonesia), China or Burma, Brahmins and others in the Bengal Army were forbidden by religious traditions to go overseas to fight in a war. Also, several regiments of the Bengal Army had been employed in endless campaigns in the Northwest, Afghanistan and Sind, resulting in serious discontent among the Indian troops as they were denied army respite, which was necessary after an arduous campaign.

The Russians were extending their territory in Central Asia and the British feared that the Russians might establish themselves in Afghanistan with designs on India. In 1839, Afghanistan was, therefore, invaded and the pro-Russian Dost Mohammed was deposed and the throne restored to pro-British Shah Shuja. But Akbar Khan, son of Dost Mohammed, again dethroned the unpopular Shah Shuja in a coup. The British Resident in Kabul was murdered and the British garrison was chased out of Kabul, overtaken at the Khyber Pass and massacred. Thus, British prestige and pride were severely jolted, which only aggravated the shaky British relationship with the Indian Soldier. In fact, a Regiment had mutinied earlier at Peshawar, as they were wary of the British who used Indian Troops endlessly to extend their empire without adequate leave, respite, pay and perks.

Here a clarification must be noted. The perception of mutiny was different in the minds of the Indian soldier and their British masters. The British often recruited the soldiers from the armies they had defeated. The Indian soldier therefore had the perception that 'allegiance' was a matter of choice and if the service conditions were not beneficial he could complain and quit. In the British mind any act of defiance violated the tenets of allegiance and compromised discipline and had to be dealt with severely according to the Indian Army Act they had concocted to ensure impeccable conduct of the Indian soldier. As a consequence, an incredible number of Indian soldiers were executed or punished severely for minor acts of defiance of orders, sometimes without trial and often by a Summary Court Martial, which was presided over only by the Commanding Officer. This did not help in improving the souring relationship between the Indian soldiers and the British. Incidentally, most of the executed Indian soldiers have greater claim to 'martyrdom' for freedom of India than any civilian listed by politicians as a 'martyr'.

During 1828 to 35, Lord Bentinck ruled India. Apart from annexing the little state of Coorg and deposing the Raja of Mysore, he suppressed 'thuggee', banned the practice of 'suttee' and introduced the use of English in administration. In 1833 East India Company ceased to trade and the Governor General of Bengal became the Governor General of India. As the British were also now encouraging missionaries to proselytize in India, the general impression conveyed to an Indian was that the British were determined to change the religious traditions and practices of their subjects by converting the Indians to Christianity. The Indian soldiers viewed these 'reforms' with great disquiet especially after the Barrackpore tragedy

In 1848, the Marques of Dalhousie was appointed Governor General at the age of thirty-five. It was during his rule that Punjab was annexed after a stunning British defeat at Chillianwallah in 1849, and later a decisive victory at Gujarat. He also introduced the 'doctrine of lapse' whereby on the death of an Indian ruler without an heir, the ruler's state was annexed by the British. This doctrine antagonized a number of Indian States. But he went a step too far when he seized the Indian State of Oudh as he regarded the Muslim King there as totally incompetent to rule. Most of the Muslim King's army was incorporated in the Bengal Army. But as many of the old Indian soldiers of the Bengal Army came from Oudh, the new Administration did not respond to their domestic woes in the villages with the same dispatch and concern as previously when the British resident could bully the Muslim King's government to take action. This inaction deprived the Indian soldiers from Oudh of their privileged position and gave rise to explosive discontent. The fuse was lit when the Indian soldiers had to bite off the ends of cartridges, which were rumoured to be greased with cow and pig fat. The Muslims, who regarded the pig as unclean, and the Hindus, who regarded the cow as sacred, were outraged.

There is no better account of the Indian Mutiny than that of Sir Winston Churchill in 'A *History of the English-speaking Peoples'* Book 4 Chapter V:

"The East India Company's Army of Bengal had long been of ill-repute. Recruited mainly in the North, it was largely composed of high-caste Hindus. This was bad for discipline. Brahmin privates would question the orders of officers and N.C.O.s of less exalted caste. Power and influence in the regiments frequently depended on a man's position in the religious rather than the military hierarchy. The Company's British officers were often of poor quality, for the abler and more thrusting among them sought secondment to the more spacious fields of civil administration. Many of those who remained at regimental headquarters were out of touch with their men and showed no desire to improve matters... There were grievances about pay and pensions....Other developments, unconnected with this military unrest, added their weight. By the 1850's railways, roads, post, telegraphs, and schools were beginning to push and agitate their way across the countryside, and were thought by many Indians to threaten an ancient society whose inmost structure and spirit sprang from a rigid and unalterable caste system. If everyone used the same trains and the same schools, or even the same roads, it was argued, how could caste survive? Indian monarchs were apprehensive and resentful of the recent annexations. Hatred smouldered at the repression of Suttee. Unfounded stories spread that the Government intended to convert India forcibly to Christianity. The disasters in Afghanistan and the slaughter of the Sikh Wars cast doubt on the invincibility of British arms. Many of the Sepoys, or Indian soldiers, considered themselves equal or superior to European troops..."

"In the year of the centenary of Plassey rumours began to flow that the cartridges for the new Enfield rifle were greased with the fat of pigs and cows, animals which Moslem and Hindu respectively were forbidden to eat. The cartridges had to be bitten before they could be inserted in the muzzle. Thus Sepoys of both religions would be defiled. There was some truth in the story, for beef-fat had been used in the London arsenal at Woolwich, though it was never used at the Indian factory at Dum-Dum. Nevertheless the tale ran through the regiments in the spring of 1857 and there was much unrest. In April some cavalry troopers at Meerut were court-martialled and imprisoned for refusing to touch the cartridges, and on May 9 they were publicly stripped of their uniforms. An Indian officer told his superiors that the Sepoys were planning to break open the jail and release the prisoners. His warning was disbelieved. Next night three regiments mutinied, captured the prison, killed their British officers, and marched on Delhi."

Actually the cavalry troopers who were stripped of their uniforms were also fettered at a garrison parade, which angered and humiliated the Indian Soldiers who witnessed the offensive proceedings. Rice Holmes in his *A History of the Indian Mutiny*, says, "It was not the inconsistency of their character that drove the same Sepoys who had risked their lives on the field of battle to protect their officers, and watched by their bedside when they were wounded, to murder them when the Mutiny broke out; it was the inconsistency with which they were treated."

The mutineers captured Delhi and killed every European in sight. The aged Mughal Emperor, a pensioner of the Company, was restored to a throne that had ceased to exercise any authority for years. He appointed Bakht Khan as Commander-in-Chief in the rank of General. Bakht Khan was a Subedar in the Bengal Artillery; he was not trained to handle large forces of all arms in battle; grand tactics and strategy were beyond his pale. Lack of military leadership and higher direction of war was a fatal weakness that could not be surmounted. Defeat was inevitable.

The Indian soldiers at Kanpur revolted and killed all the male Europeans; women and children were captured and later slaughtered by five assassins and dumped into a well. Lucknow was besieged. As Lucknow was in Oudh, kingdom of the Muslim King dethroned in 1856, those who were still loyal to the old monarch joined the mutineers in rebellion. The fighting was savage; the seige classic and resolute. It was not till March 1858, that the seige was finally raised.

The belief that mutiny was confined only to the Ganges Valley and parts of Central India is not entirely correct. In Delhi and Rohilkhund some civilians did join the mutineers; in Oudh there was a general rebellion against the British. Elsewhere, e.g. Satara, Kolhapur, Belgaum and Dharwar, there were minor 'mutinies'. A detachment of 9 Cavalry mutinied at Kalabagh on the Indus; 17th Irregular Cavalry overpowered the detachment and all the Indian Soldiers of the 9th were killed. In Bombay two were executed and six sentenced to life imprisonment on a charge of intended mutiny. At Kolhapur thirty-six were executed. On 22 January, 1858, seventeen Indian soldiers were executed at Raipur for mutiny. A Sikh Regiment at Benares and the Gorkhas at Sabatu also mutinied. Government of India, after Independence, published an authoritative account in the book "*Eighteen Fifty Seven*"; Maulana Azad, a pre-eminent Indian leader, wrote thus in his foreword to the book: '...There would have been no revolt in India in 1857, had not the initiative been taken by the disaffected Sepoys ....yet the crisis might have been avoidable had not the Government bungled in the administration of the army...the Mutiny, I'm inclined to hold, was not inevitable."

This is what Sir Winston Churchill had to say: "The scale of the Indian Mutiny should not be exaggerated. Three-quarters of the troops remained loyal; barely a third of the British territory was affected; there had been risings and revolts among the soldiery before; the brunt of the outbreak was suppressed in a space of a few weeks. It was in no sense a national movement. Or, as some later Indian writers have suggested, a patriotic struggle for freedom or a war of independence. The idea and ideal of the inhabitants of the sub-continent forming a single people and state was not to emerge for many years. But terrible atrocities had been committed by both sides. From now on there was an increasing gulf between the rulers and the ruled."

Some sensitive spot in the inner psyche of the Indian Soldier must have been terribly hurt to drive him to acts of unprecedented savagery and anger. The atrocities committed by both sides on each other were barbaric and outrageous. On the road from Meerut to Delhi the British strung thousands of mutineers on all the trees astride the road and left them to die a slow death through strangulation while vultures and crows feasted on the writhing bodies. At Benares, Colonel James Neill 'was busily hanging batches of mutineers as fast as they were brought in.' When the Government ordered Neill to move on to Allahabad, he replied by telegram, "Can't move: wanted here." The vengeance wreaked by the British on the rebels in Cawnpore was particularly cruel and appalling. This is what Sir Winston Churchill had to say on this issue: "Here Cawnpore (now Kanpur) and elsewhere the British troops took horrible vengeance. Mutineers were blown from the mouths of cannon, sometimes alive, or their bodies sewn up in the skins of cows and swine.... Nevertheless, the atrocities and reprisals of the blood-stained months of the Mutiny left an enduring and bitter mark in the memory of both countries.' So enduring was the memory that for fear of another 1857, the British hastily transferred power to Indian political persons on 15 August 1947, ten months earlier than scheduled.

Both the Indian Soldiers and the British paid a terrible price to come to terms with reality. A century after Clive had recommended, the East India Company and the Board of Control were abolished by India Act of 1858. The sovereignty of the British Crown was now imposed on India and Queen Victoria was proclaimed the Queen of India; in 1877 she was designated as the Empress of India. But direction and control lay in the hands of a Secretary of State for India who was responsible to the British Parliament. A Viceroy represented the Crown in India and was an absolute ruler bound only by the directions and policies of the British Government till 1870, when a submarine cable was laid through the Red Sea enabling the Secretary of State for India to send frequent and detailed instructions to the Viceroy. A Council of India was set up to advice the Viceroy. It was an end to civil wars, annexations or other offending or humiliating reforms. Everyone was to be equal before the law. Religious tolerance was accepted as a policy and aggressive or derisive proselytizing by the Christian missionaries was discouraged. The redoubtable Indian Sepoy had achieved the impossible in history—he had forced a mighty ruler to respect the Indian and to treat him with consideration and amity.

The question is, why couldn't the Indian soldier stage a similar mutiny before, say during the Mughal period? The notable feature of the 1857 Mutiny was that Hindus and Muslims were united in fighting a foreign power that did not regard itselves as Indians in any way. The British were here for trade and substantial profits. Any Indian industry or venture that interfered with the British aim of using their Indian Empire as a huge market for goods manufactured in Britain was expeditiously prohibited or demolished. In their blatant act of self-aggrandizement the British lost sympathy and respect from all layers of Indian society. As the Indian Soldier was their main instrumentality for holding on to India, the Mutiny rocked the very foundation of their Empire.

During the Mughal period, the conquerors had come to stay in India. They felt that their aim could best be achieved by pandering to the Muslim Indians and by playing them against the Hindus. Akbar tried hard to placate the Hindus by acquiring 500 Hindu wives for his pleasure and even floating a new religion, but nothing made a lasting impact to reconcile the two religious factions. There was always the question of the Hindus versus the Muslims, which finally gave birth to Maharatta and Sikh ascendancy to power with trappings of a movement to rid India of foreign domination.

Was the 1857 Mutiny the First War of Independence? The facts are that the Indian Soldier started the conflict because he had a legitimate grouse against his British Officers and the Government. Several Indian states that also had a legitimate or imagined grouse against the British merely took advantage of the situation and joined the rebels. The Indian Soldiers at the time did not have trained Indian commanders who could handle units or formations in battle. For this reason the mutineers sought help from the old Mughal Emperor, the disgruntled Nana Sahib, Tantia Tope, Rani Laxmibai and others to lead the rebels against the British. Had the British lost, the old Indian rulers would probably have resumed power in their own states and returned to the age-old practice of fighting each other for personal aggrandizement. There is nothing to suggest that the mutiny was pre-meditated or that anyone had a master plan for freedom or democracy in any part of India. But certainly the Indian soldier did manage to convey the message to the British that the Indian, however poor and helpless, could not be taken for granted and that he would have to be treated with respect and consideration if the British were to use him as an instrument to stay on in India.

1. ADC to the last Viceroy of British India — May 1947.

2. Return from the battlefield in Burma May 1945 with General Sir Montagu Stopford, the Twelfth Army Commander.

3. With General Stopford in Singapore — Aug. 1946.

4. Walking on the lawns of Tyersal Palace, Singapore, with Gen Stopford Aug. 1946.

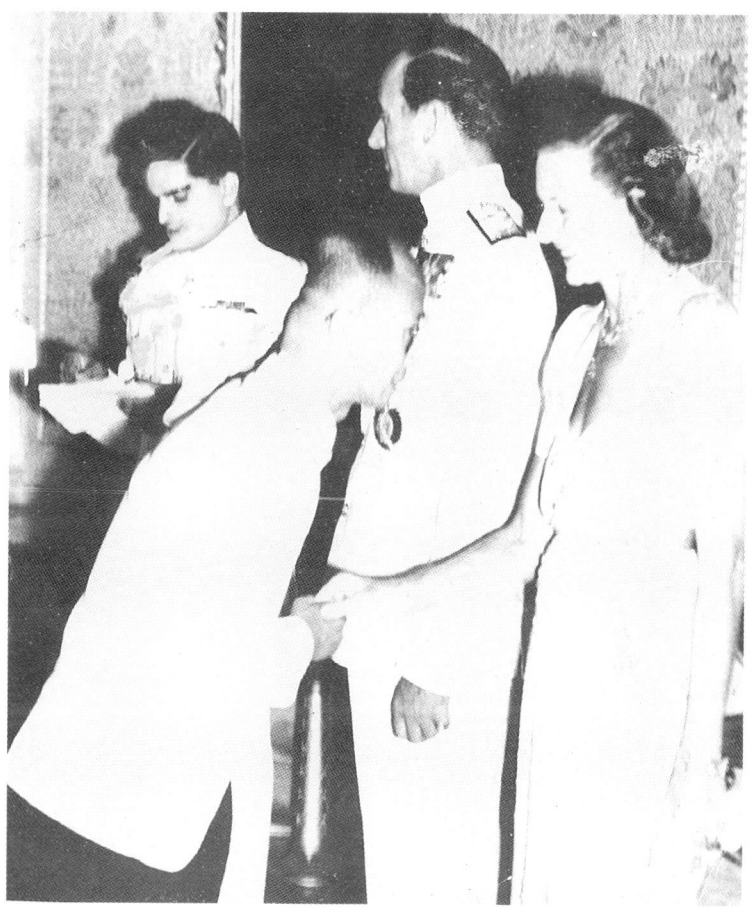

5. Introducing guests to the Viceroy and Lady Edwina Mountbatten — May 1747.

6. With Mahatma Gandhi on his first visit to see the Viceroy — May 1947.

7. Walking through rain, mud and slush with Lady Mountbatten in Calcutta — July 1947.

8. Crowds outside the Parliament House, New Delhi, on 15 Aug 1947, when the new Governor General, Lord Mountbatten, arrived to address the Constituent Assembly.

9. Lt. Col. at 26-Commanding Officer of a Battalion in the war in Kashmir — May 1948.

10. Mrs. Ann Yadav — Aug. 1948.

11. Unfurling the Tricolour at Kishtwar, Kashmir, on 15 Aug. 1948.

12. With Prime Minister Nehru in Srinagar, Kashmir, May 1949.

13. Commander of an Infantry Brigade Group on manoeuvres in the Valley of Flowers near Marsar Lake, Kashmir, 11,000ft, with a Staff Officer — June 1963.

14. & 15. Rangoon Victory Parade brochure cover with signatures of the most famous commanders in the War in South East Asia.

ရန်ကုန်မြို့

စစ်အောင်မြင်ခြင်းအထိမ်းအမှတ်

တပ်ပေါင်းစုံမိုလ်ရှုခံသဘင်

၁၉၄၅ ခုနှစ်၊ စက်တင်ဘာလ ၁၅ ရက်။

အခမ်းအနား အစီအစဉ်။

P.F. Feng Yee 馮銳
Maj. Gen. Chinese Army.
15th Sept. 1945.

The English Church
Batavia
Netherlands East Indies

DAY OF REMEMBRANCE

November the Tenth
1946

1914-1918   *Invicta*   **1939-1946**

16. Momento from Dutch East Indies with signatures of Dutch Governor-General & C-in-C and British C-in-C and the author.

Part II

After the Indian Mutiny of 1857, events in India were shaped largely by the ensuing rivalry between Great Britain and France. Obviously British Troops could not be brought in such large numbers as could ensure internal security and meet the threat perception on the borders or in neighbouring countries. All kinds of proposals were floated, examined and found impractical. The proposal to convert the East India Company's European force resulted in a 'white mutiny'. An auxiliary force was created; all Europeans and Anglo-Indians were required to serve in this force, which could be mobilized in the event of an emergency. But the imperative of keeping a large Indian Army could not be compromised.

Sir Charles Wood was Secretary of State for India during the Mutiny. In 1859 his direction to the Governor General, Lord Charles Canning was: "I never wish to see again a great Army, very much the same in its feelings and prejudices and convictions, confident in its strength, and so disposed to unite in rebellion together. If one regiment mutinies, I should like to see the next regiment so alien, that it would be ready to fire into it.' The new Indian Army was reorganized on this basis. The recruiting area of Oudh, from where the largest number of soldiers had mutinied, was more or less abandoned. A unit had sub-units of different communities or castes. Even in a Brigade usually there was a mixed battalion of Muslims and Hindus, a mixed battalion of Sikhs and Muslims and a

British Battalion; later one of the Indian battalions was sometimes replaced by a Gurkha battalion; there was also a Brigade of Gurkhas and one or two purely British Army Divisions. Many historians have commented on this arrangement as a ploy to 'divide and rule'; the author's experience as an Officer in the British Indian Army from 1941, till Independence was that this arrangement helped to unite Indians of different ethnic, caste, community and cultural origins and gave the Indian soldiers an opportunity to recognize and accept Indian diversity.

Although there was no political movement of any kind till the beginning of the Twentieth Century, the British found it expedient to progressively associate Indians with the British in ruling India to placate the Indian Soldier. Coincidentally Indian Council Acts of 1861, 1892 and 1909, which conceded just a little bit more power to Indians, came when there was a threat from the Russian, the French, the Afghans, the Boers in South Africa or the Germans, so that the redoubtable Indian Soldier could be used not only in India but in Britain's overseas possessions to counter the threat.

Alan Octavian Hume, a Scot, had already founded the Indian National Congress in 1885. Delegates who usually attended the meetings of the Congress were those who were not only well acquainted with the English language but also with western culture and political thinking. Within the Congress there were moderates, who wanted the reforms to be brought about within the British system, and those who wanted to overthrow the British administration through a revolution—both were living in a dream-world as they could not communicate their ideas to 99 per cent of the people in the Subcontinent. Nevertheless, Curzon, the Viceroy, partitioned Bengal in 1905, which provided the intellectuals in Bengal a political cause for agitation. Curzon had aimed at separating the predominant areas inhabited by Hindus, which provided most of the 'nationalists', and Muslims, who had to be placated against the Turkish pan-Islamic movement. The British were certainly disturbed as not only was the Indian soldier demanding equality and fair-play but the intellectuals were also up in arms demanding 'home rule' for the first time although they had no unity or political talent to run a huge and diverse country like India! This brought about the Minto-Morley Reforms or India Councils Act 1909, by which the Indian Legislative Council was enlarged and given more power and the Provincial Legislative Councils were to include more elected members. The Councils Act 1909 was significant as it introduced the principle of 'election' for the first time. But Morley, the Secretary of State for India, 'regarded parliamentary institutions as unsuitable for India'; Minto, the Viceroy, agreed with this view. Unfortunately, the electorate was confined to the well to do, which precluded about 85 per cent of the population in the rural areas and the cities. The Indian Soldier, who had imbibed on the British Officers' passion for democracy and gained edifying experience in his postings in various parts of India and abroad had a clear vision of the meaning and import of political freedom. These visions he shared with soldiers from other parts of India and more importantly with his village folks when he went home. So the ex-Servicemen in particular were better informed on world affairs than most of those who were eligible to become members of the Legislative Councils.

These well-informed ex-Servicemen had already begun to seek new pastures of freedom. Towards the end of the Nineteenth Century about 20,000 Punjabis, mostly Sikh ex-Servicemen from the 'famine' prone areas in East Punjab, migrated to the USA and Canada, as the Government emphasis was more on developing the Muslim dominant West Punjab. Here at home, Pingle, a Maharatta revolutionary who was involved in the 'Ghadar' movement returned to India in December 1914, with Sikh revolutionaries, mostly ex-Servicemen, to start a revolution in India. Another revolutionary,

Rash Behari Bose, joined Pingle in Amritsar. A spy sneaked the revolutionary plans to the Government. Dhananjay Keer, a biographer of Vinayak Savarkar wrote, "Some five thousand men were put on trial for treason in Punjab alone. Five hundred were tried by court-martial and executed ..." Pingle was also hanged.

Earlier, in April-July 1914, the 'Kamagata Maru', a chartered ship, sailed from Hongkong carrying 351 Sikhs and 21 Muslims immigrants to Canada under the leadership of Sardar Gurdat Singh. Under British instigation the Canadian Government refused to allow them to land on Canadian soil. The 'immigrants' had to return to India. In September 1914 the ship docked at Budge-Budge on the Hoogly. The British offered to ferry the 'immigrants' in a train to Punjab free of charge. The Sikhs refused and decided to march to Calcutta in a procession with the Guru Granth Sahib. The British police opened fire and killed eighteen. Many protesters were arrested and sentenced to long terms in jail. India was on fire.

During the First World War, the Indian National Congress went along with the Government. Gandhiji had no leadership status in the Congress at the time; in fact, at the outset of the War he organized a Field Ambulance Training Corps and the Red Cross and advised the Indians in Britain to 'think imperial'! During the War he helped the British to recruit Indian soldiers for the Army.

The Indian Soldier was employed in great strength to win the 1914-18 World War, although the British believed that the Indian soldier should not be used against Europeans except Russians (if there be need), whom they regarded as Asians! But the small population of Britain and her European Commonwealth was obviously not enough to replace the terrible casualties expected (and later sustained) in trench warfare especially in assaults against defences protected by barbed wire, mines, concentrated fire of artillery and later the Machine Gun. Though ill prepared and poorly trained for 'modern warfare', the Indian soldier fought in France, Palestine, Mesopotamia, German East Africa and elsewhere with remarkable tenacity. Indian soldiers (including Gurkhas), trained to fight in the hills of North West Frontier on the borders of Afghanistan, smashed their way through the Turkish defences and captured a vital feature in the hills outside Jerusalem during 19-21 November, 1917, which made further advance possible. Jerusalem surrendered on the 9th December 1917, after 400 years of Ottoman Turk domination—and the Indian Soldiers contributed substantially to the British Victory.

There were two Infantry and two Cavalry Divisions in France in 1914, who took the impact of the first fierce advance by the Germans; apart from high casualties, the Indians suffered enormously through lack of adequate winter clothing. By the end of the war in 1918, the Indian Soldier had not only saved the British Empire but all the Western Democracies. Over 60,000 Indians perished in the War; nearly ten thousand were decorated, eleven with the highest British honour, the Victoria Cross.

An interesting aspect of World War I was that when Turkey joined Germany in November 1914, a number of Muslim Troops of the Indian Army both in India and abroad deserted in the hope of joining the Turkish forces to fight against the British. In March 1915, a Viceroy's Commissioned Officer, Mir Mast, deserted his Regiment in France and joined the Germans; the Kaiser gave him the Iron Cross—Germany's highest medal for valour. As it happened he also had a brother, Mir Dast, in the Regiment. To get even, King George V awarded Britain's highest medal for valour, the Victoria Cross, to Mir Dast! Also, when Turkey came into the War, it was implied in German propaganda that the Kaiser had become a Muslim and that he was 'a direct descendent of the Prophet's sister'!

Politically the most significant declaration of the British Raj was that of the Secretary of State for India, Edwin Montagu in

1917. This declaration was important as it nullified the views held by Morley and supported by Minto that Parliamentary democracy was unsuitable for India, which had obviously dissuaded Indians from fully supporting Britain in her war effort and induced them not to give money and manpower generously. Montagu declared that it was the policy of the British Government to increase "association of Indians in every branch of the administration and also the granting of self-governing institutions with a view to progressive realization of responsible government in India as an integral part of the British Empire." Soon after the declaration an appeal was made to India for further military and financial help in the War. As a consequence there was an enormous drive especially in the Punjab to recruit more soldiers for the Army and to seek substantial donations to pay for the War in Europe; harsh methods were used resulting in widespread discontent among the people. Punjab was already on fire by 'revolutionary activities' in which a large number of ex-Servicemen were involved; the harsh methods used by the Administration to obtain recruits and donations only added fuel to the fire.

Fifty years after the Sepoy Mutiny, Punjab was already rebellious during the anniversary celebration. The Colonization Act, which had increased irrigation water rates and land revenue, angered the people to riot and defy the British writ. The part played by the Ghadar Party and Punjabi ex-Servicemen has already been related. During the War years the Defence of India Act took care of the extremists and dissenters, but it was feared that violence and lawlessness would continue after the War. As the Defence of India Act was to expire six months after the end of the War, Justice Rowlatt was asked to examine the situation and recommend remedial measures. Thus came into force the Rowlatt Acts, which gave the Government additional powers to deal with terrorism and was passed by the Central Legislative Council in March 1919. These Acts gave the politicians a rallying point for opposing the Government. M.M. Malaviya and M.A. Jinnah resigned their membership of the Council. Punjab, which had a very hard time during the War, revolted.

During the war years Gandhiji had been loyal to the Government; his help in recruitment and in promoting the Red Cross was much appreciated; he was conferred with the Kaiser-i-Hind, the highest award of the British Indian Government to loyal subjects. In 1916, while attending a Congress session at Lucknow, Gandhiji was informed that European planters were victimizing and tyrannizing poor peasants in Champaran-Kheda area of Bihar by forcing the peasants to grow indigo, which fetched a very good price for the Europeans. Gandhiji went to Bihar to save the peasants from the despotic European planters who not only had their own private prisons but also imposed a tax on the poor peasants on marriage, oil or sugar crushers and even to pay for the planters' holidays up in the cool of the hills! His non-violent protest did manage to induce a good deal of anti-Government feeling among the people but the planters could not be persuaded to change their ways, nor could the Government be urged to act against the tyranny of the planters.

In support of the War effort Gandhiji again visited Kheda, but the people were no longer co-operative! This is what Gandhiji said about the visit, "Whereas during the revenue campaign the people readily offered their carts free of charge and two volunteers came forth when one was needed, it was difficult now to get a cart even on hire, to say nothing of volunteers. We decided to dispense with the use of carts and to do our journey on foot. We had meetings wherever we went. People did attend, but hardly one or two would offer themselves as recruits. 'You are a votary of Ahimsa (non-violence); how can you ask us to take up arms? What good has the government done for India to deserve our co-operation?' These and similar questions used to be put to us."

Of course, the bulk of the recruits for the War came from the Punjab, which was already astir with intense revolutionary movement. The Punjab was also a province without any executive or expanded legislative council. To add to its woes, Sir Michael O'Dwyer was the Governor. Ram Gopal writes in his book, *How India Struggled For Freedom*, "He mocked at the political aspirations of the people; he was for ruthless suppression of political activities... tyrannical methods were employed in making recruitment. A typical example is of a revenue officer (Tehsildar), who used to prepare a list of all men in a village and ask each family of three or four brothers to provide one or two recruits for the war. If the fixed number was not made available voluntarily, he would resort to cruel punishment. He made the men stand naked in the presence of their women folk or pushed them between thorny bushes. Women were taken as hostages and retained until the men came forward to enlist in the army." Mrs. Annie Besant, the wife of an English clergyman, who was President of the Theosophical Society and a Congress activist in India, thought that "the hard and oppressive rule of Sir Michael O'Dwyer, his press-gang methods of recruitment, his forced war loans, and his cruel persecution of all political leaders kept the covered-up embers of resentment alive and ready to break into flames. At the special Congress of 1918 in Bombay, Punjab delegates told us how they were living over a volcano, which any act of exceptional tyranny might cause to burst." O'Dwyer's harsh rule prepared the way to the great tragedy at Jallianwala Bagh on 13 April 1919.

As stated earlier the Rowlatt Acts had been enacted in March 1919, despite strong opposition from Gandhiji and the intelligentsia. Gandhiji decided to offer 'satyagraha' "to battle against it". He formed 'the Satyagraha Sabha', a separate body outside any existing institution, as a non-violent movement against the Acts. April 6 was to be observed as the day for general strike when shops were to be closed, all activity and business suspended and prayer meeting organized throughout the Country. The strike passed off peacefully in Lahore, Amritsar and other places in the Punjab. But on the morning of the 10th April, Amritsar's Deputy Commissioner arrested and interned two well-known leaders of Punjab. When an unarmed and peaceful crowd protested the arrests and marched towards the Deputy Commissioner's house, the police blocked their passage and fired at them. Infuriated and revengeful the crowd turned into an unruly mob and killed some Europeans, including a woman missionary and set on fire a few public buildings.

The reprisals by Governor O'Dwyer were fierce and brutal. Under Brigadier General Reginald Dyer troops, armoured cars and aeroplanes were used to fire upon the mobs indiscriminately without restraint. The slaughter was unprecedented. Public flogging and whipping terrorized the people. Indiscriminate arrests were common; the administration treated animals with greater concern and care than human beings. The Indian political leaders decided to call a protest meeting in Jallianwala Bagh, Amritsar, on April the 13th, 1919. Dyer allowed the meeting of about 20,000 people to assemble in the Jallianwala Bagh, which had only one entrance or exit. Dyer entered the Bagh with two armoured cars and about 100 soldiers, blocked the exit and opened fire on the assembled crowd without warning. The firing continued for over a period of ten minutes. The inscription on the memorial there reads, 'This place is saturated with the blood of about 2000 Hindu, Sikh and Muslim patriots who were martyred in a non-violent struggle to free India from British domination.'

The consequences of the non-violent movement were not always peaceful. In 1940, a Sikh, Udham Singh, killed Governor O'Dwyer in London although Udham Singh's intention was to kill Brigadier General Dyer. Udham Singh was tried and hanged in Britain. A town on the way to Nainital is now named after him and Udham Singh is remembered as one of the martyrs in the Struggle for Freedom. Of course, the Rowlatt Acts were repealed. Gandhiji returned his Kaisar-i-Hind and Zulu War Medal; Rabindranath Tagore (recipient of the Nobel Prize for Literature) renounced his knighthood. Unlike the Sepoy Mutiny of 1857, the Jallianwala Bagh incident occurred when communications were reasonably well developed in India. Although the Indian Army had faced mass executions after numerous mutinies, this was the first time when civilians in the Punjab faced the crushing wrath of a ruthless Empire; the tragic news echoed round the Subcontinent and aroused the people to a new consciousness on freedom.

There was an interesting development in Punjab in 1921. Babbar Akalis, an offshoot group of the ongoing Akali movement for wresting control of gurudwaras from 'mahants', emerged as a terrorist group comprising largely ex-Servicemen, Servicemen on leave and some police personnel. By 1923 most of the activists were apprehended and executed or sent to long terms of imprisonment. As a consequence, in 1930, when the Army was to be reduced, the percentage of Sikh Soldiers was also reduced from twenty per cent to only thirteen.

Turkey's defeat in the War was not well received by a large number of Muslims in India. Mecca, Medina and all the Muslim holy shrines in Palestine were in the Ottoman Empire. The Sultan was regarded as a Khalifa, or secular and religious head of Islam. Britain had made it clear that Turkey would not be allowed to control non-Turkish lands and that Arabia would be set free. But the 'Khilafat' movement in India wanted to ensure that the integrity of the Sultan was not affected—in fact, 30,000 Muslims were incited to migrate to Afghanistan to distance themselves from British rule! Ram Gopal writes in his book, *How India Struggled For Freedom*, "The decade of the growth of Muslim consciousness had unmistakably suggested that so far as the Muslims were concerned, religion could not only be divorced from politics but should in fact be one of the wheels of the political chariot. With this background before him Gandhi saw in the political situation as it developed in 1919, the fulfillment of his life's mission. He told the first Khilafat conference, a joint audience of Muslims and Hindus: 'The Mussalmans have adopted a very important resolution. If the peace terms are unfavourable to them—which God may forbid—they will stop all co-operation with Government. It is an inalienable right of the people thus to withhold co-operation. We are not bound to retain Government titles and honours or to continue in Government service. If Government should betray us in a great cause like the Khilafat we could not do otherwise than non-co-operate."

Curiously Jinnah did not support the Khilafat movement. When peace terms for Turkey were announced on 14 May 1920, Gandhiji launched his non-violent non-co-operation movement to oppose it. Gandhiji, adept at methods he had practiced in South Africa, swept urban India and the intelligentsia in a rebellious storm of non-violence. Down South in Malabar, Moplas of Arab descent, inspired by Khilafat movement, burst into violence; after over two thousand had perished in fighting the British, more than 38,000 surrendered; but as the Moplas wanted a purely Muslim state, the Hindu-Muslim unity Gandhiji was able to forge, received a jolt. The experiment appears to have been a costly illusion as Jinnah gained by it.

The Khilafat as also Gandhiji's non-violent non-co-operation movement had some success till Mustafa Kemal Ataturk proclaimed a Turkish republic with capital in Ankara. Thus the Istanbul government of the Sultan ceased to exist. Ataturk was secular, much to the distress and surprise of the Muslims in India, who now renounced their past associations with the Khilafat to solicit sympathy and preferential treatment from the British. Maulana Mohammed Ali had presided over the

Congress in 1923 and showered praise on Gandhiji. When Turkey dethroned their Sultan, who had no right to style himself as the 'Calipha' in the first place, Hindu-Muslim unity in India suffered a serious setback and the Maulana gave vent to his true feelings. Ram Gopal writes in *How India Struggled For Freedom*, "The same Maulana said a year later, when the inspiring object of Turkey had disappeared, 'However pure Mr. Gandhi's character may be, he must appear to me, from the point of view of religion, inferior to any Mussalman even though he be without character.'" The words were sharp-edged daggers that pierced Hindu hearts and the Hindu Muslim riots that followed surprised only the gullible—and the 'secularists', a meaningless sobriquet used and misused for political pretences before and after Independence.

To pacify the Hindu Muslim turbulence, Gandhiji undertook a twenty-one day fast with residence in Maulana Mohammed Ali's house! But there was no change. Madan Mohan Malviya, theretofore an ardent Congressman and the famous founder of the Benares Hindu University, changed his flag and presided over the Hindu Mahasabha. Jinnah stepped out into limelight again and revived the Muslim League. He enunciated the political demands of the Muslims and ridiculed the presumptions on Hindu-Muslim unity. Of course the Congress suffered and splinter groups and communal parties thrived and dominated the elections to the central and provincial councils in 1926. One such splinter group, the Swaraj Party, with C.R. Das as the leader came into prominence with a demand for immediate independence. This was viewed with a good deal of trepidation by the intellectuals who knew that India could not out hold on its own and that some other European power could walk in if Britain left. The Author's father was in the Civil Service at the time, a Magistrate, and his British colleagues teased him and called the Hindus naïve and gullible. The British had every reason to laugh at the politicians' fragile attempts to unite to grab power, a game that continues to this day.

It was stipulated in the Government of India Act of 1919, that it would be reviewed in all its aspects after ten years. This resulted in the appointment of a commission under Sir John Simon who came to India in 1928. As the Commission had no Indian members, it was resented and opposed by all Indians. This gave Gandhiji an opportunity to launch a non-violent non-co-operation stir again. Initially the emphasis was on the boycott of foreign goods especially cloth, which was consigned to fire all over urban India. Later the focus shifted to the ongoing agitation against the salt tax. On the eve of the movement Gandhiji wrote his now famous letter to the Viceroy on 1 Mar 1930, and commenting on the British rule, said, "It has impoverished the dumb millions by a system of progressive exploitation and by a ruinously military and civil administration which the country can never afford. It has reduced us politically to serfdom. It has sapped the foundation of our culture, and, by the policy of disarmament, it has degraded us spiritually. Lacking the inward strength, we have been reduced, by all but universal disarmament, to a state bordering on cowardly helplessness..." In the context of Indian history and Gandhiji's ardent belief in non-violence, Irwin, the Viceroy, gave a short and somewhat contemptuous reply.

Gandhiji started his famous second non-cooperation civil disobedience movement on 12 March 1930, by a march to Dandi. The salt law was an oppressive measure to collect indirect taxes from the poorest of the poor as a very large population of India ate their chappatis with salt as they could afford nothing else; often salt was used to give a taste to 'sattu' or 'dalia' or 'chatni' made of ground mint and dhania or raw mango or bark of a tree or some wild herb. Dandi beaches were on the Gujarat Coast, 200 miles away from the Sabarmati Ashram where Gandhiji lived and preached non-violence. With 75 select disciples he marched triumphantly to the coast and thousands gathered on the roadside to greet and cheer him. Nothing like this had ever been seen in India before.

His entourage swelled to huge proportions. He arrived at Dandi on 5 April; the salt law was to be challenged and broken on 6 April, the day on which a 'strike' was declared in the Punjab leading to the black day on which Brigadier General Dyer with armoured cars and troops fired, without warning, on a peaceful crowd, largely pilgrims from outside for the Baisakhi celebrations on 13 April 1919. The Government allowed Gandhiji to have his way in manufacturing salt.

Of course the call to breach the law and manufacture salt was given to all who could muster courage to do so and the response was good. People tried to manufacture salt from little bits of saline earth; mill workers went on strike, British goods were torched and meetings were held to sympathize with the movement. The police repression was brutal. One of the most ugly chapters of Indian history is the barbarous and excessively inhuman behaviour of the police especially when their senior police officials are not around—it happens to this day. The police excesses were so sickening that Gandhiji had to complain to the Viceroy. No action was taken—just as none is taken now. Gandhiji decided to march to Dharsana Salt Works but on 5 May he was arrested and imprisoned in the Yervada Jail.

The British were used to mutinies and, latterly, to civil disturbances in India and they had the capacity to deal with them. But in 1929-30, Afghanistan was astir again and the old British phobia of Russian (and German) designs on India afflicted the British defence planners. In the North West Frontier Province, the Frontier Gandhi, Abdul Ghaffar Khan, a leader of great moral and physical courage, was agitating for political reforms. His arrest on 23 April, 1930, before he could respond to Gandhiji's call for civil disobedience, angered his Pathan followers. Violent mobs collected in the narrow streets of Peshawar city to demand the release of their leader. Troops were called out in aid of civil authority and faced the galling wrath of the belligerent Pathans. British troops and armoured cars opened fire on an unruly mob in the narrow confines of the City streets, killing a few and wounding many more agitating Pathans. More troops were now needed to deal with the infuriated mob. 2nd Royal Garhwal Rifles had had a rough time on the previous day. Now two platoons from the Battalion, who had been in and out of vehicles in the heat since the previous day, were ordered to move as reinforcements. They refused to embus and requested release from Army service. Fearing the worst, the British temporarily withdrew all troops from the City. Thinking that the British rule was about to end, tribesman stormed into the City. Peace was restored only in August the following year.

(Incidentally, the Author was commanding B Company in 1st Royal Garhwal Rifles during the Hindu-Muslim riots in Peshawar in Jan-Mar 1947, before his posting as ADC to the Viceroy—more of it later.)

2nd Royal Garhwal Rifles was disarmed and sent to Abbotabad. An enquiry revealed that only the two platoons that refused to embus were unhappy as they had had a rough passage with missile-throwing and abusive Pathan mobs the previous day. Despite the hostility of the Pathans, the platoons were not ordered to fire on the mob. In the event all the NCOs were tried by a court-martial and awarded rigorous imprisonment from life to three years each. (During the Second World War after the fall of Singapore in March 1942, most of the Battalion joined the Indian National Army.)

The events in 1930 alarmed the British. Not only the Indian Army, but also political parties were agitated over equality and freedom for India. There was a major revolt in the North West Frontier Province; some tribesmen were even demanded the release of Gandhiji! Fascism was on the rise in Europe and Japan. Russia had an eye on India and socialism had caught on among the Indian intellectuals. The need for the Indian Army to garrison South East Asia and the Middle East were a pressing strategic imperative as also the matter of internal security, as without a contented 'instrumentality' it was impossible for the British to rule in India. The move to placate Indians through the Simon Commission had failed. But the Indians had to be involved in a dialogue to find a solution. To end the impasse, the British Government decided to convene a Round Table Conference in London in November 1930 and invited representatives of all political parties in Britain and prominent political parties and persons of varying shades of opinion in India. The Indian National Congress declined to attend.

The Round Table Conference endorsed the recommendations of the Simon Commission for a federal structure at the Centre with representatives from the provinces and Indian states; the Governor General was to retain defence and foreign affairs with special powers to act on finance, law and order, public officials, minorities and appropriation of revenue. Of course, Europeans were to be given special status and protection in trials by courts. As the means for settling Hindu-Muslim animosity remained unresolved, another Round Table Conference became necessary.

In the Government of India Act 1919, the qualification for voting for representatives to the Legislative Assembly was that only those who paid revenue income tax could vote; and for the Council of State that the voter had to be in possession of substantial property, or had at some time been a member of the Legislature or Local Legislative Councils. Education as a qualifying factor was now added. This precluded 86 per cent of India from exercising any franchise. By definition this was not a step towards democracy—only a measure to placate the vociferous politicians and fool the Indian soldier.

The Congress was to observe January 26, 1931, as Independence Day. Gandhiji and members of the Working Committee in jail were released on the previous night. Thus the political stalemate was set in motion again as Ramsay McDonald, the British Prime Minister was anxious to resolve the Hindu-Muslim dilemma. Gandhiji sought an interview with Lord Irwin, the Viceroy, and the discussion between the two continued intermittently for a fortnight. At the end, the famous Gandhi-Irwin pact was signed on 15 March 1931. The civil disobedience movement was withdrawn and defiance of the law was to cease; the pending prosecution or proceedings against the offenders in the recent movement were to be withdrawn; some concession for making salt to those on the coast were made; and the Congress agreed to attend the next Round Table Conference. But the bureaucracy continued to behave despotically as it does to this day.

The Second Round Table Conference met in London from October to December 1931. Gandhiji was chosen by the Congress as their representative to attend the Conference; the Government nominated Madan Mohan Malviya and Sarojini Naidu. The Congress was keen to send Dr. Ansari with Gandhiji, but the Viceroy excluded him, as apparently the Muslim delegates insisted that the Congress represented only the Hindus! At the Conference each representative of a community wanted special concession for his community; there was no consensus on the communal divides. The Conference was a failure.

Gandhiji returned to India on 28 December 1931, in the midst of political turbulence. Nehru and Abdul Gaffar Khan were in jail; martial law prevailed in Bengal. The new Viceroy, Lord Wellington, who had been Governor General of Canada and before that Governor of Bombay and Madras, pursued a very repressive policy when civil disobedience was revived; he enacted several ordinances which gave the Administration extensive despotic powers. Gandhiji too was imprisoned. And as the Second Round Table Conference had failed to agree on the communal tangle, the British Government announced the controversial 'Communal Award' based on its perception of social structures in India.

At the time India was hopelessly divided on communal, caste, tribal and trade lines. The British perceived different electorates for different communities and tradesmen. Christians, Muslims, Sikhs, Hindus, zamindars, industrialists, depressed classes, planters and others were given representation in the Councils and Legislatures. The Muslim League accepted the Communal Award. Gandhiji, however, did not accept the division of the Hindus into higher caste and depressed castes. On 20 September 1932, he started his fast unto death to protest against the Award. The Government ignored the protest, but some senior Congressmen deliberated for six days at Poona to find a way out to save Gandhiji's life. The British Government accepted the Poona Pact draft drawn by the leaders, which enabled Gandhiji to break his fast. But the Government made only cosmetic changes to the Communal Award.

(The Author's father, who was at the time a senior Civil Servant, said, "The communal and caste divide in India is a ground reality. In the absence of any political structures, a caste provides a sense of belonging and social security and sustains an individual at birth, marriage and death; it is an obligation for a family of the same caste to be represented at the rituals for these events. The lower castes are normally tradesmen in the same village who serve the higher castes in one form or another with suitable remuneration and assurances of concern and help during difficult days. The only way to break this equation is give the depressed classes good education, vocational training and separate representation in elected bodies. The same applies to communal minorities. The Communal Award by the British should be supported and not opposed. As the politicians represent a very small percentage of enlightened Indian public opinion they are not therefore in a position "to represent the problems and aspirations of more than 80 per cent of the people".) (Note: Although rejected then, it is now being implemented in the form of reservations for Dalits and backwards!)

The Third Round Table Conference in November 1932, was a farce. Neither the British Labour Party nor the Indian National Congress attended the Conference. The recommendations of the Conference were contained in the White Paper presented to the British Parliament. But the Indian leaders found the proposals conservative and unprogressive. Thus the British Government was obliged to appoint a Joint Select Committee of both Houses of Parliament with Lord Linlithgow (future Viceroy of India) as the Chairman in April 1933, to examine and review the recommendations. This Committee was assisted by 21 delegates from India, who, as expected, submitted two separate memoranda to the Committee, one by a Muslim, the Agha Khan and the other by a Hindu, Sir Tej Bahadur Sapru. Nevertheless, both Houses of the British Parliament approved the report of the Joint Select Committee as Government of India Act 1933, but all politicians in India opposed it. The Act received Royal assent in August 1935 and came into force in April 1937.

In short, a full responsible government was to be established in the provinces by the Act; the Federal Legislature were to have representatives of the provinces and the Indian States; but the departments of defence, foreign affairs, and ecclesiastical matters were reserved to the Governor General. Sind and Orissa were created as two new provinces while Burma was incised from the Indian Empire. The Federation was also to include the Indian States. A Federal High Court was instituted although direct appeals from the Provincial High Courts to the Privy Council in London were permitted under some circumstances.

The need for the overseas deployment of the Indian Army has already been elaborated. The responsibility for meeting the finances involved had now to be fixed. General S.L. Menezes writes in his book, *History of the Indian Army, Fidelity & Honour*, "There was some correspondence with Whitehall as to the financial arrangement for this overseas deployment. For this and other outstanding financial issues the Garran tribunal was appointed which gave its award in 1933. An annual grant of two million pounds was to be made by Britain for this purpose from 1 April 1939, it being one million pounds before that. By 1936 this overseas commitment had increased to two brigades in Egypt, and a brigade each for the Persian Gulf, the Red Sea, Burma and Singapore...A subcommittee was set up under Major General Henry Pownall to report on the current defence problems of India. This noted that India had a major contribution to make to imperial defence..." To give India responsible governments in provinces was a small price to pay in exchange for the defence of the vast British Empire.

But the mutinies and discontent had by no means ended. General Menezes writes, "While the Chatfield Committee was deliberating a multiple murder of four British officers (including the commanding officer) and three VCOs occurred in November 1938 in 4/2nd Punjab in the battalion training camp outside Nowshera. Two other British officers were severely wounded. While individual troops, such as in 5/8 Punjab in 1928 and 1929 (one assailant was refused leave, and the other failed in promotion examination), this was the largest multiple killing of Britons since the mutiny in the 5th Light Infantry at Singapore in 1915. This unit had previously been the 74th Punjabis, "Punjabized" from the Madras Infantry in 1902. In 1905 the subedar major had been shot, in 1932 a murder had occurred in the unit, and in 1936 a VCO had been shot. On this occasion, while in training camp, the observance of Id had been postponed by a day on account of an Army/Air Co-operation demonstration for the brigade. The postponement of the observance was announced at 4:30 p.m. Though Id would normally have been observed the next day, the quarter guard was still manned by Muslims, despite there being Sikh and Dogra companies in the battalion... During the night a Punjabi Mussalman soldier, who was distressed by the postponement, ran amok, and killed and wounded officers and VCOs as already indicated." Had the soldier been a civilian he would be honoured as a martyr today and his statue garlanded on all anniversaries!

On 1 September 1939, Germany invaded Poland. In response Britain and France hesitatingly declared war on the Reich. Without consulting the Central Legislature, the Viceroy, Lord Linlithgow proclaimed on the same day that war emergency existed in India. The Viceroy's despotic highhandedness angered the Indian National Congress and they resigned from the ministries they held in seven provinces despite Gandhiji's advice to support the war. But the Muslim League under Mr. Jinnah was delighted. A little later Mr. Jinnah declared at a League session at Lahore that their aim was an independent state for the Muslims. Thus India started the Second World War on an uncertain note.

Contingents of Indian Army were already overseas. The Brigade in Egypt was gradually made up to what became famous as 4th Indian Division. General Menezes in his book quotes Chenevix Trench's view on the Indian troops, "In Cairo and the Delta they set an example which was to be followed by hundreds of thousands of Indian troops in the Middle East, of being the best behaved and best disciplined of all Allied contingents." General Menezes writes, "At the end of May 1940, a plan to assist Afghanistan against an attack by the Soviet Union was approved by Britain, entailing the raising by India of five infantry divisions (6th, 7th, 8th, 9th, and 10th), and one armoured division (31st), over the next twelve months. In the event, three of these divisions had later to be offered for Iraq, and one for Malaya, necessitating further expansion to replace them." Of course, the strategic situation at the time was very grim for Britain as Hitler had streaked through Holland and Belgium into France forcing the British Expeditionary Force to flee through Dunkirk to the safety of the British Isles; indeed it was a remarkable achievement to evacuate about 340,000 soldiers and others in less than 900 ships mostly small craft provided by volunteers. But a sizeable Indian Army was already in position in the Middle East and the Far East to blunt any Axis thrust towards India. Once again Indian Soldiers were already in position overseas to save the Western Democracies.

Britain's first victory of the War was as Sidi Barrani in Libya in December 1940. The Commander of the Western Desert Force was Maj Gen O'Connor with 7th Armoured Division (famous as Desert Rats), 4th Indian Infantry Division (the Eagle Division), two Infantry Brigades and 7th Royal Tank Regiment-about 31,000 men, 120 guns and 275 tanks in all. 4th Indian Infantry Division supported by 7th Armoured Division smashed the Italian defences at Sidi Barrani. The Commander-in-Chief, Field Marshal Lord Wavell, was to write later, "This ended the first phase of the operations, which may be called the Battle of Sidi Barrani. It had resulted in the destruction of the Greater part of five enemy divisions. Over 38,000 prisoners, 400 guns, some 50 tanks and much other war material had been captured. Our own casualties were only 133 killed, 387 wounded and 8 missing." The British were very lucky to have such outstanding Indian troops fighting for them while the bulk of the British Army was still licking its wounds after Dunkirk.

No sooner was the Sidi Barrani victory assured when General Wavell, the Commander-in-Chief in Middle East, moved 4th Indian Division to join 5th Indian Division already poised in Eritrea for the campaign in Abyssinia. Sir Winston Churchill writes in the *Second World War, Vol. II*, "The Division went partly by sea to Port Sudan, and partly by rail and boat up the Nile. Some of them moved practically straight from the front at Sidi Barrani to their ships, and were in action again in a theatre seven hundred miles away very soon after their arrival." Only the incomparable adaptability of the Indian Soldier could have achieved this remarkable military feat of moving from one front to another, where the terrain was utterly different, and then going into action straightaway on arrival.

Sir Winston Churchill continues, "Meanwhile the campaign in Abyssinia had progressed. Karen resisted obstinately. The flanks of the position could not be turned; only direct frontal attack was possible...the battle proved stubborn and cost us 3,000 casualties... On the 20th (March) General Wavell telegraphed that the fighting had been severe. The enemy had been counter-attacking fiercely and repeatedly, and although their losses had been extremely heavy and they had achieved only one success there were no immediate signs of a crack.... The attack was renewed on March 25, and two days later the Italian defence broke and Karen fell...10,000 prisoners surrendered on April 1...The victory at Karen was mainly gained by the 4th and 5th British Indian Divisions. I paid them the tribute that their prowess deserved.

"Prime Minister to Viceroy of India"

"The whole Empire has been stirred by the achievement of the Indian forces in Eritrea. For me the story of the ardour and perseverance with which they scaled and finally conquered the precipitous heights of Karen recalls memories of the North West Frontier of long years ago, and it is as one who has had the honour to serve in the field with Indian soldiers from all parts of Hindustan, as well as in the name of His Majesty's Government, that I ask Your Excellency to convey to them and to the whole Indian Army the pride and admiration with which we have followed their heroic exploits."

Of course, immediately after the victory, 4th Indian Division was 'rushed' to the Egyptian front where a German offensive was in the making under a new commander, General Erwin Rommel, about whom Sir Winston Churchill said in the House of Commons in January 1942, "We have a very daring and skilful opponent against us, and, may I say across the havoc of war, a great general." The outstanding performance of Indian Soldiers against General Rommel's army has not been given the credit it deserves.

The operations in Middle East precipitated a crisis in Central India Horse, a cavalry Regiment stationed at Hyderabad (Deccan). The Regiment had three squadrons, each comprising, Sikhs, Punjabi Mussalmans and Hindu Jats. The official version mentions only the Sikh squadron as having 'refused to embark' for the voyage to Egypt in July 1940. The squadron was 'disbanded' and its personnel tried by a Court Martial: four were executed, one hundred sentenced to life imprisonment and four to lesser terms of R.I. The unofficial version from retired personnel of the Regiment is that as the Indian element of the Regiment was to go through the Arabian Sea, known to be infested with U-boats, and the British Officers were to fly to Egypt, the whole regiment less the Officers refused to embark to protest against racial discrimination. The Punjabi Mussalmans and Hindu Jats were prevailed upon to relent, but the Sikhs, suspected of having connections with the revolutionary 'Kirti' movement, refused to budge. All India Ex-servicemen Action Committee met in 1985 at Jagraon, Punjab, and interviewed some of the next of kin of those martyred in the Regiment; the Action Committee took up their case and successfully pleaded for the recognition of the martyred as 'Freedom Fighters'. Indeed the mutiny in Central India Horse was a major turning point in the British attitudes and reprehensible discriminations between Indian and British troops. From then on the British knew that they could not take the Indian Officers and Soldiers for granted and a serious attempt was made to elevate their status to equal, as far as possible, with the British Officers and Soldiers. In fact, the Hindu and the Muslim members of the Viceroy's Executive Committee were asked to address Indian Officers and Soldiers to reassure them that things were on the mend. Later, the debacle in Singapore and Burma emphasised the urgency to address and mend British attitudes and discriminations towards Indian Soldiers and Indian Officers.

Maj. Gen. J.F.C. Fuller writes in his book, *The Second World War*, "...by launching an undeclared war on the United States, at one blow Japan solved all Roosevelt's difficulties by galvanising every American to his support. Her (Japan's) inexplicable stupidity was that, by making the Americans the laughing stock of the world, she struck more at their dignity than at their ships." Sir Winston Churchill writes thus about the event, "It was Sunday evening, December 7, 1941. Winant and Averell Harriman were alone with me at the table at Chequers. I turned on my small wireless set shortly after the nine o'clock news had started. There were a number of items about the fighting on the Russian front and on the British front in Libya, at the end of which some few sentences were spoken regarding an attack by the Japanese on American shipping at Hawaii, and also Japanese attacks on British vessels in the Dutch East Indies...No American will think it wrong of me if I proclaim that to have the United States at our side was to me the greatest joy...So we had won after all!"

The Author was attending a Gunnery Course on Manora Island off Karachi. A war with Japan was certainly expected as a Regiment of Heavy Anti Aircraft Artillery had been moved hastily in Oct 1941 from Karachi to Calcutta with a Battery to defend the Digboi oilfields in Assam. Certain Indian Army formations earmarked for the Middle East had also been sent to Burma, Malaya or Singapore. But the general consensus was that the Japanese would find it difficult to operate through the thick jungles of Malaya or the mountains and jungles on the Burmese border. The die-hard British declared after two pegs of Scotch that the Japanese were a savage yellow Asiatic race who had gone wild in China but would have their pants taken off if they clashed with a modern European power. The humiliation wreaked on the Europeans by the Japanese in Shanghai was still rankling in British hearts and minds. Everyone was convinced that the Royal Navy at Singapore with *HMS Prince of Wales* and *HMS Repulse*, two of the most powerful and modern battleships afloat, could take care of anything the Japanese may send to start a battle in South East Asia. But nobody had reckoned that the Japanese Air Force would be efficient and audacious enough to attack the British battleships. With the American Pacific fleet destroyed at Pearl Harbour and the British battleships sunk off Malaya the Japanese Navy was now supreme in both the Pacific and the Indian Oceans.

This is how Sir Winston Churchill received the news of the sinking of the British battleships: "I was opening my box on the 10th (Dec) when the telephone at my bedside rang. It was the First Sea Lord. His voice sounded odd. He gave a sort of cough and gulp, and at first I could not hear quite clearly. 'Prime Minister, I have to report to you that the *Prince of Wales* and the *Repulse* have both been sunk by the Japanese—we think by aircraft'. So I put the telephone down. I was thankful to be alone. In all the war I never received a more direct shock." The Japanese now had a virtually unopposed passage for the invasion of Malaya and Singapore.

Before overrunning Malaya and Singapore, air supremacy was essential for the Japanese. After concentrating their Air Force in Thailand, they struck systematically at all airfields in Malaya and Singapore. For every British aircraft lost in the air, four were destroyed on the ground. After supremacy in the air, their army occupied Singora, Patani and Kota Baru in the north-east using the rail, road and the sea to best advantage. On the western side of the isthmus the strategic Victoria Point was taken and the defences of 11th Indian Division were threatened. The Japanese overran the resistance at Kota Baru airfield and brought their Air Force forward from Thailand to support their army and bomb Singapore. The Japanese found no difficulty in outflanking British defences of 9th Indian Division stretched from Kuantan Port on the east coast to the railway line as the Japanese had trained in Jungle Warfare and they sliced through the Malay jungles much to the surprise and astonishment of the British commanders who had considered the jungles as impenetrable. Positioned in depth in Johore Baru was 8th Division; the Japanese encircled its Brigade on the flank. Indians Divisions and an Australian Brigade fought well but the Japanese were superior in tactics and in the air.

This is what Maj. Gen. Fuller has written, "The rapidity of their (Japanese) advance was largely due to their tactics, which were vastly superior to their enemy's. Whereas, for the greater part, the British (meaning Indians also) soldiers had been trained for war in Europe or Africa and knew nothing about jungle fighting, the Japanese were adepts at it. Whereas the British (and Indian) soldier was loaded down with equipment-pack, gas-mask, steel helmet, etc.—and depended for supply on mechanical transport, the Japanese wore a singlet, cotton shorts and rubber-soled shoes, and being rice-eaters could live off the country. Their two principal weapons were the Tommy gun and light 2-inch mortar. They made extensive use of bicycles, and their transport was the light, two-wheeled, man-hauled cart, similar to those they had used in Manchuria thirty-seven years earlier." By the end of January 1942, the Japanese had captured, destroyed or pushed out of the isthmus all British/Indian and Australian troops. The island of Singapore was now threatened from the North—and not from the approaches by sea, on the basis of which all defence on the island was sighted!

Sir Winston Churchill, the British Prime Minister, was of two minds: should Singapore be defended to the last man and the last round, or should Burma be reinforced to save the supply road to China and for the defence of India. But events moved so fast that decisions taken in London could not be implemented in Singapore.

In his book, the *Second World War*, Sir Winston Churchill gives the message he received from General Wavell, the Supreme Allied Commander of the Far East theatre-

"General Wavell to Prime Minister 16 Jan 42"

"I discussed the defence of island when recently at Singapore, and have asked for detailed plans. Until quite recently all plans based on repulsing seaborne attacks on island and holding land attack in Johore or farther north, and little or nothing was done to construct defences on north side of island to prevent crossing Johore Straits, though arrangements have been made to blow up the causeway. The fortress cannon of heaviest nature have all-round traverse, but their flat trajectory makes them unsuitable for counter-battery work. Could certainly not guarantee to dominate enemy siege batteries with them..."

The fate of Singapore had already been sealed on the day the battleships Prince of Wales and Repulse were sunk by the Japanese. Using iron barges brought with them for the purpose, two Japanese divisions crossed the Johore Straits and established a bridgehead between Kranji Creek and Pasir Laba on the night of 8th/9th February. After repairing the breach in the causeway, Japanese light tanks joined the battle. On 14 February, the three water reservoirs in central Singapore were captured—and water was Singapore's Achilles' heel. The Japanese demanded unconditional surrender. On 15 February General Percival surrendered about 85,000 Indian, British, Australian and Malay Officers and Men and over one million civilians of mixed race in the city. It was not the humiliating defeat that mattered but Britain's inability to protect the subject people in its colonies. There is little doubt that powerful modern forces could have been raised in India to counter the growing Japanese strength, but the British were reluctant to raise large armies in India for fear of another 1857. After all it was the poor toiling people in the colonies, deprived of dignity and freedom, who made Britain rich and gave its people a high standard of living. These subject and defenceless people now felt betrayed and abandoned.

Burma was not only an outpost for the defence of India but it provided a strategic road link to sustain China against Japan's unprovoked aggression and indescribable savagery. Two weak Indian Divisions held Burma over a wide front; Australians refused to divert their troops on the way by sea from the Middle East to Australia. Assured of victory in Malaya, Japanese captured Kawkareik Pass in Dawana Hills, on the border between Thailand and Burma on 21 January 1942. Moulmein in South Burma was soon captured. British/Indian troops offered some resistance on the River Sittang, but the Japanese had mastery of the air and superior skill in fighting in the jungle. To salvage a desperate military situation, General Alexander of Dunkirk fame was appointed to command all troops in Burma on March 5. On 7 March 1942, General Wavell, now Commander-in-Chief in India, complained to the British Prime Minister that, "Communication with Burma has been subject to long delays in the last two days; wireless seems to have broken down altogether and I am without any message from Alexander. I gather from naval message received this morning that decision was suddenly taken about midnight last night to abandon Rangoon, turn back convoys en route, and carry out demolition. Wired Alexander at once to inquire situation, but have had no reply. Will inform you as soon as I have official news."

There were only two arterial roads that ran north-south in Burma: Rangoon-Prome-Mandalay and Rangoon-Toungoo-Mandalay. With mastery of the air and infiltration tactics, the Japanese raced up these roads. The British/Indian/Burmese/Chinese troops, hopelessly deficient in weapons, ammunition and training in jungle warfare did put up a stout resistance in withdrawal, but despite General Alexander's commendable military leadership nothing could hold out against the Japanese juggernaut. Kalewa on the Chindwin was reached on 15 May and as the routes beyond were jungle tracks, all heavy equipment was destroyed by the British/Indian troops before crossing the mighty Chindwin. Beaten, exhausted, sick, wounded and bedraggled the troops were glad to cross over into India on 28 May. But the plight of the countless refugees was much worse.

Ram Gopal writes about the refugees, "What shocked and humiliated India most was the British rulers' racial discrimination in the treatment accorded to British and Indian evacuees from Hong Kong, Malaya, Singapore and Burma. To quote from Indian National Congress Report of the General Secretaries, 'The Indian refugees had to face starvation and death. Children, old men and women fell by the roadside, uncared for and even uncremated. Healthy young men and women were wrecks when they succeeded in reaching the frontiers of India. The British evacuees, on the other hand, were pampered and their lives made as soft and cosy as the British administration in India could make them. The distinction in treatment was carried to the absurd length of setting apart roads, one for the whites and the other for the coloured to travel by. The one for whites was a well-metalled road along which after every few miles were arrangements for feeding, resting, etc. In vivid contrast to this, the inhuman and insulting treatment of tens of thousands of Indians rankled deeply in Indian mind. The cup of India's degradation seemed to be overflowing."

Unfortunately General Percival was also indifferent to the fate of Indian Soldiers after the surrender at Singapore. He wanted the European POWs to be billeted in barracks suitable for them while the Indians could be housed in Changi Jail. The rural Indian is a fiercely proud and sensitive individual; the racial discriminations hurt his pride. The British had bungled the operations and as a consequence the Indian Soldier had suffered a humiliating defeat at the hands of an Asian power the British had always underestimated and decried. There was already disaffection among the Indian Commissioned Officers as they were denied the same status and privileges as the British Officers. General Menezes quotes Field Marshal Auchinleck's views after the latter had spoken, at the end of the War, to the Indian Officers who had revolted against the British at Singapore, "The policy of segregation of Indian officers into separate units, the differential treatment in respect of pay and terms of service as compared with British officers and the prejudice and the lack of manners by some, by no means all, British officers and their wives, all went to produce a very bitter feeling of racial discrimination in the minds of the most intelligent and progressive of the Indian officers."

The execution of four VCOs/ORs from Central India Horse in 1940, for a justifiable offence was widely known in the Army and resented. Britain's inability to defend her colonies was a factor, which had to be taken seriously. The disappointments and uncertainties induced about 25,000 Indian Officers and Soldiers in Japanese bondage (out of about 60,000) to raise the Indian National Army. Captain Mohan Singh was chosen by consensus to be the General Officer to command this force with Headquarters at Mount Pleasant where, before surrender, Indians and Asians were not permitted to enter!

In India there was consternation among the British. The British feared that the entire Indian Army might follow the lead and join the Indian National Army. Every Indian Officer of the rank of Captain and above was asked for his views on the catastrophe. A 'josh' group was formed and some Indian Officers were asked to visit Indian units to express the view that the record of Japanese imperialism in Manchuria, Korea and China was so outrageous that no serving Indian Officer could ever trust them not to behave in the same way in India. The 'josh' groups were permitted to express their wish for equal status with the British and that the British must concede freedom to India after the War. There was panic in British and American leadership also on the future of India should the Japanese relentless thrust continue westward. Sir Winston Churchill records in his book, the *Second World War Vol. IV*, "It was felt by almost all my colleagues that an offer of Dominion status after the war must be made in the most impressive manner to the people of India." Britain had to win the War and it simply could not be done without the famed warriors from India.

President Roosevelt was of the view that a 'temporary Government', 'headed by a small representative group, covering different castes, occupations, religions and geographies—this group to be recognized as a temporary Dominion Government. It would of course represent existing Governments of the British provinces, and would also represent the Council of Princes, but my principal thought is that it would be charged with setting up a body to consider a more permanent Government for the whole country—this consideration to be extended over a period of five or six years, or at least until a year after the end of war. I suppose that this central temporary governing group, speaking for the new dominion, would have certain executive and administrative powers over public services, such as finance, railways, telegraph, and other things which we call public services.'

Sir Winston was also of the same view, which he had cabled to the Viceroy on 16 Feb 1942 "My own idea was to ask the different communities of India—Hindus, Moslems, Sikhs, Untouchables, etc.—to give us their best and leading men for such a body as has been outlined. However, the electoral basis proposed, which was the best we could think of here, may have the effect of throwing the whole Council into the hands of the Congress caucus. This is far from my wish." He clarifies further in the book, "This conception of a Constituent Assembly for which each community and race would pick its foremost leaders was the method I should have followed, at this time and later. It would have avoided dealing only with party politicians." Sir Winston was right as there was no political party at the time, which could make a political appeal to 80 per cent of the Indian people who lived in rural India.

Of interest also is the cable sent by Sir Winston Churchill to President Roosevelt on 4 Mar 1942, "We are earnestly considering whether a declaration of Dominion status after the war, carrying with it, if desired, the right to secede, should be made at this critical juncture. We must not on any account break with the Moslems, who represent a hundred million people, and the main army elements on which we must rely for the immediate fighting. We have also to consider our duty towards thirty to forty million Untouchables, and our treaties with the Princes' states of India, perhaps eighty millions. Naturally we do not want to throw India into chaos on the eve of invasion." Sir Winston erred in saying that the Muslims were 'the main army elements as they were only 37 per cent of the Indian Army; the rest were Sikhs and Hindus.

The Author, son of a Civil Servant, was an Indian Army Captain in Mar 1942, and he and his father were of the view that those politicians who were clamouring for freedom at the time had neither the expertise nor influence among the people to govern a country the size of India in the face of Japanese threat and the desire of Muslim leaders to split the British Indian Empire on communal basis. The impractical demands and obduracy of the politicians in rejecting the British offer of substantial self-governance through Sir Stafford Cripps in 1942, delayed freedom by over 5 years and paved the way for the partition of India. Also Indian leaders would have gained five years experience in running a responsible government in India in collaboration with expert British administrators. This historic blunder resulted in the slaughter of nearly two million Indians during the partition; it also laid the foundation for the continuing hostility between secular India and Muslim Pakistan, which has prevented both countries from making any substantial progress in 55 years of independence.

Bipan Chandra writes in his book *Modern India*, "The failure of the Cripps Mission embittered the people of India.... The All India Congress Committee met at Bombay on 8 August 1942. It passed the famous 'Quit India' Resolution and proposed the starting of a non-violent mass struggle under Gandhi's leadership.... Early in the morning of 9 August, Gandhi and other Congress leaders were arrested and the Congress was once again declared illegal...The Government on its part went all out to crush the 1942 movement. Its repression knew no bounds. The press was completely muzzled. The demonstrating crowds were machine-gunned and even bombed from the air.. Prisoners were tortured. The police and secret police reigned supreme. The military took over many towns and cities....India had not witnessed such repression since the Revolt of 1857....After the suppression of the Revolt in 1942, there was hardly any political activity inside the country till the war ended in 1945." Unfortunately Bipan Chandra has grossly exaggerated the reality as the protests were confined largely to Eastern U.P., Western Bihar and were not extensive or large in nature. But the British repressive measures were certainly brutal.

So far as the Indian Officers and Soldiers were concerned there was no impact of the 'Revolt' on them. The Indian Officers in particular realized that India was gravely threatened by the Japanese and that the "Quit India' movement, which was confined mostly to the district of Ballia and Eastern United Provinces, some areas of Bihar and a few towns, was more of a slogan voiced by a very small fraction of about 400 million Indians than a practical proposition under conditions of war. About 250 rural stations were destroyed, 50 post offices were burned down, a good bit of the railway lines was uprooted and extensive damage was done to some rolling stock and railway engines in a very few isolated places. It was manifestly absurd to believe that the Japanese would leave India alone if the British were to quit in 1942. In fact, the terrible riots before and after Independence in 1947, proved that there was no one in India who could prevent a communal holocaust except the Armed Forces. Obviously India could only be run through the instrument of the Armed Forces who were at the time firmly resolved to defeat the Japanese with British help rather than indulge in slogan mongering. The fact that there was never any dearth of recruits for the armed forces was a clear indication that an overwhelming majority of Indian People felt the same way as the Armed Forces. Also, the outstanding performance of Indian Troops in battle against the Japanese was clear proof of the Indian soldiers' resolve to support the British in winning the War before asking the Indian Empire to wind up and concede freedom.

But the formation of the Indian National Army was indeed the biggest revolt since 1857. Although its fighting value was questionable in military terms, the psychological impact on the USA, Britain and India was immense. The Mutiny in 1857 had failed, as there were no trained leaders to fight the British. Now trained Indian Officers were in command of the best-trained troops in the British Empire. These realities made an enormous impact on the British politicians. Sir Winston Churchill, never too fond of India, now had serious reservations on the expansion of the Indian Army and certainly on the expenditure on defence of India being debited to the British Exchequer. In his book, the *Second World War*, Sir Winston writes, "No great portion of the world population was so effectively protected from the horrors and perils of the World War as were the people of Hindustan. They were carried through the struggle on the shoulders of our small Island. British Government officials in India were wont to consider it a point of honour to champion the particular interests of India against those of Great Britain whenever a divergence occurred. Arrangements made when the war was expected to be fought out in Europe were invoked to charge us for goods and services needed entirely for the defence of India. Contracts were fixed in India at extravagant rates, and debts incurred in inflated rupees were converted into so-called "sterling balances", in other words, British debts to India were piled up. Without sufficient scrutiny or account we were being charged nearly a million pounds a day for defending India from miseries of invasion which so many other lands endured...I declared that these questions must remain open for revision, and that we reserved the right to set off against this so-called debt a counter-claim for the defence of India, and I so informed the Viceroy." Of course, no one in the Indian Armed Forces agreed with this claim.

Sir Winston Churchill continues, "But all this is only the background upon which the glorious heroism and martial qualities of the Indian troops who fought in the Middle East, who defended Egypt, who liberated Abyssinia, who played a grand part in Italy, and who, side by side with their British comrades, expelled the Japanese from Burma, stand forth in brilliant light. Nevertheless, upwards of two and half million Indians volunteered to serve in the forces, and by 1942 an Indian Army of one million was in being. Although this policy of a swollen Indian Army was mistaken in relation to the world conflict, the response of the Indian peoples, no less than the conduct of their soldiers, makes a glorious final page in the story of our Indian Empire."

Of course, Sir Winston Churchill makes no mention of his refusal to apply the declaration of the Atlantic Charter to India's aspirations for freedom. Although many benefits had accrued from the British rule in India, poverty, illiteracy, disease and unemployment were still rampant. In two hundred years India had been systematically milked of its riches; its land and people were harnessed for exploitation by British business community; its soldiery was used recklessly and callously to defend the British Empire. Employment was provided to a large number of Britons with higher pay, perks and provision of much better creature comforts than those to Indian Soldiers. India was turned into a great citadel of the British Empire, a firm base from where the richest deposits of oil on earth in the Gulf region could be defended and the trade routes to the Far East and Australia could be secured. In fact, defence of India meant the defence of British colonies in the Far East, New Zealand

and Australia and Britain herself. There was no need for India to be grateful but Britain should have expressed its gratitude to India for the enormous sacrifices made by the Indian people for the defence of the Realm and for enriching their Island Nation. It was not India that was in 'debt' but Britain.

Why did the Japanese not invade India in 1942 after their spectacular military successes in Burma? Maj. Gen. J.F.C. Fuller provides the answer in his book, the *Second World War*, "Though the British had been in Burma for over a hundred years, so little attention had they paid to its strategic defence that but three mule tracks, frequently impassable during the monsoon, traversed the Indo-Burmese frontier. Within Burma itself, except for the Rangoon-Myitkyina-Lashio and the Rangoon-Prome railways, all trunk communications running south to north were still by river, mainly the Irrawaddy.........Both the British and Japanese problems were, therefore, one of communications..." The Japanese had to build up their communications to sustain an operation through the thick jungles and steep mountains between India and Burma.

While Japan was building up its resources in Burma to attack India, feverish activity was going on in India not only to meet the expected Japanese onslaught but also to liberate Burma. For these operations South East Asia Command was created on 15 Aug 43, with Admiral Lord Louis Mountbatten as the Supreme Allied Commander; his HQ were first in India and then shifted to Kandy in Sri Lanka (then Ceylon). Under Lord Mountbatten were Commanders-in-Chief Navy, Army and Air Force. On the army side, Lt. Gen. Sir Oliver Leese was C-in-C XI Army Group, comprising, among others, Fourteenth Army under Lt Gen Sir William Slim with IV Corps deployed in area Kohima-Imphal-Manipur-Tammu and XV Corps under Lt Gen Christison deployed on the Arakan front. A Chinese Army with an American Brigade were in the Hukawng Valley on the Ledo Road. Substantial supplies were also being sent to China by air over the 'hump'. These large forces had to be sustained by air, road and rail from depots in India. As a consequence there was very little goods or other civilian traffic on these links, which deprived Bengal of the foodstuffs it needed to ward off a famine. Bipan Chandra writes in the *History of Modern India*, "In 1943, Bengal was plunged into the worst famine in recent history. Within a few months over three million people died of starvation. There was deep anger among the people for the Government could have prevented the famine from taking such a heavy toll of life. This anger, however, found little political expression." Who says India did not pay a heavy price for the Allied victory? More than 25,000 Indian Soldiers perished on the battlefields and 3 million Indians died of starvation so that the western democracies might live. (The Author was in the Arakan at the time and saw the terrible famine conditions and suffering of the people in Bengal—more of it later).

In January 1944, XV Corps in the Arakan crossed into Burma and captured Maungdaw. The Japanese reacted by cutting off the maintenance lines to 7th Indian Division at Sinweya. Lord Mountbatten had promised the troops that if they were to get cut off, as in the past, they must stay put and fight it out in a 'box' (organised for all-round defence) and that he would make sure that they were supplied by air. The new tactics paid off. On the Ledo Road front, the Chinese-American troops were also on the offensive, sustained by air-supply. 3rd Indian Division, called 'the Chindits', under a brilliant general, Orde Wingate, was air-dropped or ferried in gliders into Katha area behind the Japanese troops operating against the Chinese-American forces in the Hukawng Valley. 3rd Indian Division was sustained entirely by air and provided a model for operations in future years.

But early in March 1944, before the British offensive could gain momentum, the Japanese launched their offensive into India. With 33rd, 15th and 31st Divisions; Gandhi and Bose

Brigades of the INA were to move behind 15th Japanese Division as 'Occupation Troops'. The aim of 33rd and 15th Divisions was to isolate and then capture Imphal; 33rd Division also had the subsidiary task of cutting off 17th Indian Division in area Tiddim and then to destroy it. 31st Japanese Division was to cut the Imphal-Kohima road and after capturing Kohima to seize the main Allied road and railhead base at Dimapur, thus cutting off supplies to the Chinese-American troops in the Hukawng and Salween Valley areas; further into India airfields were to be captured, thus to cut off air-supply to China and prevent the completion of the Road Ledo-Myitkyina-Lashio. It was a daring plan executed with the expected Japanese ruthlessness, but it lacked flexibility and the Japanese commander lacked common sense and imagination. But they were no different from other Asian powers that boast about 'supreme sacrifice in battle' and thus they tend to reinforce failure for the sake of prestige and braggadocio. There was rigid control over the tactics of lower commanders and three important Principles of War, the Japanese almost always neglected viz. Economy of Effort, Flexibility and Administration.

In the event 17th Indian Division at Tiddim and 20th Indian Division (Author's Division) at Tammu were withdrawn, after they had put up a good fight, into previously prepared defences of IV Corps 'box' at Imphal. General Slim, the Fourteenth Army Commander, decided to fly out all unnecessary administrative personnel from the 'box' to reduce the strain on logistics. About two and a half Divisions with their Artillery were flown in to reinforce the defensive position of IV Corps. General Slim wanted the Japanese to fight with stretched out and vulnerable maintenance communications while IV Corps was sustained by air in a compact defensive position with no danger to its Lines of Communications.

Japanese 31st Division raced north of the turbulent Chindwin astride axis Myingwe-Ukrul-Maram and Homalin-

Soma-Jessami-Kohima to carry out their task. The troops were highly motivated and eager to liquidate Kohima and seize the huge base at Dimapur, while some elements of the Division were to cut off the rail and road to Ledo and the Kohima-Imphal highway, so that the other two Divisions moving up, with INA Brigades, could overwhelm IV Corps in and around Imphal. As it happened the Japanese did isolate IV Corps at Imphal. But Kohima proved a difficult nut to crack. It is quite remarkable really that Kohima survived the Japanese onslaught as it had only the following troops when the Japanese struck on 3 April 1944:

> 1 Assam Regiment
>
> 3 Assam Rifles (Seven companies – Para Military)
>
> Shere Regiment from Nepal (Poor equipment)
>
> Three Companies of Indian Infantry (Mostly from the Transit Camp)
>
> One Company of British NCOs and Men from the Reinforcement Camp
>
> Two Companies of Burma Regiment
>
> Two Platoons 5/27 Mahratta Light Infantry
>
> A Detachment of 'V' Force (Used for gathering intelligence – proved valuable in war)
>
> Administrative personnel and the Military Hospital.

On 6 April, 1944, while the Japanese were already in contact with the defences of Kohima, 4th Battalion of British Royal West Kent Regiment (4RWR) from 161 Indian Brigade was sent to reinforce the Kohima garrison—the intention was to send the whole of 161 Indian Infantry Brigade but the Japanese had by then cut off the Dimapur-Kohima road!

XXXIII Indian Corps had only 2nd British Division under command at the time and it was preparing for amphibious operations against the Japanese on the Arakan coast; it was located in the Bangalore-Belgaum area in South India. (Incidentally, the 2nd British Division was an old formation which was on its way to join the Eighth Army in North Africa, but was diverted to India as India had no British troops to take care of the political situation in the Subcontinent.) Lt Gen Montagu Stopford was the Corps Commander (the Author was his ADC when the Gen assumed command of the Twelfth Army). Gen Stopford was commissioned in the Rifle Brigade in 1911. He was awarded the Military Cross in the First World War. In 1939 he was given command of 17th British Infantry Brigade and sent to France under Maj. Gen Bernard Montgomery. Gen Stopford was awarded the DSO for operations against the Germans. After Dunkirk he was given command of 56th British Infantry Division in England for a bit and then transferred to the Staff College, Camberley, as the Commandant—he had been an instructor there earlier. In 1943 he was promoted to Lt Gen and given command of XII Corps in Britain. Gen Stopford's father had commanded the Corps, which landed on the Turkish coast at Suvla Bay in the First World War; as the whole Gallipoli operation was a fiasco Stopford's father also suffered humiliation. Gen Stopford was determined to redeem that humiliation. As Lord Mountbatten, the Supreme Allied Commander South East Asia, was the father of Amphibious Operations and was keen to lodge a sizeable force behind the Japanese in the Arakan, he asked for a 'clued up' general to command the operation. Gen Stopford had a very high reputation as a professional soldier and he was sent to command the forces which were to land on the Burmese shores. But, just when he thought he had nothing to do as the assault craft promised to SEAC were allotted to Anzio operations in the Mediterranean, his Corps HQ and the 2nd British Division were ordered to move 'Eastward'. He left by plane from Poona on 23 Mar 44, for Comilla where Gen Slim, Fourteenth Army Commander, gave him the following tasks (taken from The Account of Operations of XXXIII Indian Corps, original copy with the Author):

(a) Immediate Task: to prevent Japanese infiltration or penetration into the Brahamputra and Surma Valleys or through the Lushai Hills.

(b) To keep open the main Dimapur-Kohima road L of C to 4 Corps.

(c) To be prepared to move to the assistance of 4 Corps and to help in all possible ways to destroy the enemy West of R. Chindwin.

Also from the Account, "During the eleven days of the siege the garrison (at Kohima) had had little or no sleep. The men were utterly exhausted and could not have continued the fight much longer in spite of food, water and ammunition dropped by air. The value of the stand of 4 RWR made at Garrison Hill was fully appreciated when 2 Div began their final assault. Had the salient of Garrison Hill (held by 4RWR) and Piquet Hill (held by 1 Assam Regt) been lost the capture of Kohima would undoubtedly have been an even harder and more costly operation than it later proved to be. Their defence against a much numerically superior enemy had been costly and 4 RWR marched out with only 250 strong." Lord Mountbatten was to call it a decisive battle of the War—certainly it was a turning point in the war against the Japanese. Although 4th Battalion the Queens Own Royal West Kent Regiment or 4 RWR has received the encomium it deserves, the Indian units which were there from the outset and had displayed unprecedented tenacity and courage in the face of murderous onslaught by the Japanese have been ignored. This is the kind of discrimination that was resented by the Indian Soldier during the Raj.

The battles at Kohima and Imphal were won as the Japanese had long stretched out maintenance communication links which could be bombed from the air and rendered ineffective, whereas the Indian/British/American/Chinese troops could be supplied from the air—'like Father Christmas, down the chimney'. Of course, air superiority is a vital pre-requisite for such operations.

2nd British Division was the only European formation in the Fourteenth Army and XXXIII Indian Corps. The Division had done some training in Jungle warfare near Belgaum in

South India when it was suddenly moved to Dimapur for the relief of Kohima. It takes a while to get used to fighting in the jungles and mountains; the Division did not have an opportunity to get acclimatized before it was committed to battle against highly motivated Japanese troops in the Kohima area. Even after the relief of Kohima the British Division was sluggish in operations as compared with the highly skilled Indian Divisions. General Stopford, who was himself British Service, was constrained to remove the General Officer Commanding the British Division and the Division itself was relegated to a subsidiary role for the rest of the War. (This was not the last time the General removed senior commanders from their posts!)

Maj. Gen J.F.C. Fuller writes in *The Second World War*, "Thus, except for the clearing up of a considerable number of Japanese detachments, Burma was recaptured in one of the most remarkable campaigns of the entire war. Remarkable in that few other theatres of the war presented so many obstacles to organized fighting. Heat, rain, tropical diseases, mountains, rivers, swamps, and all but total lack of roads seemed to have marked out Burma as one of the few regions in the world where powerful and highly equipped armies could not fight. Yet, in the last campaign, half a million men were employed, and, as we have seen, armies of considerable size freely moved from north to south and west to east over high mountain ranges, broad rivers, and through dense forest and jungle at no mean speed. That this was possible was due to many factors, and, besides leadership and soldiership, the three outstanding were air power, medical care and engineering." To this must be added the fact that only Indian Soldiers with their incomparable courage, tenacity and hardiness could have achieved this astonishing feat in military history; in fact, the life-style of the Indian Soldier was so simple that he could subsist in battle on foodstuffs that were not difficult to deliver, thus imposing much less strain on the maintenance organisations as compared with European troops.

Now for the clearing of "a considerable number of Japanese detachments" mentioned above by General Fuller. On 28 May 1945, XXXIII Corps was converted into the new Twelfth Army under command of Lt. Gen. Sir Montagu Stopford KBE CB DSO MC and a few days later the Author joined him as his only ADC from 20th Indian Division, which had fought its way down to Tharrawaddy. Rangoon had already been captured and the Port cleared by 6 May 1944. It was decided to locate Twelfth Army HQ in the famous Judson College. The Army Commander and his personal and principal staff lived in the Wright Brothers buildings on the Lake. As Fourteenth Army was preparing to pull out for an amphibious assault on Malaya, all operational responsibility in Burma was handed over to Twelfth Army "to prosecute the war against the enemy in Burma; to take over operational and administrative responsibility in liberated Burmese territory; and to be responsible for Internal Security and law and order.' The Chief of Civil Administration, Maj. Gen. Hugh Ranse, lived in the Wright Brothers building and was a part of Gen. Stopford's staff. He was later appointed Governor of Burma.

At the end of May the remnants of Japanese 15, 28 and 33 Armies as also other elements and civilians were either trapped in the Pegu Yomas or were east of the Axis Toungoo-Rangoon. To deal with this assortment, Twelfth Army had the following troops:

17th, 20th and 26th Indian Divisions

82nd (West African) Division (located in North Burma for operations if needed)

6 Infantry Brigade

268 Indian Infantry Brigade

254 Indian Tank Brigade

IV Corps under Lt Gen Sir Frank Messervy comprising 5th, 7th and 9th Indian Divisions and 255 Indian Tank Brigade

Force 136 and V Force (Proved very useful in collecting Intelligence)

In support were Patriot Burmese Forces under Gen Aung Sen (whose office was next to the Author in Judson College).

The Japanese breakout from the Pegu Yomas started on 19/20 July 1945. Twelfth Army formations were deployed with brilliant military intuition to deal with them. A 'plan' for the breakout was recovered from a Japanese Officer and there was some discussion whether this plan was 'planted' or genuine. Nevertheless General Stopford could not be persuaded to change his mind as the existing deployment had taken into account the possibility of the usual Japanese ruse to give misleading information through 'plants'. The Japanese were killed in very large numbers when they tried to force their way through to cross the Sittang River. The figures of Japanese killed between 19 July and 4 Aug, when the operations virtually came to an end were: counted dead 6271; claimed killed by guerrilla forces 3200; prisoners 710. Twelfth Army casualties during the same period were 95 killed and 322 wounded! There was sporadic fighting till 15 Aug 1945, when the Japanese surrendered. The History of the Twelfth Army gives details of the Japanese strength in the Pegu Yomas, "After sifting all available evidence (from documents produced by the Japanese after the war), the strength of the force involved was assessed at approximately 19,000. The figure of 30,618 was Japanese estimate of the whole force cut off and of this figure 15,744 were casualties."

General Menezes writes in his *History of the Indian Army*, "The mainly Indian 14th Army, under General William Slim, repulsed the Japanese, and then inflicted on them the biggest defeat that their ground forces suffered in the Second World War, the Japanese suffering much greater casualties than in the Pacific at the hands of the Americans." Louis Allen writes in his book, *Sittang, the Last Battle*, "X Day is what the Japanese in Burma called it. In the calendar it was 20 July 1945, just over three weeks before the war in the Far East came to an end. On that day, thousands of Japanese troops belonging to

28 Army came out of the rain-sodden fastness of the hills of Pegu Yomas and attempted to break through the cordon of British and Indian Divisions which held the line of the long road that led from Mandalay to Rangoon. It was the very last battle which the British Army fought in the Second World War, the last battle of the Japanese forces in South-East Asia, the last battle of a united Indian Army before partition into India and Pakistan split up for ever one of the finest armies in the history of warfare." It was not the Fourteenth Army but the Twelfth who fought these last battles. Of course there were some British units in the fray but no British Divisions; also it was not the last time the united Indian Army fought the 'last' battle—the operations in French Indo-China and Dutch East Indies, where these Indian Divisions were sent a little later, were as intense as the battles in Burma—the Author was a witness! Nevertheless, General Stopford felt he had redeemed his pledge and avenged his father's humiliation at Suvla Bay – he was later elevated to KCB and four stars for the impeccable conduct of the operations by his Twelfth Army. Of course, it was in Burma that Japan lost the war as it was here that the largest Japanese forces were smashed and pursued by Indian Troops under British command. The defeated, bedraggled and frightened Japanese survivors ran for safety to Siam, but were waylaid and killed in thousands. (The Author was privileged to witness these operations as the only ADC to the Army Commander who had planned and conducted them and the Author was greatly impressed by his General's professionalism and aplomb in battle.)

The devastating effect of strategic bombing of mainland Japan predominantly by carrier based US aircraft, cannot, however be overlooked. 160,800 tons of bombs were dropped on Japan to destroy the Japanese potential to wage war. Maj. Gen. J.F.C. Fuller in his *Second World War* quotes the Tokyo Radio broadcast of June 9, 1945, which reads, "At Tokyo, 767,000 dwellings had been destroyed and 3, 100,000 persons had been rendered homeless. At Nagoya there were 380, 000 homeless and 96,000 buildings had been destroyed; Yokohama, 680,000 homeless and 132,000 dwellings destroyed; at Kobe, 260,000 homeless and 70,000 buildings destroyed; at Osaka, 510,000 homeless and 130,000 dwellings destroyed." With the defeat in Burma and the systematic destruction of her homes and industries, Japan was already on her knees. The Emperor and the Japanese Navy wanted peace. But on July 16, much to the ill fortune of the world, Albert Einstein's dreaded formula on the release of energy on splitting an atom was successfully tested in a stretch of bleak desert in New Mexico, USA. Mr. Truman, President of the United States of America and Mr. Winston Churchill, Prime Minister of Great Britain, were conferring at Potsdam when they were informed about the successful detonation of the first atom bomb. They decided there and then to use two such bombs to force Japan to surrender to their terms and to save further casualties in war. President Truman announced on August 6, "If they do not now accept our terms they may expect a rain of ruin from the air, the like of which has never been seen on this earth." On this decision Maj. Gen. J.F.C. Fuller comments in his book, The Second World War, "If the saving of life was true pretext, then, instead of reverting to a type of war which would have disgraced Tamerlane, all Mr. Truman and Mr. Churchill need have done was to remove the obstacle of unconditional surrender, when the war could have been brought to an end immediately."

On orders of Mr. Truman, Hiroshima was selected as the first of two targets and on August 6,1945, a B-29 US bomber flew over the town at 8:15 a.m. when children were in school and workers in their factories, and released its deadly cargo over the densely populated Japanese city. The atom bomb, dangling from a parachute, duly exploded at hundreds of feet above the ground zero. Thus, in the fraction of a second about 180, 000 men, women and children were charred to death and 62, 000 houses lay in ruins, while 4.4 square miles of the city was completely burnt out.

Two days later, on August 8, 1945, the second atom bomb was dropped on Nagasaki. The terrain helped to save most of the 260, 000 inhabitants and only about 40, 000 were killed. Maj. Gen J.F.C. Fuller writes, "Thus, by means of two projectiles, a quarter of a million human beings were slaughtered and maimed, and to crown the event, on this same day – 9th August – President Truman broadcast to his fellow countrymen the following pious words: 'We thank God that it has come to us instead of to our enemies, and we pray that he may guide us to use it in his way and for his purpose."

On August 14, 1945, the Emperor of Japan accepted the provisions of the Potsdam Declaration. Maj. Gen. J.F.C. Fuller comments in his book, The *Second World War*, "Thus force triumphed over wisdom, the animal in man over the human, and for the sake of the future the brutality of the Potsdam decision to use the atomic bomb demands a moment's thought. ...By the Western Allied Powers the war in the Far East, as in Europe, allegedly was fought in the name of Justice, Humanity and Christianity; yet it was won by means which mongrelized war and thereby mongrelized peace." General Fuller ought to have realized that Governments designate themselves as "Secular" to avoid strictures based on religious commandments and sentiments.

F.W. Perry writes in his book, The *Commonwealth Armies: Manpower and Organisation in Two World Wars*, "Without the Indian Army, Britain would have been quite unable to meet her many commitments in the Middle East and Far East." General Menezes in his book on the Indian Army quotes Field Marshall Auchinleck, "I think the English never cared; the English who lived in England, the politicians, I don't think they ever took any interest in India at all. I think they used it...they couldn't have come through both wars if they hadn't had the Indian Army. I think they never really understood it."

Part II

The War in Europe had ended with the defeat of Germany in May 1944. The burden of fighting the War against Japan now lay heavily on the Indian Soldier who had withstood the Japanese onslaught into India with remarkable tenacity. Under the outstanding leadership of Admiral Mountbatten and General Slim the Japanese Juggernaut had not only been smashed but pushed back into Burma. Before the final battles were over, Field Marshal Wavell, Viceroy of India, visited England in June 1945, to finalize his plan for 'Indianisation of his Executive Council', which Churchill approved on the eve of a general election in Britain. The plan envisaged that except for the Viceroy and the Commander-in-Chief all appointments in the Viceroy's Executive Committee were to be held by an equal number of Hindus and Muslims. As Jinnah wanted all Muslims in the Council to be his nominees, the whole plan foundered on his obduracy.

Japan surrendered on 15 Aug 45, but the Indian Soldiers were needed for 'imperial' duty in Far East and Middle East and had to be kept in good humour with positive steps for freedom. In February 1946, the Royal Indian Navy revolted against the establishment demanding better service conditions and a status equal to the British Royal Navy. The Royal Indian Air Force was also rebellious. There was disaffection among the intellectuals over the trial of the Indian National Army personnel and serious demonstrations in Calcutta demanding their release. Britain's Officers and Soldiers in India and the Far East were wary of the War and eager to go home for a 'White Christmas'. And there was the Atlantic charter with its promise of freedom with American pressure that it must be implemented. Britain herself had been ravaged by the War and she was in no position to hang on to India where an Army of two million with highly experienced and skilled Officers could stage another 1857! In fact, from the time of the formation of the Indian National Army very detailed plans had been prepared for action in case the Indian Army became 'unreliable' or in the event of a 'mutiny'. For that reason the Signal Regiment was never totally Indianised nor were Indian Officers permitted to operate the Ciphers used for encoding secret messages till 1946. In the Operations and Intelligence Directorates Top Secret documents on Internal Security were not shown to Indian Officers.

As soon as the new Labour Government came to power in Britain in July 1945, all political prisoners in India were released. Fresh elections to Central and Provincial Assemblies were held in 1946 on the basis of the Government of India Act of 1935, and Indian Ministers took charge of the Administration in the Provinces. The new British Government conceded India's right to self-determination – there was clearly no other option!

In March 1946, the new British Labour Government wisely decided to send a Cabinet Mission, to negotiate with Indian politicians on the terms for transfer of power to Indian hands. An elected Constituent Assembly was to frame the Constitution but in the meanwhile an interim government was to be formed with the help of all the chief political parties. The Muslim League claimed to be the sole representative of the Muslims in India although it had lost the elections in the North West Frontier Province and Punjab. The Congress claimed to be a 'secular party', a stand rejected by the Muslim League. When no agreement was reached after protracted negotiations, the Muslim League called for 'Direct Action', which instigated Hindu-Muslim riots in Bengal and the Frontier; the riots carried on till independence and partition. Nevertheless, in September 1946, an interim Cabinet, with Pundit Nehru as the head, was formed by the Congress on Lord Wavell's invitation

Wavell had seen Atlee in December 1946 with a new plan, which in effect was a phased withdrawal from India. The British Prime Minister regarded the plan as more military than political and made up his mind to replace Wavell. As the British Government had declared its intention to quit India by

June 1948, it decided that a younger man with charisma might do better In transferring power to Indian hands by June 1948 than Wavell. The Viscount Mountbatten of Burma, who, as a Rear Admiral, was commanding a Destroyer Flotilla in Malta, was selected to be the new Viceroy of India. The King insisted that Lord Mountbatten be give a clear directive on what he was required to do and Lord Mountbatten confirmed on arrival in India on 22 March 1947, that "His Majesty's Government are resolved to transfer power by June 1948".

Lord Mountbatten's aim was quite clear: to transfer power to Indian hands in a united India and if that were not possible to split the British Indian Empire into India and Pakistan as desired by the Muslim League. He worked very hard to keep India united, but as Pundit Nehru was adamant on becoming the first Prime Minister because he represented the largest political party, an ambition also shared by Mr. Jinnah, partition of the British Indian Empire on Hindu-Muslim basis was the only answer. The question that remained to be answered was, when?

Mr. Jinnah had called for Direct Action in August 1946 to protest against the number of vacancies allotted to the Muslims and the reluctance of the Congress to accept his nominated members in the interim government. That was the beginning of the mayhem that spread throughout India—but particularly to those regions, which are today Pakistan and Bangladesh. Regrettably Mr. Jinnah was responsible for the slaughter of over two million Muslims and Hindus during the Partition only because he wanted to teach the Congress a 'lesson'. Some historians have asserted that no effort was made to quell the Hindu-Muslim riots. They are prejudiced, ignorant and wrong. There were about two Infantry Divisions in Calcutta alone, but there were not enough troops to take care of every single town and village in the whole of India. When people decide to kill each other in a senseless orgy, no government on earth can do much to prevent them. There was no dearth of appeals issued by the so-called leaders in Delhi, but this had no impact on the people who were possessed by the devil to seek revenge for the loved ones they had lost. The situation in May 1947, alarmed the Viceroy. He decided to go to the Punjab and the North West Frontier Province to make a personal assessment of the situation and then decide how to deal with it. (The Author had already briefed Lord Mountbatten on the gravity of the Hindu-Muslim riots in Peshawar and the NWFP where the Author was stationed before he joined the Viceroy as ADC.)

At Peshawar Sir Olaf Caroe briefed him on the situation in the Frontier Province, which was alarming. A mob of over 50,000 had gathered astride the railway line east of the Provincial Assembly Building and Lord and Lady Mountbatten took the risk and stood on the railway embankment to wave at them. The mob screamed for the immediate creation of Pakistan. Caroe had arranged a 'Jirgah' of tribal chiefs at Landi Kotal or the Khyber the next day. The Viceroy (accompanied by the Author as the ADC) and the Governor attended the 'Jirgah' (without the ladies) where rifle and sword brandishing tribal chiefs threatened to invade Hindu-India if Pakistan was not conceded immediately! The speeches and the slogan shouting were bloodcurdling! (The Author was the only Hindu present in the huge rally and he was more amused than frightened. There were many realistic scenes from the film 'Bengal Lancers'.) On the way back to Peshawar the motorcade was waylaid by Jamait-e-Islami students who demanded the immediate creation of Pakistan.

From Peshawar the Viceroy flew to Rawalpindi where General Sir Frank Messervy, the Army Commander, was full of woes. At his behest Lord Mountbatten visited Kahuta and saw the terrible carnage in a Gurudwara. Sikh men, women and children who had taken refuge in the Gurudwara were hacked to pieces and as many as could fill the well there were dumped in it and the rest just scattered all over. The stench of the decaying bodies was unbearable, but Lord Mountbatten stood there with eyes full of tears and made up his mind that the only answer was to split the British Indian Empire and transfer power to Indian and Pakistani hands, as soon as possible, to stop the awful brutality that pervaded a peaceful land. Messervy advised Mountbatten 'to get out before it was too late'. (The Author told them that there could be a civil war if action was not taken immediately to resolve the issue.) On return to Delhi the Viceroy sought permission of the British Government to visit London to discuss an early transfer of power.

15 August was selected for transfer of power as Lord Mountbatten had accepted Japanese unconditional surrender on that day and it also happened to be the date on which he was appointed Supreme Allied Commander of South East Asia. When he returned to India, Pundit Nehru told him that the astrologers had determined that 15 August as a day was inauspicious, but that Midnight 14/15 was all right—hence Freedom at Midnight. But Pakistan demanded freedom on the 14th and Lord Mountbatten had to fly to Karachi in the morning to 'hand over' power to Mr. Jinnah and then fly back to Delhi after lunch. At Midnight 14/15 August, Lord Mountbatten and his personal staff listened to Pundit Nehru's speech, 'Tryst With Destiny', on the radio in Government House. After the ceremony in Parliament House, Pundit Nehru, Sardar Patel and Rajendra Prasad came to Government House to call on the new Governor General. The Muslim ADC having gone to Karachi, the two remaining Indian ADCs to Lord Mountbatten hosted a champaign party to usher in freedom and Lord and Lady Mountbatten and his British Staff attended the party with Pundit Nehru, Sardar Patel and Mr. Rajendra Prasad as the guests.

15 Aug had a busy schedule. Pundit Nehru, the new Prime Minister, had to unfurl the new Indian National Flag on the ramparts of the Red Fort—a practice carried on by successive Prime Ministers today. The Governor General was

to attend the Constituent Assembly and unfurl the National Flag near the India Gate War Memorial on the Kingsway (now Rajpath). All this had to be done when movement on the roads of New and Old Delhi was virtually impossible as Delhi had been invaded by millions of revellers who were jam-packed on all major highways.

The Viceroy had three Indian ADCs; on 14 Aug when he went to Karachi he left behind the Muslim Naval ADC who had opted to serve with Jinnah. The Air Force ADC had gone ahead to Parliament House to oversee the protocol and arrangements on the podium. The Author was in the state carriage, which was trying to ply through a solid wall of humanity. At every two yards the ADC had to get down from the carriage and beg the crowd to give way to the Governor General. The crowd was seized by a spontaneous outburst of indescribable ecstasy and madness. A number of people managed to reach up and kiss Lady Mountbatten's hand or touch Lord Mountbatten's feet. They shouted repeated slogans, 'Pundit Mountbatten ki jai' (victory to Pundit Mountbatten).

The drive in the state carriage to India Gate was indeed a hassle. The crowds were denser and there was a good deal of commotion among them to shove and push their way to get a closer glimpse of their new Governor General and his Lady. When the mounted Body Guards tried to position themselves close and round the carriage, Lord Mountbatten ordered the ADC to make it clear to the Body Guards that they were not to do so. After many halts and joyous scenes, the crowd dancing or shouting pro-Mountbatten slogans, the carriage managed to reach India Gate to find that Pundit Nehru had almost been 'lynched' by an adoring crowd. Mountbatten took him on board the carriage, with Indira Gandhi and Mrs. Sarojni Naidu, to save Nehru from his admirers. As it was impossible to step out of the carriage, Lord Mountbatten ordered his ADC (the Author) to somehow get to the Flag Mast and unfurl the Tricolour. Indeed it was the most prestigious and unique order in history when the Head of State requested his ADC to unfurl the National Flag to symbolize the birth of a new free Nation. The ADC was literally hurled or carried by the spirited crowd to the Flag Mast and in the process lost most of the accoutrements on his splendid uniform. But he unfurled the Tricolour with great pride and emotion – the second Tricolour to be unfurled on that First Day of Freedom – and attained immortality for himself in history! On his return after unfurling the Tricolour, the state carriage started moving towards King Edward Road, which had a thinner crowd than Kingsway (now Rajpath). But, of course, with all the 'refugees' on board the ADC had lost his place in the carriage and had to run behind it and in front of the accompanying Mounted Body Guard all the way to Government House through the South Gate. When the movie of the episode was shown at Government House, Lord and Lady Mounbatten and the Staff roared with laughter!

At last India was free! What a joy to behold!

Part III

Reminiscences

It was in 1936 that I first met Indira Nehru Gandhi. Earlier in the year her three cousin sisters had joined Woodstock School in Mussoorie, when I was a student in the 8th Standard. Indira's mother, Kamla, was gravely ill in a TB sanatorium in Switzerland and Indira awaited her father's release from jail in Dehra Dun before going on with him to visit her mother. She was four years older than I and looked a good bit like my eldest sister. Those were the years when I was stuck on sports, cars, hikes and film stars. To my disappointment, I discovered that she had no interest in any of my fads. She was inordinately self-conscious and reticent. I thought she was rather small and frail, but attractive. She had a disconcerting habit of suddenly lapsing into silence and looking at you intensely with big probing eyes. Once jokingly she said that her nose was too big for her face and when I offered to bite off the extra bit she screamed at me in violent rage – thereafter I was afraid to say anything offensive to her right till the end. Of course, she had a distinct class about her and she was proud of her heritage, but she was not a person one could cultivate on the first meeting. She appeared to be contemptuous of the British but her mannerisms and style were very western. When she spoke of freedom I perked up a bit and asked her how we were going to get it. "My father will get it for us," she said definitively! This was the beginning of my vague interest in politics.

On his release from jail, Pundit Jawaharlal Nehru visited my School. Everybody made a fuss of him. I was sitting in the Library when he came there to autograph his book, *Letters from a Father to His Daughter (or Glimpses of World History)*. He had schooled at Harrow in England and obtained a degree in Natural Sciences from the Cambridge University. Before he returned to India in 1912, after seven years, he was called to the bar. As a Barrister, he joined his father who was already in the profession at Allahabad. Indira introduced me to him and despite my youth, I could feel at once that he was in a class much above the rest. Pundit Nehru had an inspiring presence. He was inordinately handsome and dignified. There was no bitterness about the jail or the British, but he was obviously concerned that his wife's condition had deteriorated while he was imprisoned.

Later in the year, when I went home on winter vacation from the School in December I told my father that I had met Nehru. I asked him about the 'freedom movement' as my history teacher, a Welsh Lady of missionary background, had told me that the Government of India Act of 1935 would give all the freedom India wanted. He said, "There is a good deal of upheaval among the intellectuals for self-rule. The British have conceded what they call 'full responsible government' in the major provinces. Burma has been taken away from India and two new provinces of Sind and Orissa have come into being. But there is very little democracy in all this as there is no universal suffrage. Those who pay land revenue and income tax can vote to elect members to the Legislative Assembly. To vote for members of the Council one has to have substantial property or one must have been a member of local Legislative Council or a Legislature. That leaves out more than 85 per cent of Indians from a share in any 'full responsible government'. But the Act will satisfy those who are vociferous for self-rule, as all they want is status and political power. The electoral rules do not make them the true representatives of the farmers, who provide the soldiers, or the labour that is exploited by the businessman. The British Government is obliged to pander to the politicians' ego as fascism is on the rise in Europe. Both Germany and Italy say that they must have an empire to milk just as the other European powers have. With upheavals in India and with a defiant Indian Soldier it would be impossible for Britain to defend her vast Empire unless some steps were taken to fulfill her promise of self-rule for India. But, incidentally, in this Act the ultimate authority of the Governor General remains unimpaired, so there is no freedom in real terms for anyone."

Of course, I had written to my Father that I had also met Indira Nehru at the School – in fact, I was so excited that I had written to him almost straightaway and posted the letter on my way down to the Hostel. When I reached home my Father told me that Indira was Nehru's only child. If Indira claimed that her father was going to get us freedom, it was because Nehru was a prominent leader of the Indian National Congress. He said he knew Nehru from his Allahabad days. Apparently Pundit Nehru was a socialist and his vision of a solution to world problems lay in socialism. My Father explained that 'socialism' was born out of a troubled mind of those Europeans who found it difficult to follow the magnanimous and humane teachings of Lord Jesus Christ. He had preached that 'it is easier for a camel to go through a needle's eye, than for a rich man to enter into the Kingdom of God', which was difficult to reconcile with capitalism and imperialism. The whole aim of capitalism and imperialism was to get rich at the cost of someone else, i.e. exploitation self- aggrandizement or national-aggrandizement sustains and promotes imperial capitalism."

"So does unbridled socialism; its self-aggrandizement was in terms of power and perks to those who sit on top and manoeuvre the proletariat. The assumption that the state will own all land and business and generate wealth is not workable without a benign dictator—and benign dictators do not exist. If socialism were an answer to prosperity, all Christian nations would have opted for it. To obviate any criticism on this score western Christian Governments found it expedient to call their governments 'secular', so that no one could accuse them for abandoning the basic tenants of their faith in pursuing their economic and moral policies, or for inflicting colonialism and imperialism on other people. In fact, Lord Jesus Christ wanted his followers to give up their wealth and possessions and follow him. But the priests in the West found it expedient and profitable to emphasize that Christ was there so that one could seek remission of one's sins through him. This theory also enriched the priests and the Church who promised to pray for the remission of a person's sins on donation of huge sums of money to the "Indulgence Fund" —which was opposed by Martin Luther who founded the Protestant Faith." Those were my Father's views and he was was firmly against any proselytizing through the barrel of a gun, but I found in later years that it was more realistic to be tolerant and understanding on this issue. Also, I thought that the missionaries had done rather well in reaching out to the poor and the downtrodden with good education, health care and vocational training. After all I was myself a product of education in a missionary School and a unique example of phenomenal success through that education.

My Father was opposed to conversions. "Those who proselytized to 'heathens' worked on the assumption that they were superior in intellect, money and power. Our poverty, illiteracy and helpless colonial status made the rich western countries feel that they were better human beings than we. They imposed their faith and ideas on the vulnerable and the gullible with impunity. The act of conversion was the conquest of a human being, which pleased them and pandered to their ego – and served a long-term political agenda for their country. Politically, of course, the converted people sometimes formed Islands of Dissension. Wherever the conquerors imposed their writ by force of arms over a majority community, their aim was to weaken the majority by conversions to the ruler's faith. It is not difficult to see that in times of crisis the converted generally supported the country that had converted them. This was amply demonstrated in all the Opium Wars in China. Do you think that the Spaniards or the Portuguese could have cared two hoots for the spiritual health of the highly civilized but helpless American Indians during the savage inquisition? Millions were slaughtered because they refused to convert and for very good reasons. We had the same problem in Goa and earlier, during the Mughal period and before, in our own Country."

My Father believed that politics and religion were inseparable and as I grew up and acquired a Master's Degree in History I realized that he was not far off the mark.

Occasionally my parents would dilate on religion. As I was in a Christian School, they were apprehensive that I may convert not out of conviction, but through persuasions of a complex prevalent among colonial subjects that one way to equality with the ruler was to accept his religion–it was an historic reality. He explained that all religions could be examined under three specifics: Spirituality, Morality and Practice. "Spirituality," he emphasized, "was invented to enforce credibility and morality–the love and the wrath of God expressed in coercive terms persuade the credulous to tread the righteous path. Morality generally conformed to specified Commandments. Strangely Truth is not a Commandment in most religions but it is fundamental to all Indian indigenous faiths. The purpose of the Commandments or religious edicts is to persuade man to a peaceful co-existence as a social animal. Incidentally, when the Commandments could not be enforced through a religious decree, the Romans converted them into a 'penal code' with appropriate punishment for flouting them. That could be a reason why some intellectuals think that religion was contrived as a policeman to maintain law and order by a ruler in his realm – there is a good deal of truth in it. Where Spirituality and Morality falter, however, is in Practice. The best way to examine a religion is to see how it is practised by a majority of those who subscribe to it. That is where India scores as all its indigenous faiths have practicability and scope for complete inner (and spiritual) satisfaction without hurting anyone else. We are not a religion in mourning; nor do we urge our followers to wage a holy war. The aim is to prepare man to face the ups and down of life without undue elation or depression. Ours is a take it or leave it religion—enormously liberal and pluralistic. Apart from a few aberrations in history people of indigenous faiths have never tried to convert people by the sword, or dubbed anyone of alien faith as a heretic fit for execution. In fact, in some Indian faiths the believer can conjure up a thousand Gods, or only One, or, if he chooses, none, without affecting his Spirituality or Morality. But that does not alter or modify our spiritual aim. The pursuit of Truth is our way to Paramatman or the Supreme Being and the other deities are merely guides and inspirations to help us on our way."

My Father was a graduate in science from the Allahabad University and a scholar of history. He always emphasized the maturity of our religion and its ancient origins. "Remember ", he would say, "Our indigenous faiths have been structured by great thinkers, sages and outstanding philosophers through thousands of years for answers to life's infinite problems, uncertainties, joys, pathos and human and social upheavals and, of course, to the enduring quest for an understanding of God. You must understand, my son, that our Faith was evolved through a collective effort over thousands of years. Our sages meditated in the inspiring, peaceful and creative solitude of the Himalayas. They pondered over every issue before exhorting the people to follow their philosophy for a happier, peaceful and contented life. But we respect any religion that worships God by any name. We are not rigid. We are ordained to do our duty. We do not covet other people's wealth and possessions. If we have to take up arms it is only to defend 'dharma' or a righteous cause and justice – never for self-aggrandizement. We are totally pluralistic in our approach. Hinduism is based on tolerance and truth and all religions are sacred to us."

"Neither capitalism nor socialism as perceived in the Christian West suits our way of life," my Father used to say. " We are a different people with different values. We have to evolve our own political systems for generating wealth that can be evenly distributed. We have to put a ceiling on greed and promote our ageless tradition of sharing with the deprived to make their lives worth living. Poverty cannot be removed by presuming that those pampered to grow rich at the top will voluntarily allow their wealth to percolate down to the poor in our village. But it can be removed by involving the rural people in generating wealth. Even the British have realized this and in the 'Rural Uplift' schemes we are trying to do just that now." Notwithstanding my Father's views on religion and colonialism he was an ardent admirer of the British and he would often extol their achievements in consolidating and uniting India as no other ruler had ever done in history.

My Mother often talked to me about spiritual matters, which had a more lasting impact on my psyche and ideas than my Father's views. She laid emphasis on festivals and rituals. She used to say that foreign faiths are not connected with the reality of India although the difference in scriptures is one of perception, not substance. We all worship the Almighty in one way or another. For us, Basant Panchmi, Holi, Dusshera and Diwali are unique festivals of boundless joy and love. They are at the right time of the year seasonally for indulgence and enjoyment. No other religion inspires such an uninhibited expression of joy and family values as our festivals. You can store up joy and love in your inner being and the sub-conscious activity of the mind will guide your thinking and action in daily life. Our rituals and festivals unite families and forge bonds of affection for mutual trust and dependability. The rituals and worships give the young an idea of how to respect the old and the wise and provide an opportunity to the families to renew their bonds of affection. Our theme of worship may appear to be based on mythology and superstition, but the aim is to inspire the devotees to pursue goals for the betterment of themselves and to condition their minds to an amiable and charitable disposition. Without these rituals with common celebrations and worship, it is not possible to have a united, strong and peaceful society in our Country. In any case, is there any religion in which one can conjure up God in either the male or the female form? We do not start the day by saying there is evil in us and that we need forgiveness for our sins. Why should we when we do not sin? We seek the Truth for a righteous path. We purify and strengthen our body and mind through yoga for peace and happiness. Hinduism stands for liberalism and pluralism. We can set up a stone on a plinth for concentration and focus and use it as the media to communicate with the Almighty. Only the obtuse will dispute its obvious practicability. If foreigners have ruled our Country and forcibly converted our people, it is because our greedy rulers had abandoned the righteous path ordained in our scriptures. Also because, my Mother would add, we want 'shanti' or peace not war or forced conversions.

Most Hindu families who visited us at the time thought that Emperor Ashoka had sent out Buddhist thinkers and teachers about the year 240 BC to Syria, Egypt and Macedonia which had a profound effect on the religious philosophy of the people outside India. Till then largely Greek or other mythology obsessed them, and a reasoned faith with moral and social values was alien to them. The Law of Universal Causation was the Buddha's unique contribution to a totally new perception of a well-deliberated religion. His emphasis lay on the enlightenment of the individual who could attain "Nirvana", Salvation or happiness, through right belief, resolve, speech, conduct, livelihood, effort, mindfulness and right meditation and thus, through his own efforts, absolve himself from the cycle of rebirth and unhappiness. His doctrine lay between the two extremes of sensual pleasure and bodily torture. The Buddha (567 – 487) laid no claim to any divine inspiration and discouraged speculations on divinity, or the Kingdom of God. His approach was simple and practical and found substantial agitation in the great intellectual minds of his time – and today. There is little doubt that his teachings also found expression in later-day religions in many parts of the World.

My Grandfather's homiletics also had a profound effect on my life. He was a landlord with the largest land holdings in our Village. He was over six feet tall and well built with a personality no one could challenge or ignore – not even the British whom he respected and admired enormously. He observed all the Hindu rituals and whenever a festival required a visit to the River Ganges for a holy dip, he went with a retinue of friends and servants – he used to say that it was also a social occasion when one could meet distant relatives and friends.

He observed a rigid schedule for the day – up before first light, a cold-water bath from the well inside our 'haveli' (mini palace for residence) and an hour of meditation before some yoga exercises. For breakfast, he normally had a glass of milk or lassi with almonds, which had been soaked overnight in Ganges water in a copper bowl, and one or two thick chapatti's of bajra or a mix of wheat and gram flour with white butter allowed to melt and soak into the hot chapatti. But he was very particular about being thoroughly relaxed before a meal.

If he had been through any kind of stress or tension when he arrived home for a meal, he would place a face towel rinsed in cold water for about a minute each on the back of his neck, then under each armpit and the genitals. He would always sit on the floor to eat, shake his body to loosen up and then meditate for a minute or two to bring his thoughts to rest. He used to say that the heart was not so strained when one was sitting on the floor as it was when one was sitting on a chair. After a meal he would rest for a short while and then smarten up, tie his turban, take his thick walking stick and walk briskly to the 'ghair', located about a kilometer away on the outer fringes of the Village.

The 'ghair' was a high-walled enclosure, which had stables, barns, pens, granary and sheds for farming implements, bullock carts, rath, a coach, a buggy and a motorcar. Horses, cows, buffaloes and bullocks were kept in the 'ghair' and servants took care of them. Other farmers also had 'ghairs' on the outer periphery to circle the village. The 'ghair' provided the first line of defence against any attack on the Village and its walls had turrets with loopholes. My Grandmother made sure that food was sent to all the servants working in the fields or the 'ghair' from the 'haveli' three times a day; their wives came to see my Grandmother for help which was never refused. My 'Dadi' or 'Nana' was the best Quartermaster I ever knew and indeed, she was a woman not only of exceptional beauty but rare substance.

Every morning my Grandfather inspected his estate. By then servants and bullocks who had to work in the fields had already left. From the 'ghair' my Grandfather would take a different horse every day from his stable of half a dozen horses to inspect his fields. In my family we were all excellent equestrians. In fact I had my first pony when I was only four. My Grandfather was my instructor in horsemanship. If I fell off the horse and cried he would tell me not to be a baby and to get back on to the saddle without fuss and bother. He taught me how to hold the reins and to keep my feet firmly in the stirrups. He showed me how he could make his horse trot, canter, gallop or stop and told me to do the same. He instructed me on how to change the lead foreleg of the horse on a figure of eight. I was terrified of making my horse jump over an obstacle till he showed me how I could maintain my balance and help the horse to go over an obstacle smoothly. I feared and hated him, but I also had a great deal of respect and affection for my Grandfather and whenever I left him to join my parents it was not without a tinge of sadness.

My Grandfather had his fads. He regarded the Himalayas to the North as sacred. The Himalayas, he would say, are the abode of God and our great saints and sages; our most hallowed temples and shrines are located there; our great rivers spring from there and sustain our forests, agriculture and commerce. His bed was always arranged North – South with feet pointing South. While meditating or eating he faced North. He would point to the needle of a compass and tell me to respect the wondrous magnetic force of Nature that keeps the needle pointing North. 'Let your mind and body conform in harmony to this unseen celestial magnetic force and be blessed.' When I studied Science in Woodstock School (where the facilities were excellent and assessed as the best in India at the time), I realized that my Grandfather was right – by sleeping aligned to the magnetic field of the Earth one could have the polarity of the atoms in one's body correctly re-arranged through induction.

All utensils in which water (including water from the Ganges for medicinal purposes) was stored for drinking were either made of copper or lined with a thin copper sheet. Apparently, copper primed water was a prophylactic against rheumatism, gout, cramps and even cancer. During summer, the drinking water was kept in earthen pots to chill it – the pores in the earthen pot were supposed to suck in impurities! Periodically the earthen pots were cleaned with fresh water and put out in the sun to regain their intrinsic quality. Brass utensils were shunned like the plague for food and drinks, but brass urns were used for storing grain or cattle-feed. We had three largish courtyards inside the 'haveli' and in the centre of each we had a potted 'tulsi', a herb like the mint or balsam, placed on a three foot high pillar. Every morning after a bath my Grandmother and Grandfather watered the plant. A couple of 'tulsi' leaves and a tablespoonful of Ganges water was used as first aid for colds, cough, fever, diarrhea or stomach ache and the like – and the amazing part was that it worked!

During my winter vacations, I often went out with my Father on his tours to the villages. The way in which the Village Pradhans and the Elders conducted themselves, though illiterate 'natives' to the Western World, was a lesson in dignity and self-respect. They were neither for nor against the British. All they wanted was to be left alone to run their own affairs according to their traditions and rituals. The panchayati system was in vogue and whatever the five Elders decided in a village was final and irrevocable. But whenever human frailties crossed the line, there was a need for a 'Raja' or the Ruler to settle the issue. The belief in the British dispensation of justice was absolute. A well-organized administration at the district level and Common Laws throughout the Indian Empire, my Father said, was a wonderful gift from the British, as indeed was the Army and the Central Services. The British also unified India for convenience of administration and defence and in the process laid a strong foundation for Indian nationalism, as we know it today.

In School most of the time we were only two Indians and one or two Anglo-Indians in a class of 32; the rest were Europeans, mostly boys and girls of American missionaries. There were a few British, Australian and New Zealand kids also. All my teachers were Europeans and they were all very good in their jobs. As kids, nobody seemed to notice the shades of difference in the colours of our skin, but the European

Americans were always contemptuous when they spoke of the 'niggers' in their country. The European missionary parents and some Europeans Staff of the School treated us Indians with irritating condescension. A large number of European missionaries or their wives came up to Mussoorie for the summer to escape the scorching heat of the plains and their children in School left the Hostel to live with them. Even my friends who moved to live with their parents never asked me to a meal although the European kids were asked often to a Sunday lunch after the Church Service. Apparently, the reason was that I did not eat beef as a Hindu. But the Indian Christian boy in my Class in the Hostel was also not asked out! It occurred to me even then that the European Americans had a very serious racial problem to resolve, as there were no easy answers to mutual hatred and prejudice between them and the non-Europeans in their Country. But the integration of European and non-European Americans in their Army today, without affecting their fighting potential or camaraderie in battle, is a truly remarkable achievement in racial equality.

Nevertheless, I loved my School and had a very happy and adventurous time scouring over the mountains and wading across cold streams in search of wild flowers, butterflies, ferns, beetles and tadpoles. I enjoyed being a Boy Scout; I learnt many things, including first aid and cooking, which were useful to me in life. The lessons in Map-Reading and Fieldcraft and patrolling at night in commando games to locate and raid an 'enemy' camp were of considerable help to me in assimilating the more advanced training in tactics at the Indian Military Academy. I went to Halloween parties, to picnics by moonlight, or for romps across the mountains without worrying about the colour of my skin. But at about 15/16 years of age, the girls shied off from mixing with us particularly at parties and picnics. In inter-school get-togethers in Mussoorie, the Anglo-Indian children, at times darker than anyone of us, did not mix with the Indians and were surprised to see us with European boys and girls. As we grew older the pinpricks of racial prejudices were nettling and provoking and at 17, in the final year at school in 1938, I began to understand how humiliating it was not be free—or not to be fair enough to pass off as a European! Somewhere in my psyche all this left a scar that never healed.

At home my family tried to ape the British in some ways, but not in all. Our house was furnished in the most modern style prevalent at the time with furniture and furnishings in the latest design. My parents used to order new furniture from a favourite firm in Bareilly whenever my Father was transferred from one district to another. Although my Mother was illiterate she was an exceptionally gifted artist and a remarkable woman in the management of the house, the care of her children and in the steadfast observance of all the Hindu festivals and rituals. Visitors to the house always complimented her on the choice of her curtains, the embroidery on tablecloth or serviettes, or the splendid murals on the veranda walls she had so artistically drawn of Radha and Krishna dancing in celestial joy. Although we normally used chairs, for prayers and meals we sat on mats on the floor. Our crockery and cutlery were of fine quality, bone china and silver, all from England, but used only for guests as we ate our meals served in round steel or silver 'thalis' with small bowls for dal, vegetables and curd. My mother was a strict vegetarian and no meat was allowed inside the house. She instructed my Father to ensure that I was not served beef at the School Hostel and for all the years I was in boarding my parents paid an extra charge for mutton. When I told my Mother that I used toilet paper and not water in school she nearly threw me out of the house and threatened to withdraw me from there. The main reason for sending me to Woodstock School was that it was a European establishment and not an Anglo-Indian one.

'Anglo-Indian' was a derogatory term in those days, as the Anglo-Indians were largely descendents of a plebeian British father and a nondescript Indian mother. But the contributions of Anglo-Indians to the efficient running of the Indian Railways, the Post and Telegraph, the Customs and Inland Waterways was truly stupendous and exemplary.

My Grandfather had wished that I should study with Europeans and get acquainted with their ways so that I could do well in a Colonial India. My parents had toyed with the idea of sending me to England for studies but decided that they would do so for college education as I might be alienated from them if I went too early. I realize now that without the education at Woodstock School I would never have held the most prestigious and enjoyable appointments later in life. I am immensely grateful to my parents for ensuring that I had a good start in life. In fact, it was at Woodstock that I acquired the essential skills for communicating with others in a convincing and genial manner, which was really the secret of my outstanding performance as a student on numerous courses in India and abroad and later as an Instructor in top Defence Institutions such as the Artillery School, the Defence Services Staff College, what is now the War College and the Jungle and Cdo Warfare School, and as the Commanding Officer of four different Infantry Battalions, two Brigades and the Jungle and Commando Warfare School between age 26, when I became a Lt Col, and 46, when I took premature retirement as a substantive Brigadier. My outstanding skill in 'communicating' was a crucial factor in my selection as the first Indian Officer for appointment as ADC to a very senior British Commander in the field during World War II and later to a Viceroy of India. I would say that my ability to communicate effectively with my fellow human beings from anywhere in the world was Woodstock School's greatest gift to me.

Although I could not ever get close to my Father, as he was stern and forbidding, I never faltered in my love and respect for him. My mother was a most wonderful and caring mother (we were eight siblings – six sisters and two brothers) and I adored her with all my heart. But I did learn a great deal from my father. He had travelled widely in Europe and the racial discriminations there had embittered him. But when going out he always wore western clothes with tags of the best tailors in London. He took particular care to dress well and he made sure that we were equally well dressed when we went out with him. He thought the British Parliamentary System was wonderful, but he could not understand why a nation with such high ideals could justify colonies and treat their subjects so shabbily. Everyone I met praised him as a man of ideals and principles, but the lawyers and the convicted hated him, as he would not budge a micron from the law. I am quite sure I inherited his genes with pride although they did not serve me well to get on in life – I was rigid, harsh, unfriendly, horribly conceited and could not suffer fools or inefficiency; but with cultivated diligence, an uncompromising love for my profession, an impressive physique, good looks and a dream-wife, success came my way as if by some divine dispensation and I just had to wish and the wish came true till my bloated ego got the better of me and the only way I could come to terms with myself was to seek premature retirement from the Army before I was 47 years of age, as, by then, I had done everything I ever really wanted to do as a Soldier and the only compelling desire I had yet to fulfill was to spend more time loving and caring for my wife and our two lovely children. I was to learn much later in life when I joined politics that it does not pay always to go by the book, or to be rigid in one's view on matters of discipline, or in dealing with one's subordinates, or in one's attitude towards superiors– but by then it was too late to matter!

In December 1938, I had appeared for Senior Cambridge Examination to obtain the School Leaving Certificate from Cambridge University in England. Only six of us had appeared for the Examination from Woodstock School out of a class of nearly thirty. The American students were eligible for admission to American Universities after they had passed the High School at Woodstock, but we could not gain admission in a college in India with that qualification, or appear for any competitive examination conducted by the Government of India. In the event, when the results came in March 1939, only two of us had passed the Senior Cambridge Examination. My Father thought that I ought to sit for the competitive Federal Service Examination for entrance to the Indian Military Academy after I became 18 years of age later in the year. In the meanwhile, I went to Dehra Dun to attend coaching classes for the Entrance Examination under Colonel Browne, a British retired Officer from the Royal Corps of Education. It was a useful course, but the outstanding recommendation from the Principal of Woodstock School and my own excellent health and physique helped me to get top marks in the 'interview'. I stood third among the fifteen, the number of Cadets admitted to the Indian Military Academy half-yearly. I was not particularly thrilled by my laudable success as all the time I was hoping I would go abroad and study Science, my first love, at Woodstock School. But by then the War had started and my options were closed.

At the Indian Military Academy, the instructors were all British. Except for the 15 Army Cadets from the ranks who came from Kitchener's College, we, the 15 who entered the Indian Military Academy through an open competition, had never experienced the harsh discipline, which we now faced under European Sergeant Majors and British Officers. Our whole life-style was under intense scrutiny and apparently, if the Drill Sergeant Major, a smart little twerp 5 foot nothing from the British Queens Regiment, was to be believed, we were all 'flat-footed, fat-heads who waddled like pregnant ducks'! Well—was that racial prejudice or just the Sergeant Major's pomposity? We complained. The Sergeant Major stood to attention and whispered, " I can't call out and say you are the most beautiful lads, Sir, 'cause that there Adjutant on the 'ores will accuse me of being unnatural!" It was difficult to stifle a laugh, but we understood.

There was an acute difference between the attitudes of the Cadets who came from the ranks and us, who joined the Indian Military Academy through an open competition. All of us who came in through an open competition were liberal, fun loving and secular. The Army Cadets were inclined to be cliquish, petty, double-dealers and submissive to the British Staff. In the beginning, their performance in physical training, drill, weapon training, equitation and fieldcraft was much better than ours. But we were ahead of them in academic subjects and in due course caught up with them on the parade ground and in field training. My own performance at the Indian Military Academy was poor. I was inclined to flout orders and get into trouble as a Gentleman Cadet, as I had an inherent resentment against bossism and authority, an aberration that plagued me through all the years I was in the Army. I did make some friends, but I lacked those attributes that make good and lasting friends. Although I acquired all the professional skills and excelled in many of them, I was never really the Model Officer that the Indian Military Academy was trying to produce. For example, it took me quite a while to grasp the importance of strict military discipline and of unquestioned obedience of orders from a superior; perhaps my education in a school as liberal and free as Woodstock had turned me into a 'questioner' and a rebel at heart. Whatever the reason, I could never quite reconcile with the essential attributes of the Model Officer. I found that Officers with much less ability and knowledge than got on better with their Superiors, which made me unnecessarily unhappy, as professionally I was always assessed better than they and, of course, did exceptionally well and better than anyone else on all Army Courses. Nevertheless, the training at the Indian Military Academy was excellent. I became interested in professional soldiering and I resolved to improve as an Officer keeping the IMA

Regimental Sergeant Major Stannard's advice in mind, 'Keep your mouth shut, Sir, and keep your bowels moving!' Looking back, I think I ought to have kept my mouth shut on more than one occasion. But, despite all the drawbacks, I was undoubtedly the most outstanding Officer in my age and service group when I took premature retirement in 1968.

Being the only Indian Officer in a Gunner Regiment in 1941 was unsettling. The other 2/Lt was an Englishman from Woolwich and senior to me by a day. Both of us lived in extreme fear of the Commanding Officer who made it a point to bark at us whenever he saw us. A senior subaltern took charge of us; he was to teach us regimental traditions and customs and act as our confidant. We asked him if it was possible to run away from the Regiment. He laughed. 'It's the Commanding Officer, isn't it?' Surprised, we nodded. "What goes up must come down. Nothing lasts," he said philosophically. Within a week the Commanding Officer was promoted and transferred. The new Colonel was a delightful Officer and we got to know his two pretty daughters rather well.

Paddy Miller was the Quarter Master. He had risen from the ranks and was high on discipline and regimental espirit-de-corps. When we moved to Calcutta, we were in tents at an awful place called Majarhat. Staff cars in those days (Oct 1941) were small Austins and the Administrative Commandant, a full Colonel, often travelled in the car. As soon as Paddy Miller saw an Austin he would spring to attention and salute. With younger eyes we could see better and we noticed that he saluted the car whether someone was inside it or not. "Why do you do it, Sir?" we asked. He said, "I know the Colonel travels in the car. I cannot see from here, but he is a Senior Officer and I have to salute him. Suppose he is in the car and I do not salute. That would be an offence, wouldn't it? After all no one has seen God, but we worship Him just in case He is there when we go up! Right!!" Paddy's philosophy stuck with me for life.

To both of us, the new Officers, Paddy was more than just the Quarter Master. He had a sprightly sense of humour and a repertoire of 'dirty' jokes that few could equal. He teased and bullied our innocence and questioned our manhood when we refused to accompany him to his favourite Anglo-Indian bordello off Park Street, which he visited regularly twice a week. On my return from the Gunnery Course in Karachi, my colleague, the British Officer, told me that he had been to the bordello with Paddy just once for 'sight-seeing'. The Madam was apparently genuinely French, not a day less than fifty, and she hugged and kissed all the visitors and called them 'Cheri', 'Darling', 'My Apollo' or just 'My Lover'. He thought the 'gals' were quite young and pretty, too scantily dressed for his composure and much too brash in soliciting. He said he decided to keep his virginity intact till he found someone really nice. We laughed till our sides ached.

Paddy Miller had been in a Regiment equipped with 3.7 inch Howitzer, perhaps the most accurate Artillery piece ever made. Rudyard Kipling, the favourite Bard of most British Officers at the time, had lovingly dubbed the 3.7 in How as the Screw-Gun and wrote a ballad on it. Paddy, of course, knew the whole narrative by heart and urged us to memorize it –

>"Smokin' my pipe on the mountings, sniffing the mornin' cool,
>I walk in my old brown gaiters along o' my old brown mule,
>With seventy gunners be'nd me, an' never a beggar forgets
>It is only the pick of the Army that handles the dear little pets –'Tss' 'Tss'
>For you all love the screw-guns – the screw-guns they all love you!

****

>The 'moril' of this story, it is plainly to be seen:
>You ' avn't got no families when serving of the Queen –
>You 'avn't got no brothers, fathers, sisters, wives, or sons –
>If you want to win your battles take an' work your bloomin' guns!

****

Part III

Down in the Infantry, nobody cares;
Down in the Cavalry, Colonel –e swears;
But down in the lead with the wheel at the flog
Turns the bold Bombardier to a little whipped dog!"

****

One day he turned to me and said, 'You've got a name that none of us can pronounce.' My plea that I could articulate it in such a way that he could learn to pronounce it correctly did not move him. Apparently he had told the Commanding Officer that I should be nicknamed 'Ganga Din' and quoted Kipling, 'You limpin lump o' brick-dust, Ganga Din', and laughed outrageously. I protested vehemently and said I was offended. "Ganga Din was a 'bhisti', a carrier of water. I am a young professional Gunner Officer and as smart as they make 'em – not a darn 'bhisti'! To hell with you, Paddy – I don't want to be your friend."

"Wait a minute, old fellow. Just a tick." He fell silent and looked at me intently. "Supposing we call you 'Kim'? It is almost a part of your first name, as the last three letters are (Hu) 'kam'. Quite the best choice, hey Buster, as Kipling's Kimball O'Hara, an Irish lad, was both a 'sahib' and a native and he was a pupil of a Tibetan Lama. I am not a Tibetan Lama, thank the Lord, but you are my pupil and you are both a 'sahib' and a native and very substantially handsome to pass off as Irish with a little bleach. How's that?"

At first, I felt flattered. Then I shook my head. "Kim was a spy. I am not. I'll think it over," I said.

But, of course, I never had a chance to think it over. The next day the Commanding Officer, the Second-in-Command and my Battery Commander were all referring to me as 'Kim' and I was given no opportunity to protest. Even my Army Orderly came to me with a note and said he had been told to give it to 'Kim Sahib'! What cheek! But I think I reconciled with my new nickname only after all the pretty girls at the

Club and in social functions also called me 'Kim' with that unmistakable tenderness in their voice! And so the nickname stuck and for the rest of my life I was called 'Kim'. But the real reconciliation came only after I was married because my wife could put all her love and tenderness into those three letters and whenever she called me 'Kim darling', and not just 'darling', I melted and knew instinctively that she loved me with all her heart.

A British Officer from the Royal Regiment of Artillery taught us the rudiments of gunnery at the Indian Military Academy as a sort of introduction, but after becoming a Gunner Officer it was imperative that I do a proper course at the School of Artillery. So, after I was commissioned in the Regiment, I was sent on a Gunnery Course on the Manora Island off Karachi. Among the 30 odd Student Officers, we were only three Indians and the rest were British. Of the three Indian Officers, one was a Sikh, one Muslim and I, a Hindu. The Muslim Officer and I started off as very good friends till a few days later, on a Sunday morning, while strolling barefeet on the beautiful beach just below our quarters, I scribbled on the wet sand, with my big toe, the name of my girl-friend. I had met her in Mussoorie while I was a Gentleman Cadet at the IMA and, with my small savings, I had bought her a diamond ring as we were determined to get married come what may. She was keen to have a child before I went to war as she thought I was much too impetuous to survive the hazards of a battle and the baby in my image would be her life-time solace and companion. Her father was a Senior Railway Official and a devout Muslim and her mother a German who had embraced Islam. Before I had completed the last letter of her name in the scribble on the sand, my friend grabbed me by the throat. I thought I was going to blackout. I stamped him hard on his toes with my heel and then kneed him in the groin. He let go my throat and screamed in pain. Apparently my girl friend had the same name as the Holy Prophet's daughter and I had committed a sacrilege, which could not be condoned. As I was brought up to revere all religions, I deeply regretted the faux pas. But my Muslim friend did not speak to me for the rest of the Course.

My Muslim friend was not otherwise a bad guy. He had a passion for all types of films especially those with an Islamic background and he and I went out to Karachi together three or four times to the cinema and to have an Indian meal at the best restaurants in the City, as the Royal Artillery Officers' Mess catered only to the taste of the British Officers. After he broke off with me I managed to make friends with a British Officer who was equally keen on films but he did not like Indian restaurants and so we went to the Gymkhana Club – and to its fabulous bar! On two days in the week the Club had ballroom dances. My British friend had no problem in asking girls to dance with him, but as the girls were all British most of them just looked through me without responding to my request for a dance. The humiliation got the better of me and I stuck to the bar and drank more than was good for me. On dance nights we could not make it back to catch the last ferry to Manora from Karachi harbour, as the last ferry left at nine and the dances carried on till mid-night. The ferry in the morning left at 6, so we had to spend the waiting hours on the crude benches on the wharf, or tip the ferry crew for a corner to curl up in for a brief doze in the boat. By about seven thirty we usually reached our digs on the Island and as the first parade was at eight thirty, we had just about enough time for the morning ablutions and breakfast before lining up for gun-drills. Naturally, our performance on the Course till then was rock bottom. The only redeeming factor was that I was one among seven or eight, including my British friend, who were marched up before the Chief Instructor, a Lt Col, for our shocking performance. The Colonel threatened to have us thrown out of the Course and the Regiment unless we could show definite improvement within a week. That was the turning point in my career – and life. Humiliation consumed me. I had worked very hard to get a competitive vacancy for admission to the Indian Military Academy. More than 280 candidates had appeared for the Entrance Examination from all over the British Indian Empire. Only fifteen were taken and I was third on the list. Now I was among the last! How could that happen to me! Shame and despair overwhelmed me. I felt wretched.

Was I inferior to the British? No! I had been to school with Europeans. I was aware of the fact that I had an inferiority complex, but I was proud of my record in the school where I had done very well in competition with European students. The success in School had changed me from a shy and timid Indian lad with a conservative Hindu background to a progressive and modern youth who could fend for himself among the Europeans or others. Of course, I continued to be very proud of my faith and heritage. Could my faith and pride in my heritage help me to find an answer to my shame and despair?

For several hours that afternoon, I strolled on the beach in an attempt to find a way out of this awful predicament. I could not think beyond the knowledge and experience I had acquired in life till then. I only had my past to look back on for inspiration and an answer. My Grandfather had instilled in me, while I was only eight years old, that an individual has to discover himself through meditation and yoga to confront a challenge in life. It was essentially an Indian way. But I felt diffident in pursuing a routine that could make me a laughing stock if the British Officers discovered what I was doing. Nevertheless, I decided to follow my Grandfather's advice, as there was no other option.

The next morning I was up before first-light and after the morning ablutions I sat down on a small Persian carpet outside my little cottage in the Lotus Pose with my eyes shut and the bared edges of my feet firmly placed on damp earth for meditation to renew my link with the subliminal 'Atman' or the Soul within me. My Grandfather had explained to me that a prayer is not the same as meditation. A prayer is essentially a request or supplication to God. Sometimes it is a display of religiosity to impress a congregation. Often it is an entreaty to God for favours. It could also be used as a political stunt. Meditation is very personal; it is a course of action to have a peep at yourself and then link up with one's cosmos origin or with nature – religion did not come into it.

My Grandfather told me to remember that we were all a minuscule part of the Universe. The only way to establish a link with that Universe was through one's 'Atman' or the Soul. He said the 'Atman' was an infinitesimal part of 'Paramataman' or the Supreme Soul or Being, the Almighty, who had structured the Universe – and who permeated the smallest particles in nature. The link up with cosmos was like connecting a rundown battery through a charger to the main power source. Meditation did just that – connected one to the source of all quantum energy and cosmos radiation—and its dynamism showed on one's face and in one's actions when downloaded.

My Grandfather had taught me to project two imaginary beams of light from my eyes to converge on a point in my chest just above the solar plexus where, he said, the imperishable 'Atman' was enshrined. I had first to go limp, completely relax, and then concentrate before projecting the two powerful beams of light from my eyes to the effulgence of the flame (to be conceived by the mind as the flame of a candle, a 'dia' or the Olympic torch) of the 'Atman'. Once I could see the flame of the 'Atman' in my mind's eye, I was to project a powerful single beam of light from the flame of the 'Atman' to the centre of a three-inch circle on the crown of my head above the cerebrum where the Hindus normally had a long tuft of hair. I was to then transmit the concentrated beam into the cosmos to link with a brilliant frothing sea of light well above my head – in the same way as one would align a satellite dish antenna today with the transmitter in space. In practice when I did so, my body seemed to straighten out in reflex action and after a while I could distinctly feel that the beam I was transmitting as a link with cosmos was reflected back duly energized to the crown of my head. When the energy seeped into the cerebrum and into the spine, I could feel its tingling warmth as the quantum energy filtered slowly into my body. Yes, I felt as if I had been born again!

My Grandfather assured me that it was the incredible simplicity of the ritual that distracted people from its practice and not its credibility. Once that link was made between the 'Atman' and the Paramatma, a supernal quantum energy flowed down the beam through the cerebrum and the nervous system and rejuvenated one's mind and body. The practice gave one control over one's mind and the ability to concentrate a beam of light on attitudes that bring success, happiness, love and contentment. The intensity of brightness of the Atman flame was an indication of one's state of health; it was possible to intensify this brightness to prolong life. I could also direct that beam to heal an ailment. He had made me learn some 'mantras' that I had to hum. I hummed the 'mantras' in the Lotus Pose with eyes shut and I could feel the vibrations titillating in my ears and sinus. But the chanting or humming of the 'mantras' was meaningless till I learned to use them as words of command to the subconscious, so that the essence and message of the 'mantras' regulated my thinking and actions.

Of course, an important aspect of meditation and yoga exercises was that breathing had to be free and uninterrupted. Humming also made one take a deep breath. The meditations were indeed very comforting and once I got used to the ritual I found I could meditate almost anywhere and at any time. Now, at over 82, I find meditation very useful in relaxing and concentrating my thoughts in reading and writing. In fact, thoughts scattered like tiddlywinks can be collected into a cup in the brain with remarkable rapidity through meditation.

An important aspect to remember in cosmos meditation is that the quantum energy which flows down into the cerebrum rides on negative ions which are necessary to promote chemical reactions in the body. (Some believe, with justifiable proof, that it is the ions that rained down upon us which brought about evolution of life and that ever since man started living inside houses and wearing shoes to disconnect from the negative polarity of the earth, the natural process of evolution in man has been considerably retarded.) It is obvious, therefore, that to attract ions a bare part of the body must be firmly in touch with the negatively charged earth, so that the body itself becomes a negative terminal in an electrical circuit; a bared body absorbs more ions than a clothed one, and an 'ion bath' may be taken in shade with bare feet firmly in touch with, preferably, moist earth (as compared with a 'sun bath' on a beach which provides the benefits of both the sun and the ions). Bare feet in touch with a patch of moist ground, say the lawn or moist sand, provide the best conduction. Incidentally, waterways or lakes and ponds attract ions and are the best places for meditation. But it is interesting to note that people living in the lakeside Geneva in Switzerland have spells of depression in greater numbers than in other places. This could be due to the fact that the lake attracts a large quantity of ions and the people living there are denied their share, as they wear shoes and are not negatively charged through contact with the earth). Those who walk around barefoot or practise Cosmos Meditation do not suffer from depression. Apart from a 'dhoti' or a loin cloth, Gandhiji did not wear any clothes and he used to say that his 'nakedness' absorbed energy from the air and kept him healthy. My wife used to say that when she wore sleeveless and short dresses she felt full of energy.

When the morning sun rose in all its splash of colours and majesty from the watery depths of the Arabian Sea, I used to run down to the beautiful beach to perform 'Surya Namaskar', or Salutation to the Sun, a combination of Yoga postures I had learnt from my Grandfather. After a quick shower and a rubdown with a towel, I changed into my uniform and by eight I was in the Officers' Mess for breakfast—feeling absolutely on top of the world! After lunch and some rest, I spent an hour reviewing what I had been taught in Gunnery. After tea, I was down on the beach again for an hour to walk and jog. Having worked up a nice sweat, I came back to my room, read a book or a magazine for a while and then had a nice hot bath before another session of meditation. A few minutes before eight I was in the Officers' Mess for dinner. Cigarettes, alcoholic drinks and meat were off my list and I did not go to Karachi till the end of the Course. Before going to bed early, I prepared for the next day's lessons for an hour. I pursued this routine for standing first on the Course. Two months later I was the first Indian to become an Instructor-in-Gunnery. In fact, with little variation, this was the routine I followed on all future Courses in the Army in which I stood first.

Everyone in the Regiment was surprised when I was posted as an Instructor-in-Gunnery – they did not know how hard I had worked to qualify for it; but I was very disappointed in not being able to go to Burma with my Regiment. The Artillery School had moved from Manora to Clifton in Karachi when I reported for duty. I was promoted to Captain on 28 Feb 1942, when I was just over 20 years of age. The Controller of Defence Accounts questioned the Commandant of the School on my appointment and promotion as in the schedule of pay for Indian Commissioned Officer (ICOs) it was not visualized that an Indian would ever hold the appointment. The Governor General in Council had to pass an act to entitle ICOs to hold the appointment and to receive the extra allowance as an Instructor-in-Gunnery, but the amount was scaled down from Rs 250 a month to 150! The British Officers and we did the same job and faced the same risks but our pay and allowances were less than theirs.

Then there was the question of Clubs—in Calcutta and Karachi (and elsewhere) some Clubs were exclusively for Europeans. For the first time I began to feel the impact of discrimination. At the time I was not aware of all the mutinies, which had taken place in the Army for equality in status and pay and perks. Now, as I was maturing in age and experience, the humiliation of being a Class II Officer angered and disappointed me. I could not understand how any country in the World could proclaim its democratic ideals, sign the Atlantic Charter on Human Rights and yet practices racial discrimination, be it in America or Britain. But I never felt any kind of animus towards the British Officers, as the vast majority of them were extremely friendly and pleasant and I enjoyed their company; they were very dependable and supportive in battle and I was more at ease with them than with the majority of Indian Officers I met and knew before and after Independence. Nevertheless, the injustice of discrimination obsessed and angered me, but as I had joined the Army for adventure and derring-do, I was quite determined to go through the War and volunteer for any assignment in which I could gain experience of combat and face situations full of indescribable thrills and hazards of fighting an enemy as skilled and brave as the Germans or the Japanese. I was very fortunate as the Second World War and later the War in Kashmir gave me unimaginable opportunities to fulfill all my dreams.

I was still on the Course in Manora when the Japanese attacked Pearl Harbour on 7 Dec 1941, a Sunday, to achieve surprise on a day of rest observed by Christian nations. But the outbreak of hostilities did not come as a surprise. Some units had already been moved to Burma when the Japanese had made their presence felt in French Indo-China and Thailand. The British treated the Japanese with contempt, although they had backed the Japanese against the Russians at the turn of the Century. In our discussions in the Officers' Mess we thought we could take the Japs on and make a short shrift of it. Nobody had made a proper assessment of their training methods or their resolve to press home an attack despite heavy casualties. Their brutality in China was well known, but the British thought that the Japanese would be more civilized in a war against the West. The savage attack on Pearl Harbour was, therefore, a terrible shock. But all of us agreed that victory against the Axis dictators was absolutely certain now that America was in the War with us.

My Regiment was all set to move by sea to Burma when my posting orders came. The Japanese had already invaded Malaya before I left Karachi. A week before the Japanese had struck at Pearl Harbour, we had heard that Singapore was quite safe as Britain had sent two of its mightiest battleships, HMS Prince of Wales and HMS Repulse, to deter the Japanese from seeking any major gains in South East Asia. But there were those who argued that without command of the air these mighty battleships would be very vulnerable to air attacks. So it happened. The battleships set out north from Singapore to intercept a falsely reported Japanese landing on the morning of 9th December 1941. When the battleships left for Kuantan, it was cloudy but it cleared later. Soon the Japanese attacked the battleships from the air and sank them. This catastrophe had a disastrous effect on the morale of the troops in Malaya and Singapore. On 15th February, 1942, Singapore fell and the Japanese were masters of the Indian Ocean.

In the meanwhile, the Japanese had also invaded Burma. Despite the thick jungle and poor communications, their progress was rapid and alarming. In India there was consternation. While I was travelling back from Calcutta to Karachi on posting as Instructor-in-Gunnery, I took a week's leave to see my parents. All the people I met were apprehensive that the Japanese would eventually invade and occupy India. A large number of Indians felt that Britain had milked its colonies without caring for their defence. This feeling of despair aroused the politicians to demand immediate independence, as, they argued that we had no axe to grind with the Japanese and therefore why should the Japanese want to occupy a free India. I did not subscribe to this view nor did the vast majority of Indian Officers and Soldiers.

On arrival in Karachi I heard that a large number of Indian Prisoners of War in Singapore, about 25000, had decided to join the Japanese to fight for Indian Independence. Some Indian Prisoners of War had already joined the Germans in 1941, but there was no Officer among them. Now Captain Mohan Singh and other Indian Officers led the revolt. After the Mutiny of 1857, the formation of the Indian National Army was indeed the most alarming revolt against the British; the Empire was rocked visibly to its foundation! In 1857 there were no highly skilled and trained Indian Officers to lead the mutineers—now there were with all the Japanese resources behind them. Despite all the pretensions and the imperial swagger, the British could not conceal their gloom.

So, when I saw the British Officers in a panic on the formation of the Indian National Army under Mohan Singh at Singapore, I was not touched as they had taken us for granted and often treated us shabbily. It was in the morning about the Ides March 1942, when I was lecturing to a Class on the Vickers Mechanical Predictor (now called the 'computer') and as the subject was engrossing, I did not notice that the Adjutant, a British Royal Artillery Officer, was standing outside in the veranda till one of the students drew my attention to him. Normally he would have come into the classroom and spoken to me; his diffidence aroused my curiosity. I left the classroom to meet him. He spoke to me as if he was being choked and it took me a while to grasp what he was trying to say. "Do you know this fellow Mohan Singh?' he asked. No, I did not. I had heard of him, yes. We walked to the Conference Room in silence. The atmosphere inside was sombre. It was difficult to believe that the British Commandant would get up from his chair to receive me, the junior-most Officer on his staff—and an Indian at that! Gloom was writ on the faces of all those present; they attempted to conceal the notes they had taken when I sat down on a vacant chair at the table. Apparently a plan had been hatched to face another 1857, should there be need, but I was not informed. What did I think of the formation of the Indian National Army? I thought Captain Mohan Singh was provoked to raise the Indian National Army from Indian POWs at Singapore by manifest British racial prejudices, but I had not met any Indian Officer who was not determined to fight in the War till there was victory for the Allies. We knew exactly what the Germans and the Italians had done in Europe, Russia and Africa, and we knew of the savagery of the Japanese in Manchuria and China. We knew that the British had done a commendable job in integrating diverse peoples on the Subcontinent. We owed our democratic aspirations largely to British education and institutions. But the British were inclined to live in their exclusive social camps. We were kept out of those camps because we were not Europeans. That created apprehension in our mind. A more agreeable atmosphere had to be created for mutual confidence. Racial discriminations had to go.

Did we want freedom immediately? There was a very strong desire among all of us for freedom, not for the sake of getting rid of the British, but because the British themselves wanted all colonial people to be free. But we realised that we did not have the resources, national awareness or the leadership to run a country the size of India in the face of imminent Japanese threat. None of us, however, would be willing to compromise, I said, on freedom for India after the War. My words must have been a whiff of oxygen for the assembled British Officers as sullen faces transformed into smiles of relief. Suddenly everyone seemed to want to shake my hand, but I was not amused as a wasp had stung me on the right wrist that morning and I was in pain. It must be noted, however, that it was only the formation of Indian

National Army in February 1942, that shook the British. Once they realised that the INA had no impact on the loyalty or the fighting potential of the Indian Army—and that there were serious internal dissensions in the INA itself—any mention of the INA thereafter was treated by the British with contempt and dismissed.

Sir Stafford Cripps was sent to India in March 1942, as the British Government was keen to make an appraisal of the public opinion in India after the terrible debacle in Malaya and Singapore and the formation of the Indian National Army. An offer of self-rule was made without compromising the powers of the Viceroy who would continue to keep Defence and Foreign Affairs in his own hands. The politicians rejected the offer of 'the earliest realisation of self-government in India'. We in the Army thought that the rejection of the Cripps Plan by the politicians was not a wise decision. In the month that he was in India Cripps realised that the writ of the politicians, who had rejected the offer, was neither deep nor extensive. The British Government knew that they could handle the political situation with ease without affecting the conduct of the war against Japan.

As witnesses to the events of 1942, none of the Officers at the time would disagree with the British conclusions. Indian people were not 'embittered' because 80 per cent did not know what was going on. The Indian Soldiers did not want the British to leave till the Japanese had been defeated. There was no 'massive rebellion' after the "Quit India" Resolution on 8th August 1942, which was just rhetoric and not a practical proposition. There was violence, particularly in Bihar and eastern United Provinces, but at a very superficial level. Some railway stations were torched and rails removed, but in 99 per cent of the enormous Indian Subcontinent there was no stir. Unfortunately the British reacted with unbridled brutality and used excessive force to crush even minor incidences of violence. They told us that any internal security problem would dilute the war effort and prolong the war. The recruitment programme and the will to fight of the Indian Armed Forces was not, however, affected in the slightest. In fact, there were so many volunteers for the Armed Forces that a very large number had to be rejected, so that only the best could be recruited. In our view the "Quit India" Resolution was intended to gain political mileage later should freedom be offered again to India. Also, in my view, it was wrongly presumed that the British were weak and so desperate to survive that they would quit India without a murmur. That the Indian Army would respond to the rhetoric by revolting against the British in the same way as the Indian troops had done at Singapore was a grave error in political calculations. Without these presumptions, the political Quit India Resolution does not make sense. In any case, there were just a handful of competent politicians and none of us thought that they could run a country the size of India and effectively wage war against Japan. The Indian Officers were right, as even today, after 55 years of independence, the politicians cannot run a truncated India effectively. In fact the quality of administration has dropped to unacceptable levels since Independence. Nothing works – the public transport systems are in a shambles; the postal service is pathetic; telephones are dead most of the time; the railways are dirty, uncomfortable and unsafe; law and order poses security problems to the average citizen while the politicians strut around with high grade security guards at public expense and frequently go abroad for a jolly or minor medical treatment at State expense; the police are unresponsive and corrupt; the bureaucracy is interested only in pleasing their political bosses for self-aggrandisement; justice is costly and time consuming; letters of complaints or petitions to the Government are just ignored and never acknowledged; the leaders, both civil and military, misuse their position and privileges without the slightest desire to set an example. Our politicians have yet to learn that a leader has to set the pace in patriotism, discipline, integrity, honesty and willingness to face the same fatal risks as the people.

Barring Gandhiji and a very few others, the politicians in 1942, were not different from those today and nobody had the experience and skill to face the rapacious and ruthless Japanese who would have prevailed in India within days. Thank heaven it did not happen, as the Allies would have used nuclear weapons to drive the Japanese out of India! The wisdom and valour of its soldiers saved the Indian Subcontinent.

But the fact that the Army did not support the "Quit India" resolution was held against it. The so-called Nationalist Government after Independence cut its nose to spite its face and degraded the Army in status vis-à-vis the bureaucracy and the police, who had only a subordinate role to play in a Free India. Few Indians know that the responsibilities of the Indian Armed Forces for the defence of India have increased substantially since the British withdrew their protective umbrella after our Independence, whereas the status and responsibilities of the bureaucracy and the police have decreased, as elected representative of the People have replaced their authority in the Government. Despite their hyped status the civil and police services have not performed as well as during the British Raj. Consequently, corruption and avoidable law and order situations have largely hampered sustained development and an even distribution of wealth and prosperity among the people. Few development projects have been implemented fully and there is none free of corruption and distressing inefficiency. The Indian jails are overflowing with fake freedom fighters or insurgents and Mafia leaders, while some known criminals are entrenched as Ministers! Insurgency and fake freedom movements are on a much larger scale and more widespread than during any period of the Raj. Never was the Army called out with such frequency in aid of Civil Authority as now. Instead of facing the crisis with all the ample resources available to them, the State and Central Governments find it convenient to shed their responsibility by ordering the Army to do the job for them, instead of the Police, which they often use for self-aggrandisement, but do not trust. All this only goes to prove that the freedom struggle claimed by the politicians was nothing more than a traditional resentment by some against the establishment and not a revolution to unite and free India from the British.

Of course, the politicians were afraid of an Army takeover and scaled down the Army not only in status but strength. A special police force was created to take on the Army if need be. The Chinese were the first to take advantage of the degraded Armed Forces, resulting in a humiliating defeat for India in a border war in 1962. For the same reason, the Pakistanis have been fostering insurgency in parts of India in the hope that the degraded Armed Forces will one day crack and fold up. Only a militarily weakened country attracts cross-border terrorism or border violations. Also, it must be understood that weapons by themselves cannot strengthen a country unless the Soldiers who handle them in war are given their due status and respect in peace.

In the middle of 1943, I was posted to a Regiment at Feni, which is North of Chittagong (now in Bangladesh). One day the Japanese attacked the airfield; their 'Zero' fighters, which had a very high degree of manoeuvrability, protected their bombers. While the bombing was going on our Hurricane fighters (flown by British and Indian Pilots) came in from an adjacent airfield for a dogfight. The 'Zeros' shot down two Hurricanes. A British Officer and I were watching the dogfight from a slit trench. I casually remarked that "the 'Zeros' were bloody good". My remarks provoked him to hit me on my face with his fist. I retaliated immediately and punched him on the nose. The British Officer rushed off with a bleeding nose and threatened that he would make sure I was cashiered from the Army. After the all-clear siren, the Second-in-Command called me and said that I had to be marched up to the Commanding Officer for anti-British remarks. The Commanding Officer questioned me on my past associations and after ticking me off for 'disloyal remarks' told me that I was to leave the following day for the Regimental Centre at Deolali. The formation of the Indian National Army had certainly made the British very sensitive and jittery. Even a casual remark was misconstrued and Indian offenders penalised. Of course, I lost my acting rank of Captain, which humiliated me no end.

But my posting to Deolali was a landmark in my otherwise dull professional soldier's life. It was at Deolali that I met two very distinguished Soldiers—Lord Mountbatten and General Wingate, who made it possible for me to get unimaginable appointments in the highest echelons of Military Command. Had I not gone to Deolali I would never have been posted as ADC to an Army Commander in battle or as ADC to the last Viceroy of India. Nor would I have had the most thrilling experience as a guerrilla fighter with Force 136 in the Karen Hills of Burma. And if I had not been in the Viceroy's House New Delhi in 1947, I would never have met my wife. I did not meet anyone before or during my married life except my wife Ann, who was not only very beautiful to look at but indescribably delightful to know. No one else could have given me 52 years of sheer happiness, friendship, intellectual companionship, absolute support in very difficult and trying times and two wonderful children. My wife was a rare gem, not only a woman full of grace, but also a person of compassion and concern for others. My children and I loved her with all our heart. I do not regret having punched that bumptious British Officer at Feni, as otherwise I would never have had such a unique and wonderful experience of life as a young Officer and later as a Senior Officer as I did after my posting to Deolali.

While I was at Deolali I was selected as one of two Liaison Officers for the visit of Admiral Lord Louis Mountbatten, the

Supreme Allied Commander, who was coming to inspect the 19th Indian Division then training in the hills and jungles between Deolali and Nasik. 19th Indian Division gave a demonstration of close fire support from tanks for an infantry assault on enemy bunkers. Lord Mountbatten was suitably impressed and had the Division moved to fight in Burma. Obviously, I must have impressed him also, as when I met him again in Burma he recognized me straightaway and had a nice friendly chat with me.

The charismatic General Orde Wingate, who was to lead the 3rd Indian Division, called 'Chindits', to eternal fame, had fought the Italians in Ethiopia as a guerilla and his stories were thrilling and fascinating to hear. At his behest, I sought transfer from Gunners to Infantry in the hope that I might join the 'Chindits'. By the time I was transferred to the Royal Garhwal Rifles, the only non-British or Gorkha Regiment who were expected to provide a Battalion for the 'Chindits', General Wingate had, unfortunately, been killed in an air accident. But I became an Infantryman, which opened up new vistas of opportunities I had not dreamed of before.

9th Battalion of the Frontier Force had suffered severe casualties in fighting in Burma.. As I was awaiting a posting to the Chindits, which did not materialize, I volunteered to go as reinforcement to 9 Frontier Force who were in 20th Indian Division which crossed the Irrawaddy and fought its way down to Prome and Tharrawaddy. While we were at Meiktila, it was my turn to go on a routine patrol to reconnoiter enemy defences near the Lake. As I was running a fever the Regimental Medical Officer recommended to the Commanding Officer to take me off the patrol although I was very keen to go. My Company Officer, (I forget his name – call him Kasim), a newly joined Officer, volunteered to replace me. He had been gone for about three hours when there was a very loud explosion and, of course, as per Standing Orders, we immediately took up our 'Stand-to' positions. After a while, we 'Stood-down', but I kept awake wondering why there was such a loud explosion. Early in the morning, only one Soldier from the patrol came back. His uniform was torn to shreds and he had multiple splinter wounds. After the Doctor had patched him up and given him a shot of morphia before his evacuation to the Main Dressing Station of the Field Ambulance, he told us what had happened. The Japanese had booby-trapped a 500 lb aerial bomb, left behind by the Royal Air Force in 1942, which was accidentally triggered in the dark by the leading Scout. The getaway-man had survived – all others were blown to smithereens. I took out a patrol later but all I could recover were a few weapons and bits of equipment. We lost a very fine bunch of men and a good Officer who had shown great courage and promise in the brief period he was with me. I felt particularly saddened and guilty as someone else was killed in my place.

From Meiktila we chased the Japanese to Natmauk. It was very hot and very dusty. Water was in short supply, so there was no question of having a bath before going to bed. The thought of spending the night inside a dugout trench was loathsome. As there appeared to be no Japs around at Natmauk, I ordered my Batman to take out my folding camp-bed from the Jeep and put it on a little mound near my Company Headquarters, so that I could catch some cool breeze at night. He said that it would be a foolish thing to do, as I would be exposed to stray enemy fire at night. In the event, I slept on a ground-sheet near my trench with my mosquito net supported by bamboo sticks dug into the ground. As it happened a Jap patrol did come that night and raked the area with rifle and light machine-gun fire. After the first shots, I was awake and I decided to roll down into my trench. Everybody stood to and I ordered the mortars to bring down fire on the enemy. When it was all quiet we stood down and I went back to sleep. In the morning, we found that my mosquito net had quite a few bullet holes and the little mound on which I thought I would catch some breeze was churned up by enemy bullets! As my orderly was a Pathan, I have had blind faith in a Pathan's premonitions – I took him as my orderly when I was posted as ADC to the Twelfth Army Commander; but as he had some family problems I had him posted to the Regimental Centre at Sialkot when I was in Indonesia.

From Natmauk we streaked down to Allanmyo on the River Irrawaddy. On the outskirts, the Jap rear guard stood their ground. But our Air Forces had complete command of the skies and in a jiffy the enemy position was literally pulverized by our Air and Artillery bombardment. When the position was captured, we found that the Japs had bolted, but quite a few bodies of poor men, women and children mangled by our bombardment lay scattered all over the place. The carnage was horrible and very poignant – a sight I wished I would never see again. I thought that if there was a benign God how could he possibly sanction such a bloody slaughter of the innocent. For days I was troubled by the ghastly carnage and whenever a friend, a British Officer, and I talked about it, we were filled with disgust and despair; this dreadful slaughter overwhelmed me and for days I could neither sleep well nor eat a full meal. Was there a benign God as we were made to believe? Did he control all our actions or destiny? If he did, how could he allow such a horrible carnage to take place? My friend and I concluded that God was more mythical than real. So I believe to this day.

The Japanese Army on the run from the Arakan made an attempt to cross the Irrawaddy at Thayetmyo on barges and rafts. We were on the East bank of the River at Allanmyo. The River here was over a kilometre wide and as the Japanese kept to the western side till they could float down to a safe point opposite their bridgehead on this side, we had to use our binoculars to spot them. The Divisional Commander, General Gracey, decided to use 6 pounder Anti-tank guns and Vickers Machine Guns to destroy the barges or rafts, while we lined up on the bank to see the fun. Unfortunately our deep-trench loo was dug before the Anti-tank Gunners had decided to site their guns just above the loo. Early one morning while I was in the loo I heard ear-splitting bangs and saw balls of flame shooting past just above my head. After half an hour I thought I had had too much, so I took my underpants off and threw them over the enclosure. Fortunately the Gunners spotted it and stopped firing. I ran up the slope naked, as I did not have the time to put my pants on! Everybody had a good laugh at my expense! In fact, I was teased about this incident for a long time.

On the way down to Prome we had a few skirmishes and in one of them I was in a Jeep when we were ambushed. I managed to dive out of the Jeep just in time to take up a fire position behind a tree before the jeep was riddled with bullets. We reached Prome the next day and I was thrilled to see one of the most beautiful cities in Burma. We were in Prome for some days to round up the fleeing Japanese before moving on to Tharrawaddy. I had just returned to Tharrawaddy from a patrol towards the Pegu Yomas when the Adjutant met me and said that General Stopford wanted to see me. General Stopford had been our Corps Commander and I thought I was up for a high jump although I could not think what wrong I had done to deserve any punishment. My offensive British Commanding Officer had only a week before been replaced by Lt Col 'Ganga' Hayauddin, a KCIO and a Pathan, who was one of the best Officers I ever served with and who was so pleased with my work that he was going to put me up for the DSO. I learnt later that 'Ganga' Hayauddin and General Officer Commanding my Division Douglas Gracey (probably influenced by an earlier visit by Lord Mountbatten), had recommended my name to General Stopford who was in search of an ADC from the Indian Army. I learnt later that Mounbatten had indeed spoken to Stopford about my stint with him as the Liaison Officer.

When I met General Stopford, General Douglas Gracey and Colonel 'Ganga' Hayauddin were also present. General Stopford said he wanted me as his ADC. I was reluctant to accept his kind offer as I was having a wonderful and thrilling time with my Battalion chasing the Japanese who were on the run. I had a few very good friends in the Battalion and I adored my men. I honestly did not want a change. General Gracey forced the issue and said that I had no choice as I had chased enough Japs and it was now time for me to have a change. In any case, it was an honour for the Battalion to provide an ADC to the Army Commander. My Commanding Officer told me that I was the first Indian in the job.

I was flown to Mingaladon Air base where the General's Military Assistant met me and drove me to the new Twelfth Army 'A' Mess in Wright Brothers' House on the Lake in Rangoon. The General welcomed me warmly and told me not to worry too much about the job, as I would get to know the ropes as I went along. General Stopford was a very thorough professional soldier and a stickler for the rules. He set high standards by personal example. I had to dress more meticulously and smartly in uniform than I had ever done before. Once he made me walk back for over 3 miles to our HQ to put my 'puttees' on and return in a jeep within the hour!

As the ADC my first and foremost job was to ensure my General's personal safety round the clock especially when he was travelling long distances by road and air in the battlezone. I took care of his social engagements and visitors or guests and arranged all the necessary transport for the occasion. I accompanied him on all his outings especially to the battlefields and made sure that all the maps and papers I carried for him were relevant, secure and up to date, as more often than not they were marked TOP SECRET. Although a Signals Van full of powerful Wireless Sets with a senior Officer in charge accompanied us (with similar arrangements in the big aircraft), I made sure that my General could communicate with any of his fighting formations or his Headquarters at any time he felt the need to do so. As soon as I received the Situation Reports from the various formations in the field he expected me to bring the maps up to date; if there was any major enemy activity or substantial change in the operational situation, I had to bring it to his notice at once. He would study the situation and talk to his Brigadier (in charge of the) General Staff (or BGS, a very prestigious appointment that I was to hold myself in 1965) on the secrophone (secret phone), or order a conference in the Operations Room in Judson College. He did not feel the need for a Tac HQ, as many Army Commanders were wont to do in the War, as the battlefields were not very far from Rangoon. If there was a battle in progress, he made it a point to go there and to see for himself how things were faring. He used his Intelligence network as a camera that he would focus on a particular aspect to get all the information he wanted for the formulation of his plans. Quite often he would pick my brains and ask me to respond to a question without giving me the slightest idea of what it was all about. He would always ask me to leave a thousand or more cigarettes, some good liquor and other goodies in the Officers' Mess that hosted him. I had strict orders to pay the Mess Bill before we left our hosts. Stopford became my model soldier but he was too good for me to emulate. But I learnt more about soldiering, planning and fighting major battles and Generalship as his ADC than at the Staff College or the what is now the War College, where I taught as a Professor, or later in Army Service.

As I had no leave in 1944, the General asked me if I would like a break. I had long cherished a wish to serve with 'Special Forces' and I had spoken to him about it on many occasions. Now the time was fast running out if I were to see any action with them. It was nearly the end of July and the Battle of Breakout was coming to an end. Those Japanese who managed to escape the Twelfth Army onslaught were trying to get across the River Sittang by the shortest and safest route to Thailand. The task of Force 136 Group Mongoose White was to attack the enemy's L of C and prevent his withdrawal South or East through the Karen Hills. Mongoose White were having a field day killing the enemy as he persisted in crossing the Shwegyin Chaung which was a thin blue line on the map but a high-speed torrent on the ground with very thick jungles on both sides. The Army Commander thought I would have a 'whale of a time' fulfilling my wish with 'Mongoose White'.

There I went towards the end of July and joined the finest bunch of British Officers I ever met in my life; each one of them was a daredevil whose unbelievable exploits could shame James Bond. One had only to meet these Officers to understand how Great Britain conquered nearly a third of the World. The Karen Levies they had raised and trained were skilled warriors who could spring a deadly ambush on the Japanese on a whispered command; the Karens taught me how to light a fire without matches; they laughed their way through the most dangerous situations and I learnt from them how to laugh at myself when I committed a faux pas. I had to flog myself hard to keep a step ahead to prove my worth as an acceptable leader and I was thrilled when they joked and laughed about the fickleness and caprice of women because I knew then that they had accepted me as one of them. Later I was honoured when the Village Chief garlanded me with a beautiful hand-woven silk bag with a strap—which I have to this day and find it very useful for carrying my golf balls!

After I had recovered from an accident I moved on from Bolo Auk to Thaukthekhi (QB 5883 on the Burma map) on the Shwegyn Chaung. My route lay through lush green high mountains and delightfully aromatic pine forests. We avoided a few villages inhabited by the Shans, who were not all very friendly and often gave succour and refuge to the Japanese.

And as the Japs regularly patrolled the area, I had to take a strong Levy escort to accompany me. Unfortunately, soon after we left Bolo Auk, a very heavy rainstorm deluged us and the soft earth on the uphill path turned into slippery morass. Our progress uphill was exhausting and dreadfully slow. The five stitches in the gashing wound under my chin were a nagging pain and I was near collapse with sheer fatigue, but as an Officer and a leader I just had to keep pace with my wonderful Karen Levy escort.

Late in the evening, we were forced to seek shelter in a Shan village. The Headman of the village was most reluctant to shelter us, but Sergeant Harold (Karens are Christians and a large number have Biblical names), in charge of the Karen Levies with me, managed to persuade him to allow us to stay the night there as the weather was very inclement. Harold, two Levies and I stayed with him in his house on stilts, while the others were accommodated in adjacent huts on stilts. About midnight a Japanese patrol came to the village and called out to the Headman in whose hut on stilts we were sheltered from the pouring rain. The Japs insisted that the Headman lower the rope ladder so that they could climb up about 15 feet to shelter in the hut. Alarmed we took up pre-determined positions for an escape. The Japs were a noisy lot and they were jabbering away among themselves. We could assess from their conversation that there were not more than three or four of them. Harold whispered to the Headman to open the doorway and start lowering the rope ladder while we took up fire positions in the dark on either side. The Headman had my torch. As soon as the Japs saw the rope ladder by their torchlight, they crowded together. Harold prodded the Headman to shine the torch on the Japs-at that moment, the four of us moved in to open fire on the Japs with our .30 Winchester automatic rifles. It turned out that there were only three of them and our fire killed the lot. But we had to make a get-away immediately just in case there were more Japs around.

Obviously, we could not use the ladder to exit. On arrival Harold and I had planned earlier that in case the Japs came, we would jump through the recess for a loo at the back and keep on running downhill till we came to a stream. Of course, all of us fell into the cesspool below when we jumped one by one! But it didn't matter, as we were alive and ready to give battle. We ran down hill through a field full of thick maize plants to the stream below. Our rendezvous for our party was about half a mile down stream at a junction of two streams. There we took up an ambush position to wait for the rest of our party. They joined us sooner than we had expected, but we checked them in very carefully in case the Japs were using them as a ruse to find us. Harold said he had faced a similar situation before.

The rest of our party who joined us were sheltering in adjacent huts. Apparently, there were no more Japs, but the villagers were very agitated in case our action were to bring reprisal on them. Harold said not to worry, as the villagers were certain to dump the bodies in the river on the other side of the hill before first light. I felt very secure with Harold by my side to advise me.

The filth on my uniform was revolting. The four of us decided to take our uniforms off, wash everything quickly in the stream and then run on naked till we were well away from the village as we did not wish to get involved in a fight with the Japs till we had reached our destination. By first light, we reached the bog that was a dread for the locals as it was infested with some terrible varieties of leeches. As we had to get across to a safe valley on the other side everyone had to undress, take the boots off, make a bundle with the pack, wrap it up in the ground-sheet and carry it on our heads across to the other side. We crossed in two halves – one half covering the crossing of the first half till they were in fire positions on the other side to cover the second half. Our bodies were covered with muck and leeches as we waded across the murky smelly water. Once across we got down to the nasty business of de-leeching ourselves by bringing a lighted cigarette close to the blood-sucking leech or sprinkling a little salt on it. As soon as the leech dropped off we cauterized the bleeding bite with an iodine cartridge issued to us for the purpose. But we had to rush away just in case the Japs were on our trail. We speed-marched for three hours through some of the most beautiful hills, valleys and jungles I had ever seen till we reached a friendly Shan village. Harold went alone to see the Headman to find out if it was safe for us to go into the village while the rest of us took up a defensive position in a thicket and waited. The Headman came with Harold to welcome me and invited me to the village. He said he knew what had transpired and that we should have a nice hot bath while he had our dirty clothes washed and dried before the meal he had already ordered for us. Did I mind a roasted piglet? It would be a treat I assured him! We followed him to the village school where we were to stay. But Harold took no chances – he posted sentries on the in and out tracks of the village.

A hot bath and the rice and herbs stuffed roasted piglet were quite out of this world for us guerillas on an offensive mission. We declined the Headman's offer of 'good' wine! We were on the trail again as soon as we could. Before last light we reached a Karen village and we knew we were in safe hands. The Karens sing beautifully to many western tunes they were taught by the European missionaries and it was indeed a great joy to dance round a bonfire with them and drink their local brew of rice wine and eat their delicious food – speciality: chicken stuffed with rice and herbs, wrapped up in plantain leaves, placed in a hole in the ground and roasted under a bonfire – so scrumptious! Next morning, after a very restful and peaceful night we hit the trail again to Thaukthekhmi (QB 5883k on the map) where 2000 Japanese were expected to cross the Shwwegyin Chaung on rafts they were building. It was going to be a thrill of a lifetime and we hastened with all our might to join in for the kill. In the event after 106 Japs had been killed they decided to move further down for a safer crossing – but so did we and the Levies to get them!

I had the best and the most exciting time of my Army service soldiering there in the wilds 'behind the enemy lines–every single day was full of thrills and adventures. Unfortunately, the Japanese surrendered unconditionally on 15 August, and as there were to be innumerable 'victory' functions in Rangoon. I had to return to my duties as ADC for these functions on 22 August. The fighting in that area continued till 5 September 1945.

Soon after I returned to Rangoon, General Stopford decided to visit the jail north of Rangoon at Insein where women rescued from Japanese 'Comfort Battalions' were temporarily housed for counseling, medical treatment and rehabilitation. The Japanese had forcibly taken these young women from loving families and placed them at the disposal of their Officers and Soldiers for sexual abuse. A large number of these women could not reconcile with the separation from their children or families. The brutality and savagery of the Japanese was so repulsive and distressing to most of them that they became totally psychotic. When they saw the General they howled irreconcilably and raised their flimsy skirts to expose their private parts, as they were required to do for Japanese inspections. That the Japanese lust had been so debasing and inhuman was horrifying. It was hard to respect the Japanese after what we had seen on that day at Insein Jail. The Japanese would have done the same thing had they come to India in 1942, if the British had quit India as demanded by the politicians.

General Stopford loved visiting his troops. For three or four days in the week, we were visiting troops wherever they were stationed in Burma. Lashio in north-west was short of the border and was famous as a road-head into China; the Chinese and American Troops there mixed with each other with remarkable camaraderie; the Chinese produced a delightful meal which we washed down with a sweetish but potent wine distilled by the Shans. Maymyo was closer to Mandalay and a hill-station no different in layout and shops than the ones in India where the British spent their summer months.

But Mandalay was different. It was a huge beautiful ancient city, the capital of Burmese Kings, which had been totally destroyed in the battle between the Japanese and us. It had a pagoda on top of a hill with the longest flight of steps I had ever seen. Then there was the fort where napalm bombs had to be used to silence Japanese resistance. The clock tower, a bit scarred by shell-fire, stood in all its splendour in the midst of a desert of debris. Soon after Mandalay was captured an Indian barber had set up a shop under a twisted tin shed near the clock-tower and I (still with my Battalion then) paid him 1000 rupees in Japanese banana notes for a hair-cut! Our Air Force had wrecked a train full of these currency notes and we thought it was great dishing out notes in thousands to the needy! The Agriculture College built by the British just a few miles outside Mandalay was impressive, but the Japanese left it in a terrible state.

On one occasion, while we were visiting Mandalay, we were invited to a celebration of the Burmese Water Festival when I saw Burmese dances for the first time. My General was bored after an hour of it and whispered to me to get him out it somehow. I explained to the host that the General had a scheduled meeting to attend and would he mind if we left. He said he was sorry that we had to go as there were very interesting programmes later on! But the Brigadier whose command we were visiting took me to one side and said, 'Why the hell didn't you tell me about this scheduled meeting before!' I had to wink at him to keep him quiet. Apparently, the dances went on all night and some of the petite and beautiful dancers were available to those who wished to take them to bed!

Arakan is the northeast coast of Burma – 82th West African Division was located there. The 82 Div and an East African Brigade had been brought in to Burma after the scare of the Indian National Army. British Officers with British Warrant and Non-commissioned Officers down to Platoons commanded both these formations. General Stopford decided to visit 82 Div in Arakan. He asked a Regimental Warrant Officer if the African Troops had any requirements that could not be met. "Yes,' said the Regimental Warrant Officer, 'we do not have enough Pepsodent toothpaste.'

'It is not that we are short of toothpaste,' butted in the British Commanding Officer. 'My fellows like the taste and spread the toothpaste on bread and eat it!' Back in his Headquarters, the Army Commander ordered his Brigadier Administration to ensure that 82nd West African Division was never short of Pepsodent toothpaste!

Early in 1946, General Stopford was posted to Batavia to take charge in the Dutch East Indies (now Indonesia) as many of our soldiers, who had gone there to restore normalcy, had been hacked to death by the local guerrillas and an experienced General was required to handle the situation. Among those killed was one of the most distinguished Indian Officers with a DSO and bar. I went with Monty Stopford as the ADC. It was he who invited Sukarno to come to Batavia for talks, as General Stopford was also the Military Governor till he handed over charge to the Dutch Governor, von Mook, who arrived in the middle of the year 1946. A famous South African Boer writer was on Sopford's Staff as the Civil Liaison Officer. At the time Indonesia was in a chaotic turmoil. When the Dutch were ousted by the Japanese invasion in 1942, the administration and the rule of law collapsed in its totality. Sukarno, a nationalist, had been agitating against the Dutch for freedom, but during the Japanese occupation he could only grasp an opportunity to consolidate his position. He raised and trained a powerful guerilla force in the hope that when the Allies defeated the Japanese, he would take over Indonesia by force of arms and resist the return of the Dutch. Of course, the Dutch were in no position to assert themselves in Indonesia after the Japanese were defeated, but the British still had the Indian Army less the European Troops who were hellbent on returning to Blighty after Germany had surrendered. So the highly disciplined and uncomplaining Indian Troops were sent to Dutch East Indies to restore law and order there. The aim was to occupy strategic areas till the Dutch could return and take over their colony. This arrangement was not acceptable to General Sukarno and he ordered his guerillas to attack our positions, ambush our convoys and spread disaffection and chaos throughout Indonesia and its countless Islands around it.

When we arrived in Batavia, the situation was tense and confusing. But General Stopford in his characteristic manner visited all the areas where our troops were located to make a detailed assessment of the situation before making a firm plan to deal with it. I went with him. We had closer brushes with death than in all the intense battles in Burma, as the guerillas were everywhere and they sniped at us wherever we went. Nevertheless, we managed to return safely to Batavia, thanks to the agility and vigilance of the Indian Troops. The General decided to deal with the situation with a comprehensive and flexible military plan and with an invitation to Sukarno to come to Batavia before it became necessary for us to go there and fetch him – I had a small role in contacting General Sukarno and passing the message to him in a palatable and courteous form. Within a month what was still the Dutch East Indies was reasonably safe for sight-seeing and travel. General Sukarno came to Batavia (now Jakarta) and I thought he was an extremely amiable, fun-loving and charismatic leader and my General got on well with him.

There was a large Dutch population in the Indies when the Japanese came. They treated the Europeans harshly and most of the Dutch were huddled into concentration camps; some were sent to Singapore as labour for various projects. There were some, especially among Dutch women, who collaborated and lived with the Japanese – the women told us that there were forced to do so, but we did not accept them for any kind of social relationship. There were, of course, plenty of very beautiful and healthy girls who were keen to socialize with us. And for their benefit we organized a Club and called the RA Club – RA standing for Rakes Anonymous! Its membership was limited only to bachelors and our strength fluctuated between 15 to 20, depending on postings and transfers. It was the only Club I had ever known in which you could swap girl friends by consent after a week! It so happened that our Brigadier General Staff, or BGS (later Commandant of the Quetta Staff College) was a bachelor and a founder member of the RA Club, and I had an evening party with our girl friends in his room. We were having such a wonderful time joking, laughing and dancing to gramophone music that we forgot about the curfew timings. (My General had made it very clear in his Orders that there were to be no non-military personnel in our Mess or Quarters during the curfew hours (2200 hours to 0600 hours) and that none of us was to be out during that time.) After a little powwow we decided that I was to bring out the General's huge black Cadillac, complete with the stars and the flag and that the BGS would sit in front with me with his red-band peak cap and pose as the Chief, while the girls hid themselves by lying low on the back seat. We had no problem in reaching the girls home, but on our way back I had to slow down to cross a zig-zag Military Police barrier where, in addition to the two Policeman who were there previously there were now six including the Provost Marshal. They all came to attention very smartly and saluted as I picked up speed and whizzed away – obviously the two Policemen had informed their boss that they had seen the Chief! Next morning the Chief found his name on top of the curfew defaulters list! But the BGS, a brilliant Officer of very high integrity, had by then already told the Chief what had happened and taken all the blame on himself. The Chief said nothing at all to me but I know that the BGS was ticked off in no uncertain manner!

From Batavia, General Stopford was posted to Singapore as Commander-in-Chief of the Allied Land Forces and I was with him as the only ADC. When Admiral Mountbatten left Singapore, General Stopford, now promoted to four stars, took over as Supreme Allied Commander.

King Ananda Mahidol of Siam (Thailand) died on 9 June 1946, under mysterious circumstances. A Regency was appointed as Ananda's younger brother, Bhumibol Adulyadej, later Rama IX, was too young to rule. As we had an Indian Division in Bangkok, the Commander-in-Chief decided to visit Siam soon after taking over. We were guests of the King for the four days we spent there. On the day after our arrival, the King was gracious enough to give us an audience. As usual, the Commander-in-Chief said, 'I want a brief on the King's likes and dislikes.' The General Officer Commanding the Indian Division was ashamed to admit that he didn't know about His Majesty's fads, but a British Officer said he knew Princess Chumpot, a cousin of the King and we could find out about His Majesty's fads from her. He and I tore off in a car with a Military Police jeep in the lead with the siren screaming to see Princess Chumpot late in the night. She said that His Majesty the King was very fond of photography. So I spent the next few hours of what was left of the night trying to glean information on the finer points of photography, from all sources I could contact on the wireless round the world. In the event, when we met the King, he was more interested in weapons used in the war to defeat the Japanese than cameras! But we had a wonderful time attending endless parties, Thai classical dances and sightseeing huge statues of Buddha in the lotus pose and the reclining and, of course, Angor Wat, the temple complex. The urn containing the body of King Ananda was in the Royal Chapel and I was very proud to see that the priests there were Indians from Kashmir.

General and Lady Stopford had no children and therefore I became an object of special attention. Lady Stopford was particularly kind in sending all sorts of useful gifts from Britain from time to time. I was always profuse in the expression of my appreciation and gratitude. But I did not always enjoy the periodic confessions pried out of me on my life 'off parade'. Batavia was bad enough—the social life there was literally deadly but Singapore was particularly frolicsome after the war and fishing fleets of young women from almost all continents were on the prowl for young eligible husbands at any cost, as marriage was still in fashion till then. As one of the British Officers put it, 'There are now only three dangerous places on earth: Hiroshima and Nagasaki because they are radioactive and Singapore because it is female active!' There were some Officers who had two different 'dates' on a holiday; one was normal!

The Sultan of Johore's Tyersal Palace in Singapore, built especially for his British wife, Helen, who lived there for a month and then bolted with all the crown jewels, was the Commander-in-Chief/Supreme Allied Commander's official residence with a large forested compound, a huge lawn and a big spacious hall, the sort of place that looked empty with a hundred guests at a party.

As an Indian Cavalry Regiment stationed near Kuala Lumpur had decided to import some horses to play polo, I requested them (in particular Major Shiv Verma, the Second-in-Command, who was later the Colonel of my Regiment as a Lt. General) on my General's behalf to send four ponies with their grooms and attendants to our Headquarters for attachment. General Stopford, who was from the Rifle Brigade, once a 'mounted Regiment', and I knocked around a ball with a polo stick on the Tyersal Palace lawn a few times, but he did not have the leisure to do it more often. But I would get up early and exercise the ponies. When the young women Officers in our Headquarters (comprising the Supreme Commander's and the three Service Chiefs) heard about the horses with no riders, I faced a deluge of requests to allow them to ride the ponies. Only 7 had been on a horse before and I said I would have to test them before they could take a horse out and ride on their own. Three fell off the first day with fairly serious injuries, but the four who survived became the nucleus of my party for fun and outings. For a week I conducted riding coaching classes on how to sit in the saddle, the length of the stirrups, the position of the heels and how to hold the reins with a supple hand without hurting the pony's mouth. The most difficult to teach were the signals to the pony by 'voice', hands, legs and by shifting the weight of one's body. While cantering a pony brings down the hind-legs first. As it is often necessary to change the lead foreleg, if the lead hind-leg is changed first, in most cases the pony will change the lead foreleg also. I do not know to this day what amused them but they all burst out laughing as if I had recounted the joke of the year. Often with a drink in our hand, one of the girls would say 'bring down the hind-legs first' and all the girls and boys would roar with unstoppable laughter! I loved their company and had a wonderful time.

On Sunday and holidays we would go out in the General's boat to one of the numerous islands round Singapore for picnics. We would 'down' a coconut from a tree, cut a hole in it, fill it up with crushed ice and gin, lace it with a little cognac and absinthe (thought to be an aphrodisiac!), shake it well to mix it with the coconut juice and drink it! Wow! Sometimes we would go to Johore Baru and ask the teetotaller Crown Prince, who was great fun and had loaned me his Mercedes Benz of 1936 vintage with the super-chargers, to join us and dance barefoot on the lawns of his beautiful gardens on a moonlit night. Singapore was a dream-island for whale of a time and we took full advantage of it to have really wonderful and memorable fun. 'Robin' Goodfellow was a member of this 'gang' and although she could not ride a polo pony for nuts (beg forgiveness, Robin!), she was my best friend and we thought we were young enough to wait and see how life shaped for us before deciding on anything more serious – she was the only friend I ever had who was not in a hurry to get married!

The Supreme Commander always insisted that select Singaporeans be invited with European guests. An elite Singaporean, known for his riches, always came to the parties with his very petite and beautiful daughter Clara. She had asked me over to her fabulous parties a number of times; I had always declined to accept her expensive gifts, as I could not afford to give her any in return; also, I knew the Boss would scowl if he saw them. Her world was built around fantasies of Sleeping Beauties and dashing Prince Charming on rescue missions! Of course, as ADCs are always selected from among the smartest and impressively handsome young Officers, I was no exception. But it was difficult for her to comprehend that I was only an Army Captain who happened to be the ADC to the Supreme Allied Commander – certainly no Adventurer fencing my way to rescue Damsels in Distress! She telephoned me several times during the day and at night and sometimes she would call and not say a word and just get me frustrated and angry. In every way she was highly talented having had all her education in a posh school in Switzerland and she spoke English and French like a native. I was weary of her, as she was arrogant, imperious and unreasonably possessive. When I tried to avoid her she spoke to my Boss and told him that I had reneged on my promises and that she wanted to marry me! My boss did not take kindly to the first and the only complaint ever against me and I was reprimanded though mildly. It sort of spoiled things for me as I could not even dream of getting married on a Captain's salary. In any case, an English girl, Robin, a Captain in the ATS, who worked in my Headquarters, and I had vague plans of meeting up again in England and then deciding what to do with our lives. I was distressed, as I knew it was only the youth in Clara which was on the boil. I did wish for a change, as the social life was much too hectic, and I was glad when I was posted back to Regimental Duty in India.

I had also been recommended to attend the Staff College and three months Regimental Service before the Course was a pre-requisite. So, in January 1947, I left Singapore to join 1st Battalion of the Royal Garhwal Rifles who were in Peshawar (now in Pakistan). I did the first leg of the journey in a British Overseas Airways Flying Boat from Singapore to Calcutta and I thought it was the most comfortable journey ever of my over many thousands of miles by air. When I arrived at Peshawar, the Hindu Muslim riots had already started. In fact, soon after my arrival hooligans attacked Dr. Khan Sahib's house. My Company lines were next to his house. We were playing volleyball at the time. When we heard the commotion, we quickly collected mosquito-net bamboo sticks and rushed to his help. When the hooligans saw us they ran away, but they did manage to inflict quite a bit of damage on the house. Dr. Khan Sahib was brother of the famous Frontier Gandhi, Abdul Ghaffar Khan, and Chief Minister of the North West Frontier Province. Dr. Khan Sahib was married to an English lady and some British officials at the Club had told me that she was a bit 'eccentric'; I found her absolutely normal and charming. The British did not approve of Indians marrying British women and found fault with those girls who did. It was indeed an honour to meet these two great brother leaders from the Frontier Province. In our view, they were both eminently suitable to become Prime Ministers of India. Regrettably, we abandoned them to Pakistan.

Most of the three months I spent in Peshawar were out in the streets for Internal Security. The Muslims were bent upon forcing the Hindus and Sikhs to leave the Province and they set fire to their houses or killed them whenever they could get an opportunity. But we were absolutely impartial in our action, as also were the British Officers. My Company HQ was located for nearly a month in the decrepit 'Tonga Stand' shelter in front of the Government School in Sadar, as it provided an all-round view and was central to my command – but it was an Augean stable and the stench there was just revolting!

When Lord Mountbatten was appointed Viceroy of India, I joined him as ADC. I was the first Indian Commissioned Officer from the Army to be appointed ADC to a Viceroy. A Muslim Officer from the Navy and a Hindu from the Air Force were also with me, and we three were the first Indians in the appointment.

Louis Francis Albert Victor Nicholas Battenberg was born on 25 June 1900. His mother, Princess Victoria, was the granddaughter of Queen Victoria of England. His father was Prince Louis of Battenberg from the family of Grand Duke Louis of Hesse and Rhine. As Louis was his father's name, the family wanted to call him Nicky, but his uncle, Tsar Nicholas II of Russia, was called Nicky; to avoid confusion it was decided to call the new child Dickie. Before he was 44 years of age, Dickie Mountbatten had risen to become the Supreme Allied Commander of the most vital theatre of war and provide dynamic leadership to defeat the armies from the hawkish island of the Rising Sun. He celebrated his 47th birthday in New Delhi as the last Viceroy of Imperial India, the absolute ruler of 300 million people of diverse faith, culture, race and heritage. On leaving India he was happy 'to climb down without losing some of the distinction' to command the 1st Cruiser Squadron of the Royal Navy at Malta as a Rear Admiral.

He was even the British Minister of Defence in Attlee's Government in 1949. In 1955 Sir Winston Churchill, who had also elevated Dickie's father to the same appointment in the First World War, appointed him First Sea Lord. Dickie Mountbatten worked through a whole career to avenge the humiliation of his father's resignation as the First Sea Lord because he was German by descent. In 1959, Dickie Mountbatten was appointed Chief of the Defence Staff, the highest professional appointment in the British Armed Forces. He was now a five star Admiral of the Fleet, who never retired from service.

Looking back on my association with Lord Mountbatten, I think I was most impressed by his soldierly qualities when he visited 19th Indian Division in June 1945. The Division was engaged in one of the most savage battles of the war on the Toungoo-Kalaw axis where we lost a man for every yard gained. The Division had come up against what was known as 'the Staircase'. The Japanese stand was desperate and aggressive— they had counter-attacked and charged with bayonets relentlessly. 62 Infantry Brigade were in contact with the enemy. The enemy machine-gun and mortar fire was constant and shattering. 3/6 Rajputana Rifles, the Regiment of the Div Commander, Maj Gen Pete Rees, was up on a high feature left of the road while 2nd Battalion of the Welch Regiment were on the right also on a hill feature. Both positions were under Japanese observation and fire. Admiral Mountbatten followed General Pete Rees up a narrow pathway to the forward positions of 3/6 Raj Rif. Stopford was behind Mountbatten while I was behind Stopford, the Army Commander. On top of the hill Mountbatten took the lead and went round the positions of the Battalion to shake hands with the Soldiers. Apart from the fact that the Battalion was under enemy fire, at some point his entourage must also have been seen by the enemy, but Mountbatten had the same composed look I had seen on his face as the Liaison Officer when he visited 19th

Indian Division's assault demonstration at Nasik. Till then I had thought that he was just a Royal playboy, but now I knew that he was an outstanding Soldier-Leader, a Supreme Commander and a Royal Prince who was delighted to seek a moment to share the terrible hazards of war with the humblest of his soldiers in action on the battlefield.

Mountbatten was not an easy man to serve. He was a perfectionist and unless everything was done the way he wanted, he was inclined to be irritable and quick to temper. He was very conscious of his birth and Royal status, which were his powerful driving engines in life—he used to say that he had to be twice as good as the other fellow! He had learnt the art of 'Royal Showmanship' where everything had to be done or managed as if one were on stage to impress an audience. If he were required to give a public speech, he would rehearse it for hours in front of a mirror and use every prop he could think of to make his point. He was not an original thinker but he had perfected the art of surrounding himself with knowledgeable people, so that he could pick their brain to evolve his own aim. Once the aim was clear to him he meticulously considered all factors that could contribute to a plan for its achievement. Having thus evolved a plan, he pursued it with all his vigour and determination. There was no doubt that he was extremely hard working and as ADC on duty with him one was seldom let off before midnight.

But really speaking all ADCs had a wonderful time at the Viceroy's House. There were horses to ride and hounds to take out for fox-hunts with Champagne breakfast and the prettiest girls in town as our guests. Facilities for almost all games were on a lavish scale. During summer we would have huge slabs of ice floating in the swimming pool and we tried to balance our cocktail glasses on them—and then served ourselves a delightful buffet lunch—better than any restaurant or hotel could produce. Just floating around in the cool water with a girl friend was great fun that would have made the richest tycoons round the world green with envy. The finest wine, liquor and liqueurs were on the house and the ADC bar was perhaps as well stocked as best in the world. The cigars and cigarettes were of the finest quality and all on the house, and if we wanted to buy any they were at duty-free prices which were ridiculously low. There were the Mughal Gardens with finely manicured lawns and trees and splendour of roses that filled the air with fragrance that inspired love and romance, which was perhaps denied to Mughal Emperors Babar and Aurangzeb, but not to us. It was there, in the fairyland of the Mughal Gardens, resplendent in the pale silvery light of a September full moon, like an exquisite painting in soft water-colours, that I proposed to my wife Ann. When she said yes we danced round the roses and saw them nod their beautiful heads in approval and open their petals in smile to share our joy. That painting, etched forever in our minds, was the most beautiful memory of our stay in the Viceroy's House and my wife Ann and I shared it lovingly for the rest our lives.

Two ADCs were always on duty every day – No.1 with the Viceroy and No. 2 with Lady Mountbatten. The next day No. 2 took over the duties of No.1. Our day began usually at 8 am when we would take the day's schedule to the Lord for approval. By then he was either in the bathroom, where no privacy was observed and the ADC would rattle off the day's engagements, notwithstanding the noises that emanated from there; or the Viceroy would be in bed having breakfast, or standing stark naked to get dressed for the day. If he had had a row with his wife, which grew in frequency during their stay in New Delhi, he was aggressive and peevish, but not nasty. Normally the ADC escorted him to his Office and back to his suite of rooms according to his wishes. Of course, we had all meals with the Mountbattens except breakfast. During the day, according to the schedule, we informed him of the arrival of such visitors as he wished to see and then escorted the visitors to meet him, The procedure was much the same in the evening except when we had formal parties and all ADCs were present and strict diplomatic and social protocols were observed. Whenever Lord or Lady Mountbatten went out the ADC on duty accompanied them. And of course the ADCs were in the duty room till the Mountbattens retired to their rooms. With such close association an ADC generally got to know his boss better than any biographer or even a mistress or lover.

I personally preferred to be on duty with Lady Mountbatten as she was always pleasant and extremely considerate, except that she was not in good health and I was always afraid that she might faint out of sheer fatigue or exhaustion, as she very nearly did on one of her outlandish visits in Calcutta. She was also, I think, psychologically disturbed by continued rows with her husband, which was not a new phenomenon but had apparently been going on for years with questions on their fidelity to each other. We also took the day's schedule to her in the morning with the seating plan for any luncheon or dinner party for her approval. Her programmes for the day were usually outside the Viceroy's House and it was fun going to the oddest of places with her. She was the Commissioner General of St. John Ambulance and also head of the Red Cross and the Royal Society for Prevention of Cruelty to Animals while in India, which imposed onerous and very taxing duties on her. In those days the Veterinary Hospital was way out in old Delhi and she told me one morning that she wanted to go there but without informing the doctor in charge. I confirmed with the police escort that they knew where to go, but the officer said to me that the place was in a shambles. Nevertheless, we went and on the way Lady Mountbatten stopped to check half a dozen tonga horses and to reprimand the tonga drivers (through me!) for their cruelty in not taking proper care of the horses. Of course, the conditions in the Veterinary Hospital were indeed shocking and she lost her temper with the doctor. I saw her break out in a profuse sweat and persuaded her to return home without further ado. Her visit brought about drastic changes in the Veterinary Hospital later, but on that day she complained of a severe headache and she took a while to recover. As an ADC, I was close enough to her to feel very concerned and disturbed.

Like all great men Lord Mountbatten had perfected the art of putting on devastating charms to win over a person he thought worthwhile for his purpose – I heard him tell Gandhiji that the plan to transfer power was inspired by him! Yes, he did prevaricate to make a point, or for some expediency! He always dressed to look smart and imposing and he took meticulous care to keep himself fit. He seldom had more than one cocktail or glass of wine and although he had the finest stock of cigars he would take a few puffs and leave them in an ash tray—we ADCs smoked the best cigars we could pick out of the Silver Box after dinner! Of course, he always pretended to be 'the girls man', but he was never left alone, nor did he have the time to indulge in frivolous sex. There were stories that he did so when he was away and on his own in Europe or America. Whatever his failings he was a very good man who was exceptionally loyal to those who had served him. In my view he was indeed a great statesman of historical importance who contributed substantially to the glory and greatness of his Country. He was also as good a friend of India as we ever had in the British Isles.

Lady Mountbatten was indeed the more genuine of the two. Her charms and compassion were so natural that it is not possible for me to think of her except in those terms. In Calcutta, I followed her to every single maternity hospital she insisted on visiting where she would fondle a newborn babe as if it were her own. I went with her to the huge refugee camp at Wah in Pakistan. There was a little Sikh girl who had been slashed by a sword across her chest and the wound was festering; she was in dirty blood-drenched rags, clotted hair and a running nose. Lady Edwina Mountbatten reached out, with tears in her eyes, picked up the girl and kissed her on both cheeks. On that day I became Edwina Mountbatten's slave for eternity. A rather silly and romantic thought passed through my mind that had she been 20 years younger I would have challenged Dickie Mountbatten to a duel for her hand! Since then I have lavished praise on her whenever i have had an opportunity to speak about her at a forum. Of course, Lord Mountbatten would never have been able to 'bend' sufficiently to do what Edwina did—and that is why I always thought that she was too good for him.

I had known the Mountbattens for well over two years. They were very correct in public, always posing as devoted husband and wife. But each was ambitious in his or her own field and the urge to outdo the other was so conspicuous that I was surprised that a good friend had not pointed it out to them. On some occasions, when I walked in front with another ADC to attend a function, they would continue their argument and bitterly accuse each other for trying to 'hog' all attention; of course, they were all smiles when they reached the assembled guests! I got the impression that she felt that that her husband owed his princely life-style, his opulence and indeed his phenomenal success in life to her inherited wealth and her personal charm. That he was not always grateful for this asset, I thought piqued and disappointed her. If she ever thought so, I think she was justified. They were both very nice to me and I liked them enormously, but I was always embarrassed and very distressed to see or hear them squabbling with each other so often.

Lady Mountbatten was going through a change in life while at Government House. She was 'unwell' quite often with migraine and I remember on one occasion in Simla she had a terrible headache and she begged me to do something about it. I was so upset that I started crying myself and instead of telephoning the Viceroy's Surgeon, I rushed down the carpeted staircase to get him from the Dispensary and slipped and fell on my head! But my most fond memories of the Mountbattens are those when I was on duty for her in Burma, Indonesia, Malaysia or India. She deserves a place in history as eminent and honourable as her husband.

On Lady Mounbatten's instruction I called on Gandhiji at the Bhangi Colony to say that Lady Mountbatten wished to call on him. I do not know why but Gandhiji said abruptly to me that he did not wish to receive her. Of course, I was shattered as I thought I would be sacked. I got up reluctantly, saluted and as I was leaving Rajkumari Amit Kaur, who was present, asked me to wait outside the hut. After a little while Rajkumari Amrit Kaur called me. I took my shoes off and again squatted down on the floor. "Why does she want to come here?' Gandhiji asked. "She wants to call on you as she has very high regard and respect for you, Sir," I replied. He consulted his Personal Secretary and gave me a date and asked me to confirm the appointment after consulting Lady Mountbatten. I accompanied Lady Mountbatten and daughter Pamela to see Gandhiji at the Bhangi Colony. It was a very amiable meeting and on the way back Lady Mountbatten was full of praise for Gandhiji's austerity. Of course, we, the ADCs, were always very amused when Gandhiji brought his little bowl of goat's milk curd, which he ate instead of afternoon tea.

Lady Pamela Mountbatten was in her teens then and a very sweet and charming girl to know. As I was in charge of the Library, I found Pammy, as she was called affectionately, was the one who used the Library the most. Gandhiji was gracious enough to invite Pammy and me to attend his prayer meetings. Many British magazines published photographs of Gandhiji walking to the dais supported by Lady Pamela Mountbatten on one side and me on the other! It was a wonderful experience to hear Gandhiji dilate on his favourite themes in simple but stirring words. His affection and compassion were always overwhelming. Although I did not (and do not) share his views on Non-violence, I doubt if I ever had greater admiration and affection for any other person than Gandhiji.

My Father, although a British Civil Servant, also had profound admiration for Gandhiji. My Father thought that Gandhiji understood the British better than any living Indian. While I was in School, my father often quoted Gandhiji on Hinduism. Gandhiji had written in *Young India*, a paper he edited, that "Believing as I do in the influence of heredity, being born in a Hindu family, I have remained a Hindu. I should reject it, if I found it inconsistent with my moral sense or my spiritual growth. On examination, I have found it to be the most tolerant of all religions known to me. Its freedom from dogma makes a forcible appeal to me in as much as it gives the votary the largest scope for self-expression." In later life I found this to be true as religions with dogmas were imperial writs that could be forced upon conquered people with barbaric ruthlessness and savagery not only for political sympathy and administrative convenience, but as firm bases to conquer or weaken those of alien faith.

Perhaps as (through my Father) I had known of Gandhiji's beliefs from school days I was inclined to think that he was more at ease with spiritual and moral themes than politics. May be it was for this reason that he was not so politely ignored by the politicians in the negotiations with the Viceroy. Most of us who knew Gandhiji were hurt and amazed that a leader who gave substance to the political movement in India was treated with such manifest indifference at a very crucial time in India's history. Nobody seemed to value his advice in the political game of one-upmanship except Lord Mountbatten who used him discreetly for political balance and peace. When I saw Gandhiji before Independence, there was distress and anguish writ on his saintly face and he was unusually pensive and taciturn. He resolved the embarrassing situation by leaving Delhi for Bengal where Hindu Muslim riots had continued to rage after Mr. Jinnah's call for 'Direct Action'. It was a terrible shame that ambitious politicians marginalized Gandhiji in India's most glorious hour in history.

Gandhiji used to arrive much earlier than the appointed time. I found it very difficult to entertain him—till I discovered that he did not mind giving his autograph provided one paid Rs 5 for each signature – he needed the money to run his ashram! A large number of young people in foreign embassies wanted his autograph and he was gracious enough to sign in the autograph books—but I had to pay Rs 5, often from my own pocket, for each signature to Rajkumari Amrit Kaur, who generally came with him, or to Gandhiji's Private Secretary, if I went to Bhangi Colony!

Gandhiji had formally resigned from the Congress in September 1934, although the Congress continued to stick to him to exploit his name and patronage. Pundit Nehru was, in fact, the undisputed leader of the Congress. He was erudite, a thinker, a dreamer, a man of enormous pride and self-respect. His sensitive nature had obviously been pricked while he was in England as he was always trying to paint India with imaginary hues and colours on a larger-than-life canvas to project his country as better and greater than the one where he had received his education and degrees. He did not decry Britain but he projected India as a great country, a depository of world's greatest wisdom and a saviour of all the downtrodden on earth largely to add awe to his own image in international forums. His vision was in harmony with the immense culture of mythology, which had seeped into Indian hearts and minds over many thousands of years.

But Pundit Nehru's visions were too grandiloquent to be within the immediate grasp of an illiterate and poverty stricken India. Intellectually he was not willing to concede that it was the Indian rulers and the people who were to blame for allowing the foreigners to invade India and ravage our priceless literature, arts, culture and to convert us to alien faiths which gave birth to Pakistan. As a thinker of great merit he was not able to reconcile with the premise that there could be a God. He was a stout votary of secularism of his interpretation despite the fact that he conceded the birth of Pakistan on a purely communal basis—and to preserve his claim to be the First Prime Minister of Free India. I told him so after Independence, over a few drinks, much to his consternation and resentment.

He had visited Russia and was filled with admiration for the Russian system and accomplishments, but he was not willing to acknowledge that such transformations could only be brought about through a revolution, which was not possible in India. He admired socialism but in his mind he was uncertain whether it would work in India and therefore he inflicted a mixed economy and the co-operative institutions on a people who had worked a perfectly viable economic system and evolved social structures of their own for three thousand years. He believed in his infallibility, which landed us in a mess over Jammu and Kashmir and exposed us to a humiliating defeat in the border war with China in 1962. He made it apparent that he did not like the Armed Forces because, I presume, we did not support the 'Quit India Resolution' in 1942, when the Indian National Army (INA) was busy raising Gandhi and Nehru Brigades at Singapore to fight the British; also, it was obvious that Independence came to India through the Army and not his Party. He had, as a highly qualified lawyer, defended the INA Officers at their trial by a court-martial. When India became free, Nehru had to be persuaded not to reinstate the INA personnel who had been dismissed by the British. He was also not too keen to retain the ICS, but as politicians had no experience in 'governance', Sardar Patel prevailed upon him to relent. But at that time only Pundit Nehru had the charisma, the unquestioned pre-eminence as a political leader and the highest stature to hold India together and project her as a nation on the march to progress and prosperity after 700 years of slavery.

Pundit Nehru was also great fun. Whenever he had an appointment with Lord Mountbatten at a time suitable for a drink he would walk into the ADC Room as if he was one of us. Normally before lunch one of the ADC was always busy mixing a cocktail for visitors and we felt honoured to share a drink with the Prime Minister. While he chain-smoked and sipped his drink he regaled us with amusing anecdotes about his foreign visits or about his days in England or in jail. It was obvious that he liked young company like ours, who could share a drink and a joke with him, instead of die-hard self-seeking politicians or fawning bureaucrats. He wanted to be a normal person who wanted to mix and talk to people who had no political motives or designs. I got the impression that he was a very lonely person who had missed not having the love and affection of his wife. A woman I knew who claimed to be his girl friend was not very complimentary. In Lady Mountbatten he found the responsive and sympathetic friend he was looking for who could match his intellect and background. As Lady Mountbatten was herself 'lonely' because her husband was far too busy being a perfectionist and an extrovert, she found in a brooder and loner Pundit Nehru an amiable male on whom she could unload her womanly woes since the friendship between them was deep but platonic. Nevertheless, we enjoyed talking to Punditji and whenever I had to contact him I always made it a point to request him to come a little early so that we could entertain him in the ADC Room.

Sardar Vallabhbhai Patel was different. He was friendly but he never engaged an ADC in frivolous conversation. He normally arrived just in time for an appointment. While the Hyderabad parleys were going on, the Governor General had asked him to come and see him. As soon as Sardar Patel arrived, I escorted him straightaway to see Lord Mountbatten. I was just going to sit down at the desk in the ADC Room when the GG buzzed for me. I rushed back to Lord

Mountbatten's Office to find that Sardar Patel was about to leave. He said to the GG before he left, "Your Excellency, leave Hyderabad to me. I know how to deal with them. They are my people." That was Sardar Patel – blunt and brief. While Nehru lived in the past and the future, Patel lived in the present. At Cabinet Meetings, it was obvious that they did not think alike but he never contradicted Nehru in public. The whole gamut of his thinking and concern was centred on India and its security and survival. Nehru's priority was industrialization by saving money on defence; Patel placed defence of India first. Nehru was a narcissist and westernized who believed that he had an International role to play; Patel was fiercely Indian and obsessed by nationalism. Patel could foresee a threat from China in the 1950s while Nehru was propagating Hindi-Chini Bhai Bhai. India may not have suffered humiliation at the hands of the Chinese or been plagued by the ISI and endless insurgencies, or the seemingly intractable problems over Kashmir, had Nehru and Patel got on well together. Their differences were a millstone round Free India's neck and retarded our progress by 50 years. Of course, Sardar Patel deserves our gratitude for retaining and strengthening the Civil and Police Services, as our administration would have collapsed without them. It is a pity that the Administrative Academy was not named after him, as he was undoubtedly the best 'administrator' we have had so far.

Through the years as an ADC I had been a much-pampered handsome playboy with no intention ever of getting married. At times it was difficult and embarrassing to stop women from intruding into my life – that was the only problem I ever had as an ADC. Suddenly in mid June 1947, a young woman arrived from England who was utterly different from anyone I had met before. At the time I was courting the French Charge' d'Affaires talented and beautiful daughter, Simmone, and facing endless embarrassment, as she was jealous and possessive and created scenes if she saw me talking to another girl. Ann Louisa Connorton, the young woman from England, was not only beautiful and vivacious to behold, but graceful and intelligent. She was always so calm, so helpful and so willing to listen. Her skin was flawless like the English rose; her auburn hair soft and smooth like spun silk. It was a joy to partner her at dances and parties. She had worked for a year in Berlin on a paper for the British Army of the Rhine and now she was in Public Relations at the Viceroy's House. She refused to learn to courtesy to the Viceroy despite all my entreaties and in the event when I introduced her to Their Excellencies before her first dinner with the Mountbattens, she just flashed her enchanting smile and shook hands with them. She was dressed and groomed immaculately in a long evening gown and the radiance of her youthful physical beauty stunned me. I fell instantly and madly in love with this lovely woman who was soon pursued by many bachelors and the married at the Viceroy's House. But she was quite firm in her mind that she did not want to stay in India or have an affair with me or anyone else. I was equally resolved that if I were ever to marry, I would only marry her.

After our mid-night Champagne party at Government House to usher in Independence, Ann and I went to attend the celebrations at the Imperial Hotel. Tikki, the owner of the Imperial, was an old friend and he had invited us to come to the celebrations if possible just for a few minutes. By the time we managed to reach the Imperial, it was 2;30 in the morning. Tikki greeted us enthusiastically and called Ann the most beautiful girl in New Delhi! He knew we loved dancing to his Band and the Band knew our favourite Slow Foxtrots and Waltzes. Although the Band was about to pack up, when they saw us they settled down, encouraged by Tikki, to play 'Two Dreams Met'. Arm in arm, Ann and I walked to the empty Dance Floor. She had been to a Beauty Parlour earlier in the day for a facial and to have her hair done in a very attractive coiffure. In her long green evening gown with black and gold motifs and a pearl necklace, she was indeed the Beauty Queen on that first day of our Independence at the Imperial – and the revelers endorsed that view vociferously! She was radiant and graceful and in her high heels she fully matched my 6 foot military carriage. I was dressed in my full regalia – gild epaulettes with gild multi-strand aiguillette on the right shoulder and full medals – as ADC to the last Viceroy of India. The new citizens of Free India crowded round the Dance Floor to gawk at us in awe and envy. Ann and I danced cheek to cheek as if we were possessed by the Divine Spirit of Freedom. When the music stopped the revelers cheered us with a thunderous applause, cat calls and chorus, 'You love birds – happy Independence Day!'. Like professionals we bowed to acknowledge their good wishes -and shed tears of spontaneous joy. It was a very memorable experience for us and we talked about it with our children, grand children and all our friends through the years.

The first Flag Hoisting of the Tricolour at the Red Fort by Pundit Nehru was at 6 a.m. we had to leave the Imperial early so that I could change and be there on time. After that I was on duty again with the new Governor General for his Swearing-in-Ceremony. Pundit Nehru was also to be sworn in as the First Prime Minister of Free India. Of course, as ADC I was one of the principal actors for the Ceremony but regrettably I have been left out of the huge mural in the our Parliament Annexe depicting the Swearing-in-Ceremony. Incidentally, the Indian Tricolour, although already in existence, was redesigned with the Ashoka Chakra in the internationally accepted proportions in size by Mountbatten himself.

After the morning Ceremony at Government House, the Mountbattens were to drive in the State Carriage to Parliament House to address the Constituent Assembly. The crowds were so thick and jubilant that I had a difficult time in imploring them to allow the carriage to go through. Many among the crowd wanted to kiss Lady Mountbatten's hand, or touch

'Pundit' Mountbattens's feet. All the while the crowd were shouting 'Pundit Mounbatten ki Jai', and complimenting him profusely for India's Independence. During the Ceremony I stood behind Lord Mountbatten on the dais in Parliament House. Mounbatten's address was a masterpiece of oratory and when he asked me how it went off, I told him it was 'brilliant', which pleased him no end.

Later the Mountbattens were to drive to India Gate in the State Carriage to unfurl the second Tricolour as Pundit Nehru had already unfurled the first one at the Red Fort. Again the crowds were so thick and jubilant that I had a very difficult time in trying to get the State Carriage through to India Gate. When we arrived at India Gate we found that his admirers were virtually lynching Pundit Nehru—some were trying to hoist him on their shoulders. Mountbatten invited him to take refuge in the State Carriage. Obviously it was just not possible or wise for Mounbatten to attempt to get out of the Carriage, walk to the dais and unfurl the Tricolour. He said to me, "Come on, Kim, you are young – go and unfurl the Flag for me." I stepped out of the Carriage and from that moment I was literally tossed and flung by the crowd to the Flagpole. I managed to grab the halyard and pull it to unfurl the second Tricolour on that day – and made history! I doubt if an ADC had ever been ordered to carry out such an onerous and historical mission. The Guns boomed to proclaim the new Flag of Freedom as I stood to attention and proudly saluted our new ensign of Independence—and cried unashamedly with a rare thrill and joy in my heart. On that first auspicious day liberty who ever thought that there would be a supernal design to create a situation where a Soldier, a representive of the Army that ushered in freedom, would be favoured to unfurl the National flag near India Gate, the splendid memorial to brave Indian Warriors who sacrificed themselves to save democracy in the First World War (1914-1918)! That moment of ecstary has inspired all the thoughts for this book. I knew

I was born lucky but I could not dream that my lucky stars would hurl me to those lofty heights.

By the time I returned to the State Carriagge, with most of my decorations on the uniform missing or torn, Pundit Nehru, Indira Gandhi and others had already been invited by the new Governor General to take refuge in his State Carriage—there was now no place for me! Instead of returning to Government House along Kingsway, where the crowds continued to the thick, it was decided to go by King Edward Road and into Government House through the South Gate. Of course, I had no option except to run behind the State Carriage all the way, with the mounted Body Guard trotting behind me, so that I could be present in a new set of uniform for the huge reception for three thousand guests in the lawns of Government House. Was this, the jog behind the State Carriage the final act of sacrament before I could call myself a citizen of Free India—and no longer a subject of the British Indian Empire!

After the Reception there was the state dinner followed by a display of fireworks in Central Avenue. By then, I was so exhausted that I was falling asleep every time I sat down. Fortunately I had asked Ann to meet me at the fireworks display. The Mountbattens and all the guests sat on sofa sets in front of the North Block steps while Ann and I and other staff sat on the steps which had been suitably covered by a carpet. I was much too tired to see anything of the fireworks but Ann kept on nudging me whenever there was something spectacular in the sky. I had quite made up my mind by then that having shared such great historic moments together, I was never going to let go of our togetherness ever in my life—and I didn't. The more we saw of each other the more we realized that we were made only for each other.

The last time I went to Pakistan with Lord Mountbatten by air was on 29 August 1947, a day before my birthday, as he was to preside over the Boundary Commission in Lahore. There was a great change in Lahore since I had been there last. Masses of Pakistani flags adorned every pole or building we passed from the Airfield to Government House. Some of the buildings set ablaze during the partition riots lay in ugly charred ruins. All the roads and by-ways where pretty Punjabi girls used to flaunt the latest in fashion and giggle when they saw a handsome boy, looked desolate and sad. The people we saw on the roads were almost all young men who walked forlornly in their salwaar and kameez as if they had nowhere to go. Lahore was no longer a city of joy and fashion with its pomp and colour and young belles eyeing young men and teasing their way through the streets. Lahore now had the desolate air of a town in the Muslim Middle East.

Mr. Jinnah was kind enough to greet me and make tender inquiries about my Father whom he had met a few times. He invited me to stay with him in Karachi and visit my old haunts again especially in Manora Island. But I thought he was looking very tired and pale since I had last seen him a fortnight earlier – I thought his TB had taken a turn for the worst. I also met his AsDC. The Naval ADC had been with us till Independence and he and I were very good friends. The Army ADC was a term junior to me at the IMA and I met him often in Burma especially after he took over as ADC to General Bill Slim. The Army ADC was also a very good friend and we had quite a ball talking about the old days and the queer characters we had met round the world in our job as ADC. Fortunately the Pakistani Army Chief, General Sir Frank Messervy, was also there. He had commanded a Corps in battle under my Boss in Burma and despite the difference in our ages we shared many common fads in life; it was always a joy to meet him and to talk to him endlessly about the War days. On this visit to Lahore I had accidentally left my silver cigarette case, a gift from General Stopford, at the Government House. General Messervy was kind enough to inform me when I reached Simla that he would pass through New Delhi by air and leave my cigarette case at the Palam Air Force Base for delivery to me – a gesture of extreme kindness from a Commander-in-Chief, which I never forgot. After retirement when General Messervy, always young in heart, indiscreetly fondled a teenage girl and was taken to court. I wrote him a letter of sympathy and urged him to face the consequences bravely – he had a DSO and was a legend for courage in battle. He made a true confession and was awarded a suspended sentence by the Court.

After Lord Mountbatten's visit to Lahore on 29 August, we went to Simla. On the next day, my birthday, I telephoned Ann at New Delhi and told her how much I loved her and missed her. For once, it was the truth! There was a long pause of excruciating silence when my heart stopped beating a thousand times. "I too love you," she said. "Many happy returns of the day." It was the sweetest birthday gift of my life and I was so overwhelmed that I had a good cry before I rushed down to the bar and poured myself half a glass of Scotch on the rocks. Lady Mountbatten said that she had never seen me look so happy, wished me many happy returns of the day, and insisted on having Champagne to celebrate. But, of course, they did not know that I was happy as for the first time I had fallen deeply in love with a beautiful woman who also loved me. Much later when I told Lady Mountbatten about our intention to get married, she said, mischievously, "What about the others?"! When Ann and I decided to get married, I had regrettably to leave the Mountbattens. I was posted to 3rd Battalion of the Grenadiers then at Bombay.

Ann and I were married at the Cricket Club of India, Bombay on the 21st December, 1947, in a civil ceremony. All the Officers of my Battalion were kind enough to attend and join us to a Champagne lunch. The Mountbattens and all our friends sent us gifts and their congratulations. After lunch my bride and I went to Matheran, a small hill station not far from Bombay, for our honeymoon. I took my portable gramophone with records of all the dance music both of us loved. Those were moonlit nights and after dinner, we would walk down to a glade in the valley with our gramophone and records and dance cheek-to-cheek. Indeed our dreams had met. There were just the two of us with the World left way behind and out of our thoughts. Gradually we became one in thought and deed as sheer happiness, so sublime and infinite, fused us together. The more we shared our love for each other, there was always that much more to share. We vowed that should we be born again, we would fall in love with each other again and again.

My Battalion was located in temporary wartime hutment at Kurla, which had been used by refugees during Partition and left in a shocking mess. Moving into those awful huts after the luxuries of the Viceroy's House in New Delhi was an unimaginable experience for my elegant bride. We had no electricity, piped water or waterborne sanitation. Ann didn't mind using a kerosene lantern, or water from a bucket, but she didn't like the commodes or 'thunder boxes'. The great thing was that it never got her down, and it really was amazing how she adjusted herself to the primitive living conditions in a few days without a whimper. I was so terribly in love with her that I could have given half my life to find better accommodation for her. I melted indescribably when she assured me that she did not mind the awful living conditions so long as we were together. I told my children often that their mother had made an enormous sacrifice in separating from her closely-knit and loving family in England to marry me and to live in tents and wartime huts when she could have easily gone back to the ease and comfort of her home in London. But the vagaries of love are difficult to explain and equally difficult to understand.

Fortunately, my Battalion was moved from Kurla to Colaba. As the British Troops were leaving, I was selected by the General Officer Commanding Maharashtra Area, an

Englishman, to organize the farewell parade. My wife Ann was an indispensable help in drafting a short write up on each British Unit's history and connection with India and in designing the brochure-programme that was admired by everyone. The farewell parade for the British Troops went off without a hitch and the GOC of the Area, a British General, wrote me a charming letter of appreciation and thanks.

When my Battalion moved to Colaba in Bombay, we were allotted a small flat at Churchgate, our first real home together. The previous occupant had left it in poor shape. I came home early from Office the day after we had moved in and was very touched to find my bride on all fours scrubbing away the grubby floor although we had an ayah and a sweeper to do the job. Ann loved a clean orderly house and within a few days she converted our flat into a cozy and elegant home. No soldier could ever have wished for a more understanding and caring wife.

Soon after the farewell parade to the British Troops, my Battalion moved to Poona to form part of the Brigade that was earmarked for operations in Hyderabad Deccan where the law and order situation was deteriorating rapidly. Hyderabad was a princely state with a Hindu majority population and a Muslim ruler who was reluctant to accede to India after Independence. Walter Monckton, a brilliant British Barrister, was adviser to the Nizam, but the latter was more fully engaged in siring his 300 odd wives than listening to the sane advice Monckton had given to accede and accept substantial offers of autonomy by India. I met Monckton often at the Viceroy's House. He married Lady Carlyle who had been the head of Women's Auxiliary Corps of India as a Brigadier during the War. Lady Carlyle had stayed with us in Rangoon and Singapore a number of times and I got to know her quite well; but as she had divorced her first husband to marry Monckton, she was, much to my regret, a persona non grata at all official functions in the Viceroy's House. I found Sir Walter Monckton and his wife charming and very interesting and sought every opportunity to talk to them.

In Hyderabad the Razakars, a terrorist Muslim organization, devastated the poor Hindu population and forced India to intervene. Just before the intervention I had a very brief stint with our Resident in Hyderabad as his Military Assistant. The Resident also tried his utmost to persuade the Nizam to accede, but the Nizam had dreams of converting his State into a new and independent country. I did not stay long in Hyderabad as I was keen to fight in Kashmir.

On 22 October 1947 Pakistan had invaded Kashmir with a force comprising Pathans and Pakistani military personnel on 'leave'. That this was going to happen was apparent to all of us who were serving in the North West Frontier Province before Independence. But nobody took it seriously. At the Government House Mountbatten was thrilled to have an opportunity of planning Military Operations again. Troops were moved into J & K with lightening speed once the Maharaja, had, at his own behest, signed the instrument of accession. All of us in the Army were terribly angry of the betrayal by our colleagues who had gone across to Pakistan. After I was married I asked my bride if I should volunteer to serve in J & K. She said I ought to do so straightaway. At the age of 26 I was promoted Lt Col to command a Militia Battalion in J & K..

When I arrived at Pathankot on my way to Srinagar, the Provost Marshal of the local Sub Area, a Major and years older than I, came up to me at the Railway Station and demanded to see my Movement Order. I fired him for not saluting a Senior Officer. He said he thought I was a 2nd Lt from my youthful looks, but when he saw my Movement Order he promptly came to attention and saluted and apologized. He said they had been on the look-out for a Lt Col to command a huge convoy of vehicles going up to Srinagar and requested me to follow him to see the Sub Area Commander. The Brigadier was a KCIO and years senior to me. I had met him once before when both of us were Captains. He asked me if I had any experience of commanding convoys. I told him I had done it a few times in Peshawar, but could I be excused from commanding the convoy to Srinagar as I was in a hurry to get up to my Battalion. He was angry and I had no option but to take charge of the convoy which left at 4:30 in the morning the next day.

The road was in poor shape and there was no bridge across the river at Kathua. By the time the convoy crossed into J & K it was past 5 in the afternoon. There was no place to harbour, so I decided that we would carry on to Jammu. We were moving very slowly in the dark and everything seemed to going well till I heard long bursts of Light Machine Gun in the rear. I was in a Station Wagon but my Despatch Rider was moving just behind me on a motor cycle and I ordered him to take me back to see what had happened. By the time I got there, the Officer in charge of the protection party, a Captain, who had come up from the ranks, had done a wonderful job in driving away three or four Pakistani soldiers who had sneaked across the nearby border to ambush us. Some of the vehicles were damaged, but fortunately nobody was hurt. I thought that this was a good omen for my future in the war in J & K.

When I arrived in Srinagar I discovered that my Battalion had to be pieced together from Sheikh Abdullah's volunteers, largely Kashmiri Muslims, who had done a magnificent job in fighting the Pakistani invaders, but who were still deployed against the enemy in Uri and Tithwal. Colonel Biji Kaul, a live-wire and an outstanding KCIO, was Commandant of J and K Militia. I suggested to him that we might use the Militia on the same lines as Force 136. He agreed but the snags could not be sorted out before the war was over.

While I was piecing together a Battalion from the Peoples' Militia, with a Company already deployed at Uri, Biji Kaul received an urgent message from the makeshift Corps HQ at

Udhampur, to send a Lt Col to Kishtwar, as Pakistani infiltrators, Muslim refugees from East Punjab and local insurgents had wreaked havoc in the area Doda-Kishtwar-Bhadarwah. A Company of 2 Rajputs and two Companies of J & K State Forces were already there, but the Corps Commander wanted the Lt Col to take command of the troops in the area and to raise a Militia Battalion there with all haste. Early restoration of law and order in that strategically vital area was necessary as it was feared that the Valley would be cut off if the insurgents took possession of Batote or Kud, which could seriously retard the operations in the Valley. The attempts of the militants to foist an Islamic government had already been thwarted by the troops there but the situation continued to be critical. Biji Kaul decided to give me the command at Kishtwar.

I flew down to Jammu the next day. Major Rajaratnam, my 2IC, was already busy piecing together 14 J & K Militia at Jammu, the Battalion I was to command. As there was no time for the whole Battalion to be raised, I took the Battalion HQ and two hastily formed rifle companies, comprising ex-Servicemen, with me in transport to the road-head at Batote. We reached Batote the next day. Unfortunately, the Pakistani infiltrators had breached the road from Batote to Doda in several places, so we had to march with porters from Batote to Kishtwar. After an over-night halt at Batote, all of us speed-marched to Doda on the first day. As the suspension bridge over the Chenab to Doda had been systematically wrecked, I decided to camp at Khaleni. The charred hamlets, the destruction of all culverts, bridges and the telegraph line astride the track emphasized the urgency of my presence at Kishtwar to take charge of what was clearly a grave situation. Early the next morning I decided to forge ahead with Capt Gupta, the RMO, and Flight Lieut Pawar of the Air Force and a Soldier Orderly. I instructed the Subedar Major, who had joined the Militia on retirement after 32 years service in the Indian Army, to bring up the troops to Kishtwar as quickly as possible.

The four of us who went ahead of the Main Body were young and fully armed; we were determined to fight our way to Kishtwar if necessary–a bit of bravado, but that was the mood of derring-do among all of us in those days. All that mattered was the freedom of India.

My little group made it to Thatri by last light. By then we were thoroughly exhausted. A speed-march over sixteen miles of rough mountain mule-track, with all the bridges and culverts wrecked, was grueling. We expected Thatri, a tourist's delight, to provide some succor, but the State Rest House and all other buildings had been totally destroyed or burnt down by the insurgents. A patch of turf was the only place to rest our weary limbs and while one of us acted as the sentry the other three rested using our haversacks as pillows. For an hour we waited for our main column, but there was no sign of the them and no response to our repeated yells which reverberated through the unending stretch of the Chenab Valley. Hunger, cold and fatigue were irksome.

As Kishtwar was only about 8 miles away, we decided to trudge on. We had very sketchy information on the mountain-track to Kishtwar and it was pitch dark. Direction keeping was difficult. All the bridges on the streams had been destroyed. Sometimes, in the dark, we followed a track leading to the hurtling waters of the Chenab and cursed our way back to the main track. But after an hour's trudge we were lucky to find a stone and mud hut just off the track. Shafts of wavering light lanced through the numerous chinks in the patched up door. An old man had to be threatened to open the bolted door; he was an ex-Serviceman and when he saw us he was delighted to invite us to come into his hut where the only light was from the 'chulah' fire on which his wife was cooking a meal. A frightened little boy was trying to hide behind her when he saw us. The old man told us that the little one was his grandson and that his young son and his wife, the little boy's parents, had been butchered by the terrorists in the fields just above the hut. I discovered later that such tales of horror and tragedy were common in the area. We thanked him for his offer of a meal but declined to accept it as we realized that his food stocks were meagre, but we did have some herbal tea with goat's milk and no sugar to gratify our gnawing hunger. It was a mistake not to have brought a pack meal with us and I made sure that the omission was never repeated. We marched on an empty stomach, which was not a very pleasant situation on a rugged mountain track on a cold night for dog-tired soldiers with all the weight of their weapons and the accoutrements!

About three-thirty in the morning we heard the grinding of a water-mill and groped our way uphill along a stream to find it. The worker at the water-mill was at first frightened and refused to open the door but our stern threats prevailed and reluctantly he allowed us to enter and even produced a few delicious corn 'chapatis' and 'chatni' to gratify our ravenous hunger. Of course, our arrival late in the night and the fact that we were not going up to Kishtwar must have made him very suspicious of our real identity.

As the grinding noise was jarring, we requested the worker to stop the mill so that we could have a little sleep before going uphill to Kishtwar which was about a mile away. The four of us lay down on a dirty old tattered mat in the confined space next to the millstone and fell asleep instantly. Shortly afterwards, at first light, we were roused by a commotion outside. Someone was ordering us to come out with our hands up! We peeped through the cracks in the door and saw that our challengers were Soldiers from our Army. I opened the squeaking wooden door and shouted 'friends' while the other three of my party took up a firing position behind the door just in case the Soldiers were not our Army!. But the Soldiers on patrol from Kishtwar grabbed me when I stepped out of the mill. Imagine their consternation when they discovered who I was! I looked so confoundedly young that they found it hard to believe that I was the new Colonel, their Commanding Officer! Apparently the worker had slipped out and told the patrol that we were terrorists! But when the four of us looked at each other in daylight we were really dismayed, as we thought we had itchy blisters of smallpox – swarms of bedbugs in the mat had obviously feasted to their heart's content while we lay, exhausted, in deep sleep.

To locate, contain and smash terrorists in an area of over 500 square miles of steep rugged mountains was daunting and challenging. I cursed myself for accepting the assignment so coyly. There was no air or land transport; signal communications were poor and indifferent tracks only made a very difficult task appear almost impossible. But then, India had only just recently attained freedom and none of us had ever handled such intricate command problems before. My immediate superior was miles away beyond Jammu. But it did not occur to anyone of us to just sit back and do nothing. In any case, if I were to do nothing we would soon be targets of terrorist attacks ourselves. Of course, I had learnt the hard way during the Second World War that a commander who waits for things to happen, or shirks because of inadequacies in resources, always ends up in disaster and defeat. As a young Lt Col at 26 years of age, who had always been aggressive and physically vigorous, I was not inclined to contemplate such ignominy which could not only bring disgrace to me and my command but to my Country. I had volunteered to fight in J & K to serve India and I was thrilled to command such a large land mass there as a young Lt Col. My Officers and Soldiers and I shared our enormous love for and uncompromising pride in free India in full measure. I had seen the Japanese humiliated and wretched in abject defeat because they allowed the 'initiative' to slip out of their plans. I was absolutely determined to seize the initiative from the terrorists in vital areas and then go all out to destroy them after building up my resources. As the first Commander in free India to face insurgency I had no option but to fight and win as indeed my colleagues were doing elsewhere in J & K, to save our Country from the machinations of a ruthless, unscrupulous and bigoted enemy. The high morale of my troops and Officers was, of course, an invaluable asset and the real key to our fantastic successes in the intense counter-insurgency operation waged relentlessly for four arduous months.

My Officers and I evolved a simple but audacious plan to deal with the insurgents. After a thorough synthesis of all the intelligence available to me through our own sources, the police and the civil administration, I marked the most troublesome areas on the map and selected a communication centre roughly in the middle of each area as a firm base. A Company garrisoned each firm base; I used two Platoons of the Company to patrol, ambush or attack targets based on the intelligence gathered by the Company and me. In the beginning we held only a few firm bases owing to lack of resources, but when I had more trained troops we spread out to cover most of the troublesome areas. I gave orders that those who needed our help must be helped to the best of our ability, but those who sought to terrorize us must be crushed with a firm hand. Captain Piar Chand of 4 Kashmir Infantry was already in the fray since 24 Nov 1947, in the area Bhadarwah – Doda where an enemy-sponsored Islamic government was trying to take over as the Maharaja's civil administration had totally collapsed. When the Indian Army took over responsibility of the area, Captain Bhisham Bali was sent to Kishtwar with a Company of 2 Rajputs. Both these Officers were a great help to me.

Capt Gupta came with me as the RMO. He was an exceptionally energetic and young doctor and as he was blessed with an inordinate gift for healing, I used him for communicating with the people; I consulted with my Officers and decided to convey 'josh' information or well crafted rumours through Gupta to give the impression that we were masters of the situation. I also made it a point to receive or meet the elders and religious heads in every town or village I visited and I asked Capt Gupta to look into their health problems. Within a short period everybody knew that we were impartial and just in our dealings and that we were determined to restore normalcy with a very firm hand.

Of course, owing to primitive communications, a good deal of running around was necessary, but we were all young and enormously spirited to serve new India. Fortunately a Lt Col's status was higher at the time than the District Magistrate and the District Superintendent of Police and this was one of the decisive factors which enabled me to exercise my command functions without any let or hindrance when the Civil Administration was restored by Sheikh Abdullah in July 1948. In fact, the Civil Administration and the Police were so exceptionally kind, cooperative and efficient that I was very enthusiastic in commending their good work to General Cariappa when he visited us. Incidentally, one of the problems in J & K during the intractable insurgency in 1989 to 2001, was that the Army Officer had lost his status vis-à-vis the Civil and the Police Officials. No Army in the world can give of its best without a special status.

By September 1948, we had successfully smashed the insurrection in the area Doda-Kishtwar-Bhadarwah. Many developed nations have found insurgency or terrorism difficult to control despite all the conceivable modern assets in ground and air transport, communications and weapons. We were operating on a shoestring with no modern transport, communications or weapons across one of the most difficult terrains in the world with just a few hours rest on any day and without any creature comforts whatsoever. But the most indomitable weapon of war, high morale or josh, was in such abundance among my soldiers that they repeatedly assured me that all they wanted was to kill the enemy to keep Mother

India secure and free. All they needed, they said, was a plentiful supply of ammunition and nothing else. I was very touched by their sentiments. Within four months my troops were fully in command of the situation despite lack of roads for vehicular movement and a primitive communication network. Perhaps we were better off by a few slots than Emperor Jahangir's Governor in Kashmir, Dilawar Khan, who had captured the defiant Raja of Kishtwar in 1620, and produced him in chains before the Emperor. Fortunately the Raja of Kishtwar had left a very indispensable legacy for us in the shape of a huge, well-levelled elephant polo ground which was converted by us into an airstrip with expert advice from Flight Lieut Pawar, IAF, who had accompanied me from Jammu for this task. One day, without any warning, a daredevil IAF pilot on his way to Srinagar, circled round the airstrip till we got everyone off it, and then landed his Dakota on it! He had a little problem taking off, but he did so by hairbreadth, much to our relief!

By any standards the performance of 14 J & K Militia, the Gujjar Company of 2 Rajputs (replaced by a Company of 1 Para later) and two Companies of J & K State Forces, was most impressive. Captain Piar Chand had been engaged in crushing the insurgency from the start. He was an outstanding and fearless J & K State Forces Officer who did most of the running around with me. In a letter No.337 dated 22 Aug 1948, to 50 Para Brigade, our immediate superior formation, I wrote to recommend Piar Chand for the Distinguished Service Order, a British decoration, as our own had not till then been instituted. This is what I wrote:

1. Capt Piar Chand, 4 KASH INF, was sent to this area on 24 Nov 47, in command of a Company of Garrison Police (State Forces) to restore law and order in DODA District. He came under command of Indian Army from 25 Jan 48.

2. Captain Piar Chand's work during the 9 months he has been in this area has been worthy of outstanding merit and

great praise. He was sent here at a time when the whole of this area was torn by communal strife and hatred. Civil Administration was non-existent. An enemy sponsored Muslim Government had been established in this area. Open warfare between Hindus and Muslims on the one hand and between forces of law and order and the rest on the other, was in progress. Many villages had been burnt down, and in exploded communal frenzy the locals had destroyed most of the bridges and roads in this area.

3. Captain Piar Chand took charge of a very grave situation with confidence and firmness. He completely disregarded his own personal safety and comfort and advanced from village to village with a handful of men disarming insurgents and restoring confidence among the people. His small force was often attacked by large and fully armed 'JATHAS'. But Captain Piar Chand pressed on his advance often through deep snow, against bitter opposition and over the rugged steep mountains of this area. Indeed he became a source of inspiration and encouragement to his men.

4. The entire credit for restoration of peaceful conditions in this area (meaning the stretch from Bhadarwah to Doda) must go to the person of Piar Chand. He has saved the lives and property of hundreds of people in this area. His name must inevitably become a legend to those who had resigned all hopes of existence and safety and to whom Piar Chand brought hope and prosperity.

5. I recommend Captain Piar Chand for award of the Distinguished Service Order or its equivalent. "

Of course, Piar Chand, was a J & K State Forces Officers and nobody was interested in pursuing his case for a gallantry award, which he deserved so fully. Later he distinguished himself in battle and deserved a bar to his gallantry medal, but that also was ignored – such were the inexcusable caprices of the War. in J & K in 1947-48!

The Army Commander, Lt Gen K.M. Cariappa. OBE, (later the first Indian Commander-in-Chief of the Indian Army) rightly decided to visit us by air to congratulate the troops and the commanders on their magnificent achievements. He was the first VIP to land in a two-seater aeroplane on our airstrip. We were thrilled to receive him with all the respect and honour we could muster. After the usual preliminaries, he told me that he would like to have his pack lunch he had brought with him away from the others, as he was keen to discuss a Top Secret operational matter with me. The two of us settled down on a Kashmiri carpet I had borrowed for the occasion to munch our sandwiches and to share a bottle of beer under a magnificent old chinar tree. The General asked me if I could carry out a 'strong raid' across the Umasi La at the end of Oct, 1948. I was not surprised as Biji Kaul, promoted to Brigadier, who had visited us a little earlier to express his profound appreciation of our achievements and had warned me that I may be asked to operate across the Umasi La. Of course, an Army commander's wish is an order. Having just turned 27, I was young and impetuous enough for any derring-do. My soldiers were champing at the bit to canter out and crush the Pakistani aggressor wherever we could find him. General Cariappa was duly impressed by my enthusiasm and said he would do all he could to help.

In a nursery rhyme we had learnt as kids that 'a battle was lost for want of a nail'. We had nothing for high altitude or snow conditions -not even a full quota of an extra issue of clothing for winter! Nevertheless, despite our shortages we were determined to fight and win—nail or no nail! The Ordinance had nothing to help us, so we did not feel let down. Of course, as I was absolutely determined to take the enemy by surprise I gave no indication to anyone in the Battalion that we were going to operate at high altitude under snow conditions despite our shortages in equipment. I trained the companies in the tasks I had in mind for them and prepared them generally for operations at high altitude under snow conditions. In any case, not notwithstanding the high altitude and the snow conditions in Oct/Nov 1948, we were determined as Officers to lead the troops from the front – those were the fine traditions of the Indian Army. We knew Zorawar Singh had crossed the Umasi La sixty years earlier on horses in summer. I was the second commander in history to go over the Umasi La and the first in history to do so on foot in Oct/Nov 1948, under winter conditions. Zorawar Singh never came back—we were determined to return with a whacking big victory for Indian Arms. In those days we did not take counsel of our fears.

In the second week of October 1948, I discussed my plan in detail with Captain Piar Chand. I wanted him to go to Arthal the next day with a Company and to send a Platoon immediately on arrival to Machail, 10,000 feet high, the area where Sapphire Mines were, and to seal off all routes to Zanskar, as Surprise was all important for success. He was also to collect woollen garments like cholis, tight pajamas, light shawls and the like for 300 hundred men and scout round for porters and ponies to accompany us across the Umasi La.

About a week after Piar Chand had gone, 14 J & K Militia less one Company slipped out of Kishtwar well before first light on the Ram Rasta—so named as one had to invoke Lord Ram for safety when walking over a wooden plank stuck into a sheer cliff face—a thousand feet below, the Chenab roared its way to Pakistan! When I reached Arthal by nightfall I was delighted to find that Piar Chand had done a marvellous job in collecting the woollies, but he just could not get enough porters who were willing to lift our loads. That was a jolt. Piar Chand and I sat up for most of the night rehashing our loads to put the maximum number of fighting men across the Umasi La, but we had to cut short on the time factor and thus the extent of our operations. People often forget that Logistics is an important Principle of War and all Strategy and Tactics depend on our ability to sustain ourselves in battle.

On the first day we made it from Arthal or Atholi to Machail. No sooner had we arrived at Machail when a terrible snow-storm besieged us. The next day we were impaled in our shelters by the blinding snowfall. I did not believe in miracles or the supernatural but my Subedar Major did and he pushed me to appease Chandi Devi at the temple there for blessings and to extract a promise from the Goddess for clear weather for the duration of our operations across the Umasi La. At first I thought that the idea was much too bizarre and unmilitary for serious consideration, but my Officers thought that there was absolutely no harm in at least trying it out as there were no other options. So we assembled the Battalion in deep snow and witnessed the most unbelievable manifestation of mysticism and spiritualism that anyone of us had ever seen before.

The ritual for offering the sacrifice of a white goat to Goddess Chandi was at once fascinating and sacrosanct. In those remote high mountains, as elsewhere, the Goddess Kali is worshipped as Goddess Chandi as a deity who is believed to be most generous and kind in response to prayers and offerings. The man who was to supplicate on our behalf was a 'Pujari', or priest, in his early fifties who had been a devotee at the temple for more than twenty years. He was tall, handsome with a saintly aura; his mantras or incantations were remarkably musical and hypnotic and all of us fell silent as if we had suddenly been frozen to lifeless statues in time and space by some divine injunction. The Pujari sprinkled a few drops of water on the head of the white goat, which moved its head up and down, perhaps to indicate that it was ready for the sacrifice. At that moment the Pujari's son severed the goat's head with an axe designed especially for such sacrifices. The Pujari, who was now seated in the lotus-pose in front of the deity, convulsed wildly for a minute or so and froth dripped from the corners of his mouth. Somewhere in the far distance I could faintly hear the chimes of temple bells and the clarion call of a 'sankh', or conch, and then the Pujari spoke in a voice which was distinctly feminine and indescribably sublime – the utterances were from the Goddess herself! She ordained that the skies shall clear that night and remain clear for the duration of our operations and that if we were to take the Pujari's son with the axe with us, no harm would come to our soldiers who were on a mission against evil. It was an incredible and traumatic experience and all of us were visibly shaken. I thanked the Pujari and walked back to my shelter in silence and disbelief. But, behold, all that the Pujari said in a trance came to pass! The skies cleared that night and the next morning we resumed our advance to battle across the Umasi La.

(When we returned victorious from the Battle, the rearguard Platoon reported that a soldier was missing. I was enraged and threatened to have the Platoon Commander tried by a Court Martial. He hastened to the Pujari and offered a sacrifice to Chandi Devi. The ritual was repeated and the Pujari went into a trance and told him that the missing soldier was lying injured and unconscious under a huge black rock about six miles up the track to Umasi La. We recovered the soldier but his frost-bitten feet had to be amputated. The Battalion also offered a sacrifice to express our heartfelt gratitude for the divine shield which gave us profound courage to dare and win against intense small-arms fire and the bitter cold in the most challenging high altitude terrain in the world. Our success was total unique and unimaginable. The Pujari asked me to make a 'secret wish' – as there was very little left for me to do in the wilderness of Kishtwar, I beseeched the Devi for a posting to the Valley. For no apparent reason I was posted to command a Battalion in the Valley on the Uri Sector after about a month!)

When we reached the top and activated our plan to capture a Gompa occupied by the enemy, we were amazed to find that it had been abandoned minutes before our attack.

As surprise was now lost, we raced downhill through an unending landscape of huge boulders strewn across the barren rocky mountain slope. When we closed in to tackle the Sumchum Gompa, known to the locals as Ting, a hail of bullets greeted us. The sound of bullets ricocheting off the boulders and whining menacingly was an experience we can never forget. But for the protection of the boulders (and Chandi Devi !) we would have suffered heavy casualties.

Notwithstanding the heavy fire, the leading Platoon commander, Subedar Bhagwan Das, an ex-Serviceman I had recruited at Khaleni, darted from cover to cover, dodged the bullets and closed in on the enemy's machine gun post that was covering the track. When a short distance away he sprang out of cover, hurled a grenade and rushed the position firing his Sten Gun from the hip. All the enemy in the post were killed. This extraordinary display of valour by Bhagwan Das encouraged his Platoon to join him. Supported by our fire, Bhagwan Das made commendable progress in overcoming enemy defensive positions opposing our advance. The enemy fled downhill in desperation using the reverse slopes as cover. We had to pursue the enemy without breaking contact.

By last light we had fought our way to Ating. While my forward Platoon was in contact, a local captured by our patrol on the flank informed us that the enemy was assembling a convoy to carry supplies from the Padam Valley, the main granary in the area, to supply the Garrison at Kargil. This delightful news sent an extra dose of Adrenalin racing through our tired, cold and numbed bodies. As Piar Chand was up in front, I ordered him to streak down the open flank on the left with his Company less the Platoon in contact, and round up the convoy. Just in time, we managed to capture over 20 Ladhaki ponies and many prisoners who had been wounded badly-in the fighting, but despite our best efforts they died soon afterwards. The ponies were God-sent and we used them to carry our loads all the way back to Kishtwar.

When the enemy heard the firing in his rear, he fired scores of flares, which set the tall grass on fire. That was lucky as the fire gave us the warmth we needed on a bitterly cold night. The flares also helped us to concentrate our fire more accurately on the enemy positions before he panicked and fled.

My logistics had run out on me, but 14 J & K Militia had certainly carried out the 'strong raid' ordered by General (later Field Marshal) K.M. Cariappa, then GOCinC Western Command. And all on a shoestring against seemingly impossible odds. We recommended Bhagwan Das for the Victoria Cross, the highest British decoration for valour as our new decorations had not come into force by then. He deserved a Param Vir Chakra (the equivalent of the Victoria Cross) as much as anyone later in Kargil, but all he was awarded was a Vir Chakra, a paltry decoration for the remarkable achievements of a Battalion at high altitude under snow conditions and without the necessary clothing or equipment! The Commanding Officer and Captain Piar Chand had already been recommended for a DSO each for smashing a major insurgency in area Kishtwar-Doda-Bhadarwah; a bar to the DSO was now recommended for each for the Battle of Umasi La for their outstanding leadership, courage and unique military achievement against overwhelming odds. As the RMO, Captain Gupta, had done particularly well, he was recommended for an MC. But after Partition, the Army was in doldrums and unless one was in a position to peddle the achievements of a unit in the corridors of power, nothing happened. 14 J & K Militia was more than 100 miles from its Brigade HQ—too distant for anyone to hear our war drums or our whoops of joy in the celebration of a splendid victory for Indian Arms. The recommendations for awards were lost in the tortuous corridors of bureaucratic apathy. Nevertheless, 14 J & K Militia wrote two chapters of remarkable valour and historical achievement for Indian Arms in the wilderness of Kishtwar in 1948.

- General Srinagesh was kind enough to send us his congratulations; the official history mentions the operation. (Incidentally, Srinagesh became a devotee of Chandi Devi. The Battalion also contributed towards building a shelter for the devotees in inclement weather at Machail.) General K.S. Thimayya, DSO, told me later that the Battle of Umasi La did help in the victory at Zoji La and Kargil (which I did not know at the time). But the greatest injustice was that 14 J & K Militia did not even get Umasi La as Battle Honours and the exceptional and unique achievements of its Officers and men were ignored and forgotten.

In those days there was no accommodation for separated families. While I was fighting the war in J & K, my wife was frantically looking for accommodation that we could afford on my meagre salary as a Lt Col. As there was no ban on tourists, my wife decided to fly to Srinagar as a tourist. She found accommodation at Nedou's Hotel and awaited my return from Kishtwar. She had told me earlier in a very compassionate tone that if I were to get killed in battle she wanted to collect my ashes after cremation herself! When the Army discovered that she was the wife of an Officer fighting in J & K, she was issued with a notice to leave Srinagar within a week. The injustice was that wives of Officers not in Kashmir could visit the Valley, but not the wife of an Officer fighting there! My poor woman had nowhere else to go in India where accommodation would be readily available. In sheer desperation she went to Delhi and with the help of an old friend she found some accommodation and a job to pay for it. It was sad to see such sudden changes in the Army's attitudes towards the welfare of its Officers. It was then that I decided I would quit as soon as I had earned a pension.

Fortunately, I was posted back to the Valley to command another Battalion at the end of 1948. Soon after I took over command of the Battalion in the Valley there was a cease-fire. Most of us were very disappointed as our Troops were making a steady progress in evicting Pakistani Forces from the State of Jammu and Kashmir which had acceded to the Dominion of India legally. My new Battalion was almost entirely Kashmiri Muslims. I am very proud to record that every one of them was keen to fight Pakistan as the invaders had killed a large number of Kashmiris including women and children and committed rape and arson extensively. The people of the Valley felt the same way. I have no doubt that if Pakistan had vacated the areas they had occupied illegally, as they were required to do by a United Nation's resolution, an overwhelming majority of the Muslim population in the State of Jammu and Kashmir would have voted to remain in India at that tme.

Although the war in J & K had ended, Officers serving there could not ask their families to come and reside in the State. Apart from the fact that my wife was lonely in Delhi, as she did not know anyone there, whatever she and I earned was not enough to sustain her there. Fortunately General Srinagesh came to my rescue and had the orders changed. Ann was allowed to come to Srinagar and we hired a very posh and comfortable Houseboat to live in – they were so inexpensive on those days! The two years we spent in Kashmir were some of the happiest years of our life. On holidays and weekends, my wife and I went to some of the most beautiful country in the World. We would stay either in a remote Forest Rest House or in a tent on our own. We walked through valleys of flowers, lush green meadows and aromatic pine and deodar forests hand in hand, singing with all our might, "If I should fall in love again, I'll fall in love with you again," and other songs we knew. We waded through cold streams, caught fish, roasted it on open fire, and washed it down with beer chilled in the icy cold water. We chased each other up and down hill and played hide and seek till we were exhausted. Then we would sit on the banks of a stream, hug and kiss, dangle our legs, and let the water caress our tired feet. It was such great fun teasing each other and pretending we were angry and then coming together in love and laughing till our sides ached. All my wonderful dreams of love and romance now came true. Just being together in the vast wilderness and freedom of the snow-covered mountains was an ecstasy, which gave a new meaning to our love for each other. Ann was so beautiful, so very lovable, so companionable that I thought I could live without air and water but not without her. I had never known such happiness before. Although neither one of us believed in rebirths, if it were true then I was certain that we had been lovers in our previous life – and we resolved over and over, again and again to be lovers if ever we were born to a new life..

It was summer of 1949. We were up in Gulmarg for golf and hikes when Ann told me that I was going to be a father. Me – a father! I was thrilled! How wonderful! We came down to Srinagar and invited our few friends to cocktails and dinner. But I did not want my wife to have our baby in Srinagar, as the available medical facilities were poor. Fortunately, a friend, an Army Officer, offered us paying guest accommodation in his house, 100, Lodi Road, in Delhi. Before the onset of winter in Srinagar, Ann moved to Delhi. In those days the Hindu Rao Hospital in old Delhi was rated as the best and Ann decided to have our first child there. Lt Col Stan Menezes (later a Lt Gen and Vice Chief of the Army Staff) from 3 Grenadiers was posted in Delhi and he offered to take Ann to the Hospital whenever necessary. He telephoned on March 4, 1950, to say that Ann was in labour and that he had taken her to the Hospital. That evening he telephoned again to say that Ann and I had a son and that all was well. I celebrated the birth of our son with some friends and flew down to Jammu the next day as there was no direct air service to Delhi. From Jammu I went to Pathankot by road and caught the over-night train to Delhi. It was a great moment in my life to hold our infant son in my arms – he was a bonny baby so plump and cute with features so unmistakably a mix of Ann and me. Both of us loved our roly-poly baby with all our heart. A month later Ann and Arun, our son, joined me in Srinagar. Our married life was now full of excitement of having such a lovely and happy baby to care for and play with and we took him out to the mountains as often as we could. Ann, a voracious reader, gave up her books temporarily to take care of our boy. We talked endlessly about his cute smiles and the noises he made when we played with him. When he learnt to recognize us and utter a guttural sound to call us, we were ecstatic. Ann and I were happy beyond our dreams..

In December 1950, I was posted to command the 2nd Battalion of the Grenadiers located at Clement Town near Dehra Dun. The only accommodation we could get was an old decrepit cottage. While I was busy sorting out the Battalion, which was not in too good a shape after the Police Action in Hyderabad, my wife worked hard to convert the small cottage into a comfortable home for us and for our infant son, Arun. But the Battalion was in urgent need of a Welfare and Healthcare set-up for the families of my soldiers. Although my wife was wildly in love with our infant son, she organized her time so beautifully that within a short space of time other units were talking about Mrs. Yadav's model Welfare Centre. Her diligence and dedication to the welfare of my soldiers certainly helped me enormously in having an enjoyable and worthwhile stint as the Commanding Officer of a great and famous Battalion known for two hundred years as 'The Second to None'. Later, when I assumed command of the 9th Battalion of the Grenadiers, which could authenticate its history of honour and glory to the 17th Century, my wife worked with rare dedication and enthusiasm to create the best Welfare Centre for Soldiers in the Division despite the fact that we had our second lovely bonny child, a beautiful daughter, Maya, As a consequence, my Battalion was reputed to be one of the best unit in the formation. A good wife is God's gift for success as a Commanding Officer. May be I was born lucky to have someone like Ann marry a soldier!

After I had done the Staff College I was posted to Army Headquarters in New Delhi in September 1952. General Cariappa was then the first Indian Commander-in-Chief. Whenever he went on tours he took a Lt Col from his Headquarters as a Staff Officer. I went with him on a few tours in India, but I did not want to go to Nepal with him as I found that while he was very polite and correct with the Troops he was visiting, he was not always pleasant to his staff. Nevertheless, I was ordered to go. We were entertained very lavishly in Nepal by His Majesty the King who made General Cariappa a four-star General in the Royal Nepalese Army and showered him with all sorts of gifts. I do not know what happened to the gifts but I did not get my share as I used to when I was ADC to British Commanders.

Nepal was a bit jittery at the time as the Communist Regime in China had extended its hold on Tibet. The General was equally concerned and he dictated a letter to the Prime Minister during our flight from Kathmandu to Delhi setting out his apprehensions on Chinese designs. On arrival at Delhi he ordered me to deliver the Top Secret letter personally to the Prime Minister. I went to Teen Murti House, then the PM's residence (and previously the residence of the British Commander-in-Chief in India), and informed the PM's Personal Secretary, O.M. Mathai, whom I had known and disliked from my days as ADC, about my mission. Mathai was casual and offensive. He told me to leave the letter on his desk. He did not think it was necessary for me to deliver the letter personally to the Prime Minister, as there were far too many letters from Cariappa to be of any importance – something he ought not to have said to me. But my orders were clear, so I had to go back to the General and tell him what had happened. General Cariappa was most dismayed and he told me that he had not been getting on well with Pundit Nehru. He said both he

(Cariappa) and Sardar Patel, the then Minister of Home Affairs, felt that we might have trouble with the Chinese. Pundit Nehru did not think so and had already ordered a scale down of the Army. I felt sorry for General Cariappa, but I did not offer my sympathy as I knew that he was inclined to be overbearing and tactless – a weakness which also plagued me!

While I was an Instructor at the Senior Officers' Course at Mhow (1954 – 56), I was directed to write a new textbook for the Army on Jungle Warfare. After a thorough research and my experiences in Burma, I produced a very comprehensive Manual on Jungle Warfare. At the time it was the only Manual of its kind in the World and both the Commandant and the Chief Instructor were very appreciative of the hard work which had gone into the writing of the textbook. The Manual was, of course, of considerable practical value to our Troops engaged in counter-insurgency operations in the thick jungles in Northeast India. As the need was felt to train Troops in Jungle Warfare centrally before they were committed to these operations, it was decided to raise the Jungle and Guerilla Warfare School to train these Troops. As my Commandant at the Infantry School was now the Director of Military Training at Army Headquarters, I was selected to raise the Jungle Warfare School as the first Commandant. At the time I was Dean at the Defence Services Staff College, Wellington, South India, and my appointment as Commandant of the Jungle and Guerilla or Commando Warfare School and promotion to Brigadier came as a total surprise to me. But there were those who were jealous and eager to see some unimaginable conspiracy in my appointment and early promotion. Anonymous letters were sent to the Chief of the General Staff at Army Headquarters decrying my appointment – a distressing behavioral departure of Officers from the great traditions of the Indian Army in which I was commissioned. I would have quit then, but I had another two years to go before I qualified for pension.

Nevertheless, I was sent to England to see how the Royal Marine were training their commandos and to see also the training methods of the Special Forces located at Hereford. The training of the Royal Marine Commandos, especially their Speed Marches and rappelling down a cliff impressed me – the rest was the same old stuff from the training Manuals of the last World War. The Special Forces Battalion was not so forthcoming in showing their training or equipment. Apparently they did not regard anyone outside NATO, in particular the USA, as a partner safe enough for sharing anything on the secret list. Their Boat Squadron demonstration was quite interesting, but nothing new. I had served with Force 136 in the Karen Hills in Burma and knew exactly how the Special Forces operated in war. But it was a very pleasant visit and I was grateful to them for taking such good care of me – they took me way out into the beautiful Welsh countryside to an old pub for cocktails and dinner which I enjoyed very much.

Of course, Lord Mountbatten was, as always, very gracious and kind when I called to see him —at the time he was Chief of the British Defence Staff. It was largely because I had been his ADC that I was treated with a little bit of extra consideration than most other Officers from the Indian Armed Forces on visit to the UK. I had met Lady Mountbatten earlier in New Delhi before she died.

From England I went to Germany. Winter Anstey had done the Staff Course with me and he was kind enough to be my host. He was commanding an Armoured Regiment in the British Army of the Rhine and I managed to see how they were dealing with nuclear threat from the Communist Block. Winter and his charming wife, Mary, were kind enough to show me round Germany and I had a wonderful time with them. After retirement, they bought a beautiful house at Dunkeld in Perthshire, Scotland, and on my way back from America in 1988, it was a joy to stay with them again. Sadly that was the last time I saw Winter. He died in 1996. He was a gentleman, a very affectionate friend and one of the finest Army Officers on my short list. Regrettably Mary, a lady to the core, for whom I had great regard and affection, passed away in December 2002. But our links continue through our children.

On my return to India in August 1961, the Director of Military Training and I went round looking for a suitable place for locating the Jungle and Guerilla (or Commando) Warfare School. I selected Clement Town near Dehra Dun as during the Second World War, I was posted briefly at Badshai Bag in the same range of the Siwalik Hills where units were training for Jungle Warfare. I thought that it was better to train Troops in not too thick a secondary jungle, where you could see and correct fire positions and movements than in a thick primary tropical jungle where you could not. After I had the School going I went to see how the British were training their troops at Kotatingi in Malaya. Australians were also there. They had some kind of role in Vietnam, but they disclosed nothing. The British Gorkha Regiments were particularly kind to me and hosted some very lavish parties to entertain me. I found a demonstration of attack in the jungle by helicopter borne troops by the Royal Marines particularly interesting as also the use of dogs in war. When I returned to India I incorporated these in our own training schedule including the use of dogs in war.

After six weeks on my return to India the training at the Jungle (the word Guerilla was dropped) Warfare School started in full swing. Initially I trained complete Infantry Battalions, two at a time, with one Rifle Company specifically for commando operations. Later Police Battalions earmarked for counter-insurgency operations were also sent for training. None of my Officers had any experience of fighting in the Jungle, but professionally they were very good. The Director of Military Training had given me a free hand to draft the training syllabus – a unique dispensation which strengthened my resolve for excellence in training the Troops. I wrote out every single lesson plan and exercise myself: the Instructors were rehearsed in teaching these to the Troops. The various Operations of War, Patrolling, Speed Marches, Rappelling, new Ambush Drills contrived by me, Survival in the Jungle, Living in the Jungle and Commando Operations were all included in the Training Syllabus. Also included in Commando training was 'instant obedience' drill innovated by me in which a trainee was required to jump from a rope obstacle into a pond or river instantly on order. Of course Speed Marches were new to our training in the Indian Army and resented at first, but everyone got used to them after a while. Training in Commando Operations was not entirely new but skills we taught in carrying out raids, ambushes, rescue operations, demolitions or laying booby-traps were based on wholly new perceptions and drills evolved by me. I was very proud of making a very substantial contribution to training of the Army I loved and admired with all my being.

But the burden of Welfare of this huge command was, of course, borne by my wife. She did a wonderful job in creating a first-rate organization in a very short period of time. Two years later when I was ordered to raise and command 68 Infantry Brigade Group, my wife, by now a well known expert, had no difficulty in helping the first ladies of the various units under my command to set up a Welfare Centre for their unit. After Edwina Mounbatten, my wife Ann was the most welfare-conscious lady I ever met.

With absolute bliss and contentment at home, I was able to devote all my time as a Professional Soldier to administering and training my commandos. I had no interest to detract me outside my profession. Unfortunately the senior Indian Officers at the time lacked experience as unit commanders, as they had been elevated to command formations in the vacancies which had to be filled by Indians of requisite seniority after the British had left. The majority of them lacked professionalism, which was systematically denied to them during the Raj. For this reason, the mechanism of their assessment of those under their command relied largely on what their juniors could do to please them and their families by groveling or gifts. Without any doubt I was at the time the most professionally qualified senior Officer in Service having been an Instructor-in-Gunnery, Instructor on the Senior Officers' Course, Instructor at the Staff College and the creator and Commandant of the Jungle Warfare School. I had authored the Jungle Warfare Book, first of its kind, in 1956 and rewritten the standard Army Manuals on Patrolling, Defence and Withdrawal operations while I was an Instructor on the Senior Officers' Course in Mhow. As Commandant of the Jungle Warfare School I had introduced Speed Marches and wholly new doctrines for the training of Commandos, including new techniques for ambushes, counter-insurgency operations and the drills for survival in jungle country; the lesson plans for all the instructions and the tactical exercises at the School were written personally by me I had commanded four Infantry Units, held the top appointment of Brigadier General Staff and raised and commanded an Infantry Brigade Group and commanded a Mountain Brigade apart from having officiated as commander of two Infantry Divisions. My record in war was enviable. I had served too long with elite British professional Commanders and I found it humiliating to serve under Officers who were professionally incompetent and morally weak. The growing differences with my seniors, who were forever jockeying for the next rank at any cost without deserving it, and the degrading policy of the Government vis-à-vis Military Officers and Civil and Police Officers, made it abundantly clear to me (and my wife) that I was a misfit in the Army. My love for my profession was absolute and I worked hard to achieve perfection and self-satisfaction in the numerous commands I was honoured to hold. But in 1968, I ceased to enjoy Soldiering. The only option I had was to seek premature retirement. With my wife's consent I packed away all by uniforms and accoutrements in a steel box my father had given me in 1939, and retired from the Army on 28 August 1968, two days before my 47th birthday-perhaps the youngest Brigadier to seek premature retirement at that age. Soldiering was the profession of my choice. I had a unique, wonderful and glorious time for the years I had the honour of wearing the uniform of the Indian Army, incomparably the best in the World. The day I retired was the saddest day of my life till then and I cried unashamedly to reconcile with unfulfilled dreams and high expectations.

When I retired our only my son, Arun, was a Cadet at the National Defence Academy. The following year he moved to the Indian Military Academy and was commissioned in June 1970. My Father had held a King's Commission in the 14th Battalion of the Rajputs, a Territorial Army unit, in mid 1920s. I was the second and my son the third to hold a Commission in the Army. Of course, by tradition my son ought to have gone to the Rajputs, the Gunners, the Garhwal Rifles or the Grenadiers, the Regiments in which his forebears had served. Instead he asked to be posted to the 2nd Battalion of 4 Gorkha Rifles who had been with the "Chindits' and later trained under me in the Jungle Warfare School for long range penetration operations. Arun topped the entrance examination to the Staff College but he was denied his choice to do the Staff Course at Camberley as another Officer had sufficient political influence to grab the vacancy there. Instead Arun was sent to Kuala Lumpur. Although we were angry at this blatant injustice, which had become a common practice in the Army, as a good Soldier he was quite reconciled with it. He was very happy in the Battalion, which he commanded from 1990 to 1993. Then he did the Higher Commanders' Course before going to the Staff College as an Instructor. Till then we were the only father and son who had both been instructors at the Staff College, but intellectually and as a professional Soldier my son was superior to me. He was expecting a posting after completing his two-year term at the Staff College and I had hoped that he would command 68 Brigade. I had raised and vigorously trained the Brigade in the high and rugged mountains of the Kashmir Valley for two years; in the event, in 1965, with commendable ease, 68 Brigade captured Haji Pir, a strategically vital feature near Uri in Kashmir, and made history. But my dreams were shattered when suddenly, while on tour with the Staff College, our brilliant and loving son had cerebral hemorrhage during the night and was found dead in his room the next day. A promising career in the service of India thus came to an end – as also our dynasty in Army Service. My wife, daughter Maya, Arun's family and I were devastated. The Yadav family had never before faced such a terrible tragedy. India lost an outstanding Soldier and a future General of great promise.

My wife, Ann, who had so bravely held the family together during some very lean and trying years after my retirement, did not recover from the unimaginable tragedy of our bereavement. After 52 years of a beautiful love affair, a complete and fulfilling life as parents, Ann suddenly passed away on 29 March 1999. She died of a broken heart. Ann had come suddenly into my life and changed it forever, and now she passed away just as suddenly as she had come, but left to the family she had raised with such care and concern a profound vision of love and happiness. Our daughter, Maya, and her son Arjun, Arun's widow and two daughters, Nisha and Karen, and I were shattered. Tragedies seem always to come in pairs. Thus ended more than half a century of my life in which I had gone through gratifying achievements, thrilling adventures, the joys and sorrows of a play boy, exhilarating successes and paltry failures, from slavery to freedom—but I could not have come through to a full life without the love and companionship of my beautiful and loving wife, the mother and grandmother of my lovely children.

Now I wait to join my wife and our son wherever they may be.

Index

1857 Mutiny, 34, 37, 55, 56, 62, 63
1857 Revolt, 35
1857 Sepoy Mutiny, 12

Abbotabad, 79
Abdul Ghaffar Khan, Frontier Gandhi, 78, 81, 177
Abyssinia, 86, 100
Action Committee, 88
Administrative Reforms, 47
Afghanistan, 31, 59, 69, 74, 78, 85
Afghanistan and Sind, 56
Afghans, Turks and Mughals, 46
Africa, 16
African Coastal Deserts, 16
Agha Khan, 83
Agra, 40, 42
Akali Movement, 74
Akbar, 63
Akbar Khan, 56
Alexander of Dunkirk, 93
All India Congress Committee, 97
Allahabad, 122, 123, 126
Allahabad University, 126
Allamayo, 160
Allied Land Forces, 173
America, 221
America or Britain, 149
American, 25, 109, 113, 133
    Indian, 125
    Leadership, 95
    Missionaries, 132
    Pacific Fleet, 90
    University, 137

War of Independence, 1776, 31
Amritsar, 68, 73
Ananda Mahidol, King of Siam (Thailand), 173, 174
Angkor Wat, 174
Ankara, 75
Ansari, Dr., 81
Anstey, Winter, 221
Anti-Mogul Movement, 9
Anzio Operations, 105
Arabia, 74
Arabian Sea, 147
Arakan, 54, 102, 105, 160, 170
Arakan Coast, 104
Arcot, 51, 53
Arjun, 226
Armed Forces, 38, 44, 98, 99, 154, 156, 188
Army Casualties, 109
Arthal, 210, 211
Artillery School, 135, 148
Aryans, 31
Ashok Chakra, 192
Ashoka, Emperor, 47, 128
Asia, 16, 34
Asian Power, 94, 103
Assam, 54
Ataturk, 75
Atlantic Charter on Human Rights, 149
Atlantic Charter, 32, 100, 113
Atlee, Clement, British PM, 33, 34, 114
Atom Bombs, 18, 111, 112
Aung Sen, 109
Aurangzeb, 41, 43

Australia, 101, 132
Australian Troops, 91
Australians, 93, 222
Axis Blitzkrieg, 16
Axis Powers, 16, 17
Axis Thrust, 86

Babar, 40, 41
Babbar Akalis, 74
Badshai Bag, 222
Baisakhi, 14, 78
Bakht Khan 60
Bali, Bhushan, Capt., 205
Balkan States, 16
Ballia, 98
Banaras Hindu University, 76
Bangalore-Belgaum Area, 104
Bangkok, 173
Bareilly, 134
Barrackpore, 45
Batote or Kud, 201
Battalions of Sikhs and Muslims, 65
Battle in Burma, 110, 171
Battle of
   Breakout, 163
   Buxar, 25
   Plassey, 51
   Sidi Barrani, 86
   Srirangapatam, 53
   Swally Roads, 42
   Umasi La, 214
Belgaum (South India), 60, 106, 107
Benares, 61
Bengal, 40, 43, 81, 102, 114
Bengal Army, 55, 56, 57, 58
   of East India Comp., 35
   Regiments, 54
Bengal Artillery, 60
Bengal Gunners, 15
Bengal Partitioned, 1805, 66
Bengal Presidency Army, 51
Bentinck, Lord, Governor, 52, 53, 57

Berlin, 191
Besant, Mrs. Annie, 72
Best, Thomas, Capt., 42
Bhadrawah, 205, 208
Bhagwan Das, 213, 214
Bhangi Colony, 186, 187
Bhumibol Adulyadej (Rama IX), 173
Bihar, 17, 40
Bihar and Eastern UP, 153
BOA Flying Boat, 177
Boers (South Africa), 66
Bolo Auk, 164, 165
Bombay, 13, 17, 60, 196, 198
Bose, Rash Behari, 68
Botavia, 170, 171, 173, 174
Boundary Commission, (Lahore), 194
Brahmputra Valley, 105
Britain, 11, 12, 13, 14, 18, 29, 30, 33,
   42, 44, 68, 70, 74, 85, 92, 95, 99,
   101, 113, 123, 150, 174
Britain and France, 85
Britain and India, 55
Britain's Need for Indian Soldier, 13
Britain's Wars in China, 30
British, 9-13, 15-17, 19, 25, 26, 28, 29,
   32, 36-38, 39, 43, 45-47, 50, 54,
   56-58, 61-63, 68, 75-82, 88, 93-95,
   97-101, 110, 122, 127, 129, 132,
   134, 137, 149-155, 157, 160, 161,
   169, 170, 177, 188, 198, 214, 223,
Achievements, 18, 28, 36, 66
Administration, 94, 97
Air-crafts, 90
Army, 25, 52, 55, 59, 66, 86, 110,
   191, 221
Arrogance, 31
Battalion, 66
Battleships, 90
Business Community, 100
Civil Servants, 186
Colonial Positions in India, 29
Colonies, 100
Commanders, 219

Index

Crown, 25, 33, 62
Debts, 99
Defence Staff, 221
Democratic Psyche, 27
Education, 152
Empire, 25, 30, 46, 69, 70, 83, 99, 100
Empire in Asia and Africa, 29
Empire in India, 27
Expeditionary Force, 40, 85
Factory at Surat, 42
Goods, 78
Government, 29, 70, 80-82, 99, 114, 117, 123
Gunners, 52
In Ruling India, 66
Indian Army, 38, 66
Indian Empire, 17, 20, 27-30, 33, 42, 97, 117, 144, 194
Indian Government, 13, 71
Indian Troops, 93
Institutions, 30
Isles, 44, 85, 183
King, 44
Labor Party, 83
Leadership, 95
Legacies, 27
Manufactured Products, 10
Military Powers, 28
Mutineers, 52
Officers, 11, 28, 29, 47, 48, 50, 53, 58, 59, 67, 84, 88, 94, 95, 137, 140, 142, 143, 148, 151, 156, 164, 170, 171, 174, 178
Other Ranks, 39
Paramountcy, 26
Paratroopers, 34
Parliament, 62, 83
Parliament System, 136
Phobia, 78
Police, 68
Policies, 27
Possessions, 11

Power, 17, 51
Racial Discrimination, 11
Racial Prejudice, 152
Raj, 9, 11, 31, 35, 38, 46, 69, 155
Resident at Kabul, 56
Royal Artillery, 151
Royal Navy, 34
Rule, 35, 77, 79, 94, 100
Russian Design, 78
Schools, 44
System, 66
Troops, 18, 34, 53, 65, 93, 105, 197, 198
Turks, 78
Vessels, 89
Victory, 31
War Against-, 46
Brown, Col, 137
Buddha, 129, 173
Buddhist, 128
Budge-Budge (Hoogly), 68
Burma, 18, 34, 83, 89, 92, 93, 100, 101, 102, 107, 108, 111, 113, 122, 148, 149, 150, 158, 161, 168, 170, 171, 195, 220
Burma and Singapore, 84
Burma Water Festival, 169
Burmese, 54
Burmese Border, 54, 89
Burmese Forces, 109
Burmese Kings, 169
Burmese Shores, 105
Buxar, 25, 27

Cabinet Mission, 114
Cacha, 54
Cairo, 85
Calcutta, 33, 43
Calcutta and Karachi, 149
Camberley, 225
Cambridge University, 122, 136
Canada, 81
Canadian Government, 68

Capitalism, 123, 127
Cariappa, Gen., 206, 209, 214, 219, 220
Caroe, Sir Olaf, 116
Caste Marks, 52
Caste System, 32
Catherine of Braganza, 43
Censorship, 27
Central Asia, 56
Central India Horse (Hyderabad), 25, 88, 95
Champaran-Kheda Area, (Bihar), 71
Chandi Devi, Goddess, 21, 211, 212, 213, 215
Changi Jail, 94
Charles 11, 43
Chatfield Committee, 84
Chenab, 201, 202, 210
Chenab Valley, 202
Chillianwala, 57
China, 30, 89, 91, 92, 102, 103, 150, 169, 188, 190
China or Burma, 56
Chindwin, 93, 103
Chinese, 156, 190, 220
Chinese American Troops, 102, 103, 169
Chinese Army, 101
Chinese Troops, 93
Chitor, 41
Chittagong (Bangladesh), 156
Chittagong and Dacca, 54
Chola Kingdom (South), 47
Christeson, Lt. Col., 101
Christian Europe, 9
Christian Missionaries, 62
Christianity, 43, 45
Church of England, 44
Church of Rome, 43, 44
Churchill, Sir Winston, 40, 61, 86, 87, 89, 90, 91, 95-97, 99, 100, 111, 113, 179
Civil Administration, 205, 206, 208
Civil Disobedience, 78, 81

Civil Disobedience Movement, 77, 81
Civil War, 34
Clement Town (Dehra Dun), 218
Clifton, 148
Clive, 61
Coast Artillery (Cochin), 15, 25
Colonial
    India, 135
    States, 124
    Subjects, 125
    Troops, 29
Colonialism, 124
Colonization Act, 70
Comilla, 105
Common Laws, 132
Communal Award, 81, 82
Communal Holocaust, 26
Communist Regime China, 219
Congress, 17, 36, 37, 76, 81, 98, 114, 187
Congress Session, Lucknow, 70
Congress/Muslim Leadership, 16
Connorton, Ann Louisa, 191, 198, 217, 218, 219, 223, 228
Constitutional Reforms, 29
Coorg, 57
Cornwallis, Charles, 50
Council of Princes, 96
Counter-Insurgency Operations, 220, 222
Court Martial, 188, 212
Cradock, Sir John, 52
Cricket Club of India, 196
Criminal and Civil Law, 27
Cripps Plan, 153
Cripps, Sir Stafford, 16, 17, 26, 97, 153
Cross Border Terrorism, 156
Curzon, Lord, 66
Customs, 135

Dalhousie, Marques of-, 57
Dandi, 78
Dandi March, 77

Index

Dawana Hills, 93
Defence
   and Foreign Affairs, 80, 153
   and Security System, 32
   Institution, 135
   of India, 155, 190
   of India Act, 14, 70
   Services Staff College, Wellington, 135, 220
Dehra Dun, 121, 222
Delhi, 41, 60, 61, 215-217, 219
Deolali, 157, 158
Destroyer Flotilla, 115
Dharsana Salt Works, 78
Dharwar, 60
Digboi Oil Fields, 89
Dilawar Khan, 207
Dimapur, 103, 104, 107
Dimapur-Kohima Rd., 104, 106
Divided India, 41
Doda, 201, 205, 208
Doda-Kishtwar-Bhadarwah, 201, 206, 214
Dominion States, 37
Dost Muhammad, 56
Dowry, 43
DSO (Distinguished Service Order), 208
Duke of Wellington, 49
Dunkeld (Perthshire), 221
Dunkirk, 16, 85, 86, 105
Dutch East Indies (Indonesia), 18, 110, 170, 171
Dutch Population, 172
Dutch Women, 172
Dyer, Reginald, British Gen., 14, 78

East Bengal, 201
East India Company, 10, 12, 13, 25, 35, 36, 43, 57, 58, 62, 65
East Indies (Indonesia), 56
Eastern UP, 17
Economic and Moral Policies, 124

Economic System, 188
Education, 27, 44, 48, 50, 80, 124, 135, 176, 187
Egypt, 16, 84, 85, 88, 99
Egyptian Front, 87
Elections, 76, 114
Electoral Rules, 123
England, 14, 16, 34, 135, 136, 177, 187, 189, 190, 191, 221
Etawah Dist., 35
Eurasian Children, 50
Europe, 16, 29, 30, 43, 46, 51, 112, 113, 123, 136, 152
   and Africa, 91
   and America, 183
   and Japan, 79
European
   Americans, 133
   Artillery, 55
   Christian Missionaries, 44
   Commonwealth, 68
   Commonwealth Countries, 29
   Forces, 65
   Missionaries, 133, 167
   Officers, 36
   Planters, 71
   Power, 89, 123
   POWs, 94
   Regiments, 55
   Troops, 10, 18, 26, 59, 171
Europeans, 31, 39, 42, 43, 45, 123, 132, 133, 135, 144, 149, 150-152, 154, 172, 176

Fake Freedom Movements, 155
Fall of Singapore, 79
Far East, 85, 109, 112, 113
Far East and Australia, 100
Fascism, 79, 123
Federal Services Examination, 137
Festivals, 127, 128
Festivals and Rituals, 127
Field Ambulance Transport Corps, 68

First Burmese War, 56
First Sea Lord, 179
First War of Independence, 37, 63
First World War, 12, 13, 17, 21, 29, 37, 68, 105, 179, 193
Fort St. David, 43
Fort St. George, 42
France, 10, 16, 42, 45, 65, 69, 105
Free India, 188, 192
Freedom Movement, 74, 88, 122
French, 27, 43
French Indo-China, 18, 149
French Indo-China Operation, 110
French Revolution, 1789, 31, 45
Fuller, JFC, Maj. Gen. 91, 101, 107, 108, 110, 111, 112

Gallipoli Operations, 105
Gandhi and Nehru Brigade in Singapore, 188
Gandhi, Indira, 118, 121, 122, 123, 194
Gandhi, Mahatma, 14, 38, 68, 71, 72, 74-76, 79, 80-82, 85, 98, 121, 147, 155, 183, 185, 186, 187
Gandhi's Non-Violent Methods, 14
Gandhi-Irwin Pact, 81
Ganga Hayauddin, 161, 162
Ganges Valley, 60
Garrison Hill, 106
Gattan Tribunal, 84
German East Africa, 69
German Panzer Forces, 16
German (s), 31, 66, 69, 87, 105, 151, 152
Germans or Japanese, 149
Germany, 17, 18, 85, 113, 123, 221
Surrender, 171
Ghadar Movement, 67
Ghadar Party, 70
Golkonda Coast, 42
Gorkha Battalion, 66
Government of India Act of 1919, 14, 77, 80

Government of India Act of 1933, 83, 122
Governor General Bengal, 57
Governor Generals, 27
Canning, 27
Clive, 27
Curzon, 27
Dalhousie, 27
Harding, 27
Hastings, 27
Irwin, 27
Lytton, 27
Minto, 27
Mountbatten, 27
Wavell, 27
Gracey, Gen., 160, 162
Great Britain, 25, 27, 32, 65, 99, 111, 164
Great Reformation, 45
Great World Wars, 27
Greeks, 31
Guerrilla Warfare School, 220
Gujarat, 40, 57
Gujarat Coast, 77
Gulmarg, 217
Gunnery Course (Karachi), 140, 142
Gurdat Singh, 68

Haji Pir, 226
Harold, 166, 167
Harrow (England), 122
Hawkins, William, 42
Hector, Monro, Maj., 25
Henry VIII, 44
Hereford, 221
Himalayas, 127, 128
Hindu
and Muslim, 38, 52, 62, 81, 113, 208
Festivals, 134
India, 116
Kush Range, 42
Maha Sabha, 76
Muslim Animosity, 80

Index

Muslim Army Officers, 34
Muslim Riots, 76, 79, 114, 115, 116, 177, 186
Muslim Rivalries, 33
Muslim Unity, 76
Rituals, 129
Hindu, Jain and Buddhist Rulers, 44
Hindu Rao Hospital, 217
Hindukush Mountains, 31
Hindus, 33
Hindus and Muslims, 33
Hiroshima, 111
Hiroshima and Nagasaki, 18, 174
Hitler, 85
HMS *Prince of Wales*, 89, 150
HMS *Repulse*, 89, 150
Homeless in,
   Kobe, 110
   Nagoya, 110
   Osaka, 110
   Yokohama, 110
Hong Kong, 18, 68, 93
Hoogly, 43
Hugh Ranse, Maj. Gen., 108
Hukawng and Salveen Valley, 103
Hume, Allen Octavian, Founder of INC, 12, 13, 14, 35, 66
Hyderabad, 45, 198, 199, 218
Hyderabad Parleys, 189

Immigrants, 68
Imperialism, 123, 124
Imphal, 104
Imphal Kohima Road, 103
India Act of 1858, 62
India and Pakistan, 19, 29, 110
India Gate, 118, 193
India Gate War Memorial, 118
Indian
   Armed Forces, 155, 221
   Army, 10-12, 28, 29, 46, 57, 65, 69, 74, 85-87, 95, 97, 99, 100, 110, 112, 153, 171, 205, 209, 210, 220, 223, 225

Cavalry, 55
Civil Service, 28
Command Officer (ICO), 148
Councils Acts of 1861, 66, 67
Custom and Traditions, 36
Emperor, 37
Empire, 11, 18, 25, 28, 38, 55, 83, 132
Factory (Dum Dum), 59
Forces, 17, 18
Jails, 155
Kingdoms, 27
Legislative Council, 67
Military Academy, Dehra Dun, 133, 137, 138, 142, 144, 195, 225
Mutiny of 1857, 58, 61, 65
Nation State, 10
National Army, 15, 25, 95, 99, 113, 151-153, 157, 170, 188
National Congress, 13, 35, 66, 68, 80, 83, 85, 94, 103, 104, 123
National Flag, 117
Ocean, 90, 150
Prisoners of War, 25, 151, 152
Railways, 135
Sepoy Mutiny, 1857, 11
Social Structure, 46
States, 57, 63, 83
Tricolour, 192, 193
Troops, 35, 52, 55, 56, 93, 99, 106, 110, 154, 171
Indo-Burmese Frontier, 101
Indonesia, 160
Indulgence Funds, 124
Indus, 60
Industrialization, 190
Infantry School, 220
Inland Waterways, 135
Insein Jail, 168
Instrument of Accession, 199
Insurgency, 155, 156, 206
Iraq, 85
Irwin, Lord, Viceroy, 81

ISI, 190
Islamic Republics, 32
　Bangladesh, 32
　Indonesia, 32
　Malayasia, 32
　Pakistan, 32
Istanbul, 75
Italian Armies, 16
Italian Defence, 87
Italians in Ethiopia, 158
Italy, 17

Jagraon, 88
Jahangir, Emperor, 42, 207
Jain Temples, 44
Jallianwala Bagh Amritsar, 14, 72-74
James I, King, 42
Jammu, 200, 201, 204, 207, 217
Jammu and Kashmir, 21, 188, 199, 200, 204, 205, 206, 208, 215, 216
　Militia, 200, 214, 215
　State Forces, 201, 207, 208
Jamrud Fort, 49
Japan, 16, 18, 89, 110-113, 153, 154
Japan Navy, 90
Japanese, 16, 17, 25, 89, 90-93, 95, 98-102, 104-106, 108, 109, 149-151, 155, 156, 159, 161-163, 165, 168, 169, 171-173, 179
　Army, 160
　Imperialism, 95
　in Manchuria and China, 152
　Invasion, 1942, 170
　Navy, 111
　Occupation, 171
　Occupation Troops, 103
　Troops, 107
Jaunpur, 40
Jerusalem, 69
Jesus Christ, 45, 123, 124
Jinnah, Mohammad Ali, 18, 26, 33, 71, 75, 76, 85, 113, 115, 187, 195
Johore Baru, 91, 175

Johore Straits, 92
Joint Select Committee, 83
Judson College, 108, 109
Jungle and Guerrilla Warfare School, 222
Jungle Warfare School, 225

Kashmiris, 216
Kahuta, 116
Kalabagh, 60
Kali, Goddess, 211
Kamagata Maru, Ship, 68
Kamla, 121
Kanpur, 60, 61
Karachi, 117, 118, 142, 143, 148, 150, 151, 195
Karachi to Calcutta, 89
Karen, 87, 164, 165, 226
Karen Hills (Burma), 157, 164, 221, 157
Karen Village, 167
Kargil, 213, 215
Kashmir, 40, 149, 174, 190, 199, 207, 215
Kashmir Issue, 31
Kashmir Valley, 226
Kashmiri Muslims, 200, 216
Kathmandu, 219
Kathua, 200
Kaul, Biji, 200, 201, 209
Kaur, Rajkumari Amrit, 186, 187
Kawkareik Pass, 93
Khaleni, 201, 213
Khan Sahib, 177
Khandesh, 40
Khilafat Conference, 75
Khilafat Movement, 74
Khyber Pass (Pakistan), 49, 56
King Edward VII, 49
King George IV, 48
King George V, 69
Kings Commission, 225
Kingsway (Rajpath), 194
Kipling, Rudyard, 140, 141

Index

Kirte Movement, 88
Kishtwar, 201-203, 205, 210, 213, 214, 215
Kitchner College, 137
Kohima, 103, 104, 106, 107
Kohima Garrison, 104
Kohima-Imphal Highway, 104
Kohima-Imphal-Manipur-Tammu, 101
Kolhapur, 60
Korea and China, 95
Kotatingi (Malaya), 222
Kranji Creek, 92
Kuala Lumpur, 174, 225
Kuantan, 150
Kuantan Port, 90
Kurla, 197

Labour Government, (Britain), 114
Lady Carlyle, 198
Lady Mountbatten, Edwina, 118, 119, 181-184, 186, 189, 192, 196, 221, 223
Lady Pamela Mountbatten, 185
Lady Stopford, 174
Lahore, 73, 85, 195, 196
Land Reforms, 27
Landi Kotal (Khyber), 116
Lashio, 168
Law and Order, 10, 28, 51, 108, 171, 208
Law of Universal Causation, 129
Lawlessness and Terrorism, 14
Line of Control, 105, 164
Linlithgow, Lord, 83, 85
Lodi, Alam Khan, 40
Lodi, Ibrahim, 41
London, 15, 73, 117, 136, 197
London Arsenal, (Woolwick), 59
Louis Francis Albert Victor Nicholas Battenberg, 178
Louis of Hesse and Rhine, 178
Lucknow, 60
Luftwaffe, 16
Luther, Martin, 45, 124, 45

Machail, 210, 211, 215
Madras, 42, 43, 52
Madras Army, 51, 52-55
Mafia Leader, 155
Maha Bandula, 54
Maharattas, 42, 43
Malabar, 75
Malaviya, Madan Mohan, 71, 76, 81
Malaya, 18, 85, 89, 90, 93, 94, 108, 1509
Malaya and Singapore, 153
Malta, 115, 178
Malwa, 40
Manchuria, 95
Mandalay, 169
Mandalay to Rangoon, 110
Manora Island (Karachi), 89, 142, 148, 149, 195
Martial Class, 38, 46, 47
Masulipatam, 43
Mathai, OM, 219
Mathura, 54
Maungdaw, 102
Maya, 226
Maymyo, 169
McDonald, Ramsay, British PM, 80
Mecca and Medina, 74
Meditation, 145, 146, 148
Mediterranean, 17, 105
Meerut, 45, 59, 61
Meiktila, 158, 159
Menezes, Sir Frank, Lt.Gen., 34, 84, 85, 94, 109, 116, 117, 195, 196, 217
Mesopotamia, 69
Metcalf, Lord, 50
Mewar, 40
Mhow, 220, 224
Middle East, 16, 18, 79, 113, 79, 85, 86, 88, 89, 93
Military and Civil Administration, 77
Military Cross, 105
Military Operation, 33, 199
Miller Paddy, 139, 140

Mindo, 70
Mingaladon Air Base, 162
Minto-Morley Reforms, 67
Mir Kasim (Bengal), 25
Mir Mase, 69
Moguls, 9
Mohammad Ali, Maulana, 75
Mohan Singh, Capt., 15, 26, 95, 151, 152
Monckton, Walter, 198
Mongols, 31
Montagu Declaration, 1917, 12, 13, 15, 30, 31, 37
Montagu, Edwin, Lt. Gen., 29, 69, 70, 105
Montogomery, Bernard MG, 105
Moplas to Arab Descent, 75
Morley, 70
Mount Pleasant, 95
Mountbattan, Lord Louis, 19, 34, 101, 102, 105, 106, 110, 118, 119, 157, 158, 161, 178, 179, 180, 181, 184, 189, 192, 193, 221
   Administration, 173, 179, 183
   of Burma, 29, 115, 116, 119
Mughal Army, 43
Mughal Emperor, 20, 51, 181
   Aurangzeb, 20, 181
   Babar, 20, 181
Mughal Empire, 42
Mughal Gardens, 20, 181
Mughal Rulers, 44
Muslim Refugees, 201
Munro, Sir Thomas, 53
Muslim
   and Hindu, 40, 59, 65, 75, 115
   Indians, 63
   Leaders, 29, 97
   League, 33, 38, 82, 85, 114
   Middle East, 195
   Naval ADC, 118
   Population, 216

Rulers, 32
Troops, 69
Mussorie, 133, 142
Mutineers, 60, 61
Mutiny in 1857, 99, 151
Mysore, 57
Mysticism and Spiritualism, 211

Nagasaki, 112
Naidu, Sarojini, 81, 118
Nana Sahib, 63
Nasik, 180
National
   Army, 79
   Defence Academy, 225
   Movement, 61
   Parliament, 13
Nationalism, 9, 40
Natmauk, 159, 160
NATO, 221
Nawab of Oudh, 25
Nehru, Jawaharlal, 20, 21, 81, 114, 115, 117, 118, 121-123, 187-190, 192-194, 219, 220
Nehru, Indira, 123
Neill, James, Col,, 61
Nepal, 219
New Delhi, 15, 21, 157, 178, 181, 191, 195, 197, 219
New Mexico (USA), 111
New Zealand, 100, 132
Nile, 86
Nizam, 198, 199
Non-Violence, 15
Non-Violent Non-Cooperative Movement, 75
North Africa, 104
North East, 56
North East India, 220
North West Frontier, 34, 69, 87
North West Frontier Provinces, (NWFP), 78, 79, 114, 116, 177, 199
Nowshera, 84

Index

O'Connor, Maj. Gen., 86
O'Dwyer, Sir Michael, 72, 73
O'Hara, Kimball, 141, 142
Operations of War, 223
Opium Wars in China, 125
Orissa, 40
Ottoman Empire, 74
Ottoman Turk, 69
Oudh, 57, 58, 60, 65

Padam Valley, 213
Paget, Gen., 55
Pakistan, 17, 21, 116, 117, 177, 183, 188, 194, 199, 210, 216; Pakistan and Bangladesh, 115
Pakistani, 156
  Army, 195
  Flag, 195
  Forces, 216
  Infiltration, 201
  Invaders, 200
  Military, 199
Palam Air Force Base, 196
Palestine, 69
Pamela, 185
Panchayat System, 132
Panipat, 41
Param Vir Chakra (PVC), 214
Partition, 29, 114, 115, 197, 214
  Riots, 195
Pasir Zaba, 92
Patel, Sardar, 21, 117, 188, 189, 190, 220
Pathankot, 199, 217
Pearl Harbour, 90, 149, 150
Pegu Yomas, 108, 109, 110, 161
Penal Code, 27, 38, 126
Percival, Gen., 94
Persian Gulf, 84
Persians, 31
Peshawar (Pakistan), 56, 78, 79, 116, 177, 178, 200
Pete Rees, Maj. Gen., 179

Piar Chand, Capt., 205, 207, 208, 210, 213
Pingle, Marahatta Revolutionary, 67, 68
Plassey, 59
Pluralism, 128
Police and Civil Service, 44
Political
  Blunder, 17
  Freedom, 11, 67
  Movements, 30
  Parties (ty), 38, 79, 80
  Prisoners, 114
  System, 40, 127
Poona, 198
Poona Pact, 82
Population, 28
  Cultural, 28
  Ethnic, 28
  Linguistic, 28
  Religious, 28
Port Sudan, 86
Portuguese, 42, 44, 45
Post and Telegraph, 135
Post and Telegraph Services, 28
Postal System, 27
Potsdam, 11
Potsdam Declaration, 112
Pownall, Henry, 84
Prasad, Rajendra, 117
Prince of Wales and Repulse Battleships, 92
Princess Chumpot, 173
Prisoners of War, 15
Privy Council (London), 83
Prome, 161
Prome and Tharrawaddy, 158
Protestant British, 45
Provincial Assembly Bombay, 116
Provincial Legislative Councils, 67
Punjab, 13, 28, 30, 41, 57, 67, 68, 70-73, 74, 78, 84, 88, 114, 116

Queen Victoria, 62, 178, 62
Quetta Staff College, 172

Quit India, 33, 97, 153, 154, 168
   Movement, 17, 98
   Resolution, 154, 155
Qutab-ud-din Aibak, Sultan of Delhi, 31

RA Club, 172
Racial Discrimination, 149
Racism, 39
Radha and Krishna, 134
Rajendra Prasad, 117
Raipur, 60
Raja of Kishtwar, 207
Raja of Vijayanagar, 41
Rajaratnam, Maj., 201
Ram Rasta, 210
Rana Sanga, 41
Rangoon, 108, 162, 163, 168
Rangoon and Singapore, 198
Rangoon-Myitkyine-Lashio, 101
Rangoon-Prome-Mandalay, 93
Rangoon-Roungoo-Mandalay, 93
Rani Laxmibai, 63
Rawalpindi, 34, 116
Razakars-Terrorist Muslim Org., 199
Red Cross, 68, 70, 182
Red Fort, 117, 192, 193
Red Sea, 62, 84
Regiment Garhwal Rifle, 177
Reginald Dyer Troops, 73
Regionalism, 9
Revolt of 1857, 42, 98
Revolutionary Movement, 72
Revolutionary Plans, 68
Rhine, 191, 221
River
   Chindwin, 106
   Ganges, 129, 131, 132
   Irrawaddy, 160
   Shwegyin Chaung, 164, 167
   Sittang, 93, 109, 164
Roads and Railways, 27
Roe, Sir Thomas, 42
Rohilkhund, 60

Roman, 126
   Catholics, 45
   Colony, 27
   Customs, 44
   Empire, 43
Rommel, Erwin, Gen., 16, 87
Roosevelt, 89, 96
Round Table Conference (London), 80, 81
Rowlatt Acts, 1919, 14, 70, 72, 74
Rowlatt, Justice, 13, 70
Royal Air Force, 159
Royal Corps of Education, 137
Royal Garhwal Rifles, 79, 158
Royal Indian Air Force, 26, 113
Royal Indian Navy, 26, 113
Royal Marine Commandos, 220
Royal Marines, 221, 222
Royal Navy, 26, 49, 89, 178
Royal Nepal Army, 219
Royal Soc. For Prevention of Cruelty to Animals, 182
Rural Areas, 11
Rural India, 10, 17
Russia (n), 16, 149, 188
Russia and Africa, 152
Russian Front, 89
Russian System, 188
Russian, Afghanistan and French, 66
Russians, 56, 68

Sabalu, 60
Sabarmati Ashram, 77
Saivism, 44
Sapphire Mines, 210
Sapru, Sir Tej Bahadur, 83
Satara, 60
Satyagraha, 72
Savarkar, Vinayak, 68
School of Artillery, 142
Scotland, 221
Second Round Table Conference (London), 81

Index

Second World War (1939-1945), 15, 17, 18, 19, 22, 26, 29, 32, 34, 37, 40, 50, 79, 85, 86, 89, 109, 110, 149, 204, 222
Secularism, 188
Security Problems, 154
Security, 10, 28, 190
    External, 10, 80, 108, 114, 153, 178
Self-Governing Interests in India, 11
Sepoy Mutiny of 1857, 30, 37, 74
Shah Alam, Mughal Emperor, 25
Shah Shey, 56
Shanghai, 99
Shans Village, 165, 167
Sheikh Abdullah, 200, 206
Shivaji's Troops, 43
Sialkot, 159, 160
Siam, 110
Sidi Barrani, Libya, 86
Sikh Regiment, 60
Sikh Revolutionaries, 67
Sikh Wars, 59
Sikhs, 42, 43
Simla, 196
Simmone, French, 190
Simon Commission, 80
Simon, Sir John, 77
Sind, 40
Sind and Orissa, 83, 122
Singapore, 15, 18, 25, 45, 84, 89, 90-92, 172-177
Singapore and Burma, 94
Singora, Patani and Kota Baru, 90
Siwalik Hills, 222
Slavery, 188
Slim, Sir William, Lt. Gen., 101, 103, 105, 109, 113, 195
Social Structure, 81, 188
Socialism, 79, 123, 127, 188
Society, Indian, 63
Soma-Jessami-Kohima, 104
South Africa, 75
South East Asia, 16, 18, 19, 26, 34, 79, 90, 101, 105, 117, 150

South East Asian Countries, 105
South Malaya, 35
Soviet Union, 85
Spaniards/Portuguese, 125
Special Forces, 221
Spencer, Herbert, 55
Sri Lanka, 101
Srinagar, 199, 200, 207, 215, 216, 218
Srinagesh, Gen., 215, 216
Staff College Camberley, 105
Stopford, Gen, 105, 108, 109, 110, 161, 162, 168, 170, 171, 174, 179, 195
Sukarno, 170
Sukarno Government, 171
Sultan of Johore, 174
    British Wife Helen, 174
Sumchum Gompa, 213
Summary Court, 57
Supreme Allied Commander for South East Asia, 34
Suraj-ud-Daula, 51
Surat, 42, 43
Surma Valley, 105
Swaraj Party, 76
Switzerland, 121, 176
Syria, Egypt and Mesopotamia, 128

Tagore, Rabindranath, 74
Tammu, 103
Tantia Tope, 63
Territorial Army, 225
Terrorism, 206, 204
Thailand, 18, 90, 149, 164
Thailand and Burma, 93
Tharawaddy, 108, 161
Thatri, 202
Thaukthekhi, 164, 167
The Allied Powers, 112
The Allies, 16, 27, 47, 155
The Ganges Valley, 28
The Yamuna Valley, 28
Theodosius, Roman Emperor, 43
Theosophical Society, 72

Thimayya, Gen., 215
Third Round Table Conference, (London), 83
Tibet, 219
Tibetan Lama, 141
Tiddim, 103
Tipu Sultan, 53
Toungoo-Kalaw Axis War, 179
Trade Routes, 100
Tradition, 48
Transfer of Power, 29, 35, 115, 117
Tribes, 31
Truman, US Pres., 111, 112
Tryst With Destiny, 117
Turkey, 69, 75, 76
Turkey's Defeat, 74
Turkish Coast, 105
Turkish Defences, 69
Turkish Forces, 69
Turkish Pan Islamic Movement, 67
Turkish Republic, 75
Turks, 31
Tyersal Palace, 174, 175
Tzar Nicholas II Russia, 178

Udham Singh, 73, 74
Udhampur, 201
Umasi La (Pass), 21, 209, 210, 211, 212
UN Resolution, 216
United Kingdom, 11, 18, 32, 221, 32
Unites States, 32
UP and Bihar, 98
Uri (Kashmir), 226
Uri and Tithwal, 200
US Air-Crafts, 110
US Pacific Fleet, 16
USA, 99, 221
USA and Canada, 67

Varma, Shiv, Maj., 174
Vellore, 45, 51-53

Vellore Fortress, 52, 53
Victoria Cross, 69, 214
Victoria Port, 90
Vietnam, 222
Vijayanagar, 40
Vir Chakra (VC), 214
Vocational Training, 124

War College, 135
Washington, Gen., 50
Wavell,
    Field Marshall, 113
    General, 87, 91, 93
    Lord, 18, 19, 26, 86, 87, 114
    Old Warrior PM, 28, 33, 34
    The Viceroy, 32, 33
Welfare Centre (Mrs. Yadav), 218, 223
Wellington, Lord, 81
West Asia, 29
Western Desert Forces, 86
Whitegate, Orde, Gen, 102
Wingate, Gen., 157, 158
Women Auxiliary Corps of India, 198
Wood, Sir Charles, 65, 137
Woodstock School, Mussorie, 121, 134, 135, 136
Woolwich, 139
World War I, 31, 69
World War II, 135 see also Second World War
Wright Brothers, 108
Yervada Jail, 78
Yoga, 148
Young India, 186

Zanskar, 210
Zojila, 215
Zorawar Singh, 210
Zulu War Medal, 74